C++20 STL Cookbook

Leverage the latest features of the STL to solve
real-world problems

Bill Weinman

Packt>

BIRMINGHAM—MUMBAI

C++20 STL Cookbook

Group Product Manager: Richa Tripathi

Publishing Product Manager: Gebin George

Senior Editor: Rohit Singh

Technical Editor: Pradeep Sahu

Copy Editor: Safis Editing

Project Coordinator: Manisha Singh

Proofreader: Safis Editing

Indexer: Manju Arasan

Production Designer: Ponraj Dhandapani

Marketing Coordinators: Pooja Yadav and Sonakshi Bubbar

First published: May 2022

Production reference: 1130522

Published by Packt Publishing Ltd.
Livery Place
35 Livery Street
Birmingham
B3 2PB, UK.

ISBN 978-1-80324-871-4

www.packt.com

Contributors

About the author

Bill Weinman has been involved in technology since he built his first computer at age 16, in 1971. He's been coding in C and C++ since the early 1970s. He's written systems and applications for major clients, including NASA, Bank of America, Xerox, IBM, and the US Navy. Also an electronics engineer, he previously worked on the Voyager II spacecraft, audio amplifiers for SAE, and sound systems for Altec Lansing.

Since the mid 1990s, Mr. Weinman has focused on writing and teaching. His books and courses cover HTML, SQL, CGI, Python, and, of course, C and C++. An early contributor to online learning, his clear, concise writing has made his courses a popular feature on `lynda.com` and LinkedIn Learning.

Follow Bill on his website at `bw.org`.

About the reviewer

Vitalijs Vaznais was born in Daugavpils, Latvia. His favorite programming languages are C and C++, which he has been using for the last 26 years (and commercially for 24 years). He is pleased with the latest changes/evolution in both these languages and looks forward to seeing how they start to evolve.

Table of Contents

Preface

1

New C++20 Features

Technical requirements 2
Format text with the new format library 2
How to do it... 3
How it works... 4
There's more... 6

Use compile-time vectors and strings with constexpr 7
How to do it... 8
How it works... 8

Safely compare integers of different types 9
How to do it... 10
How it works... 10

Use the "spaceship" operator <=> for three-way comparisons 11
How to do it... 12
How it works... 14
There's more... 14

Easily find feature test macros with the <version> header 16
How to do it... 16
How it works... 17

Create safer templates with concepts and constraints 17
How to do it... 18
How it works... 20
There's more... 21

Avoid re-compiling template libraries with modules 23
How to do it... 23
How it works... 25

Create views into containers with ranges 28
How to do it... 29
How it works... 31
There's more... 33

2

General STL Features

Technical requirements   35

Use the new span class to make
your C-arrays safer   36
How to do it...   36
How it works...   37

Use structured binding to
return multiple values   38
How to do it...   39
How it works...   41

Initialize variables within if and
switch statements   43
How to do it...   43

How it works...   44
There's more...   45

Use template argument
deduction for simplicity and
clarity   46
How to do it...   46
How it works...   48
There's more...   50

Use if constexpr to simplify
compile-time decisions   51
How to do it...   51
How it works...   52

3

STL Containers

A quick overview of the STL
container types   53
Sequential containers   53
Associative containers   54
Container adapters   55

Technical requirements   56

Use uniform erasure functions
to delete items from a container   56
How to do it...   57
How it works...   59

Delete items from an unsorted
vector in constant time   61
How to do it...   61

How it works...   63

Access vector elements directly
and safely   64
How to do it...   64
How it works...   66
There's more...   66

Keep vector elements sorted   67
How to do it...   67
How it works...   69
There's more...   69

Efficiently insert elements into
a map   70
How to do it...   71
How it works...   73

Efficiently modify the keys of
map items 75
How to do it... 75
How it works... 78
There's more... 78

Use unordered_map with
custom keys 79
How to do it... 79
How it works... 81

Use set to sort and filter
user input 82
How to do it... 82
How it works... 83

A simple RPN calculator
with deque 84

How to do it... 86
How it works... 90
There's more... 91

A word frequency counter with
map 92
How to do it... 92
How it works... 96

Find long sentences with a
vector of vectors 97
How to do it... 97
How it works... 100

A ToDo list using multimap 101
How to do it... 101
How it works... 103

4

Compatible Iterators

Iterators are fundamental 105
Iterator categories 108
Iterator concepts 108

Technical requirements 111
Create an iterable range 112
How to do it... 112
How it works... 114
There's more... 115

Make your iterators compatible
with STL iterator traits 115
How to do it... 116
How it works... 117
There's more... 117

Use iterator adapters to fill STL
containers 118

How to do it... 118
How it works... 121

Create a generator as iterators 122
How to do it... 123
How it works... 125
There's more... 126

Use reverse iterator adapters
to iterate backward 127
How to do it... 127
How it works... 129

Iterate objects of unknown
length with a sentinel 130
How to do it... 131
How it works... 133

Build a zip iterator adapter 133

How to do it...   134
How it works...   138
There's more...   140

Create a random-access iterator 140
How to do it...   141
How it works...   146

5

Lambda Expressions

Lambda expressions   147
Closures   148

Technical requirements   149
Use lambdas for scoped
reusable code   150
How to do it...   150
How it works...   153

Use lambdas as predicates with
the algorithm library   155
How to do it...   155
How it works...   157

Use std::function as a
polymorphic wrapper   158
How to do it...   158
How it works...   160
There's more...   161

Concatenate lambdas with
recursion   162
How to do it...   162
How it works...   163

Combine predicates with logical
conjunction   164
How to do it...   164
How it works...   165

Call multiple lambdas with the
same input   166
How to do it...   166
How it works...   167

Use mapped lambdas for a
jump table   168
How to do it...   168
How it works...   169

6

STL Algorithms

Technical requirements   172
Copy from one iterator to
another   172
How to do it...   173
How it works...   175

Join container elements into a
string   176
How to do it...   177

How it works...   179
There's more...   180

Sort containers with std::sort   180
How to do it...   181
How it works...   184

Modify containers with
std::transform   185
How to do it...   185

How it works...   187

Find items in a container   188
How to do it...   188
How it works...   190
There's more...   191

Limit the values of a container to a range with std::clamp   191
How to do it...   191
How it works...   193

Sample data sets with std::sample   194
How to do it...   194
How it works...   197

Generate permutations of data sequences   197
How to do it...   198
How it works...   199

Merge sorted containers   200
How to do it...   200
How it works...   202

7

Strings, Streams, and Formatting

String formatting   204
Technical requirements   205
Use string_view as a lightweight string object   205
How to do it...   205
How it works...   207

Concatenate strings   209
How to do it...   209
How it works...   211
There's more...   211
Why would I choose one over another? 215

Transform strings   215
How to do it...   216
How it works...   218

Format text with C++20's format library   218
How to do it...   219
How it works...   223

There's more...   224

Trim whitespace from strings   225
How to do it...   225
How it works...   226

Read strings from user input   227
How to do it...   228
How it works...   231

Count words in a file   231
How to do it...   231
How it works...   232

Initialize complex structures from file input   232
How to do it...   233
How it works...   235
There's more...   235

Customize a string class with char_traits   237
How to do it...   237

How it works...   240
There's more...   240

Parse strings with Regular
Expressions   241
How to do it...   242
How it works...   243

8

Utility Classes

Technical requirements   246

Manage optional values with
std::optional   246
How to do it...   247
How it works...   249
There's more...   249

Use std::any for type safety   250
How to do it...   251
How it works...   252

Store different types with
std::variant   253
Differences from the primitive union
structure   253
How to do it...   254
How it works...   258

Time events with std::chrono   259
How to do it...   259
How it works...   264

Use fold expressions for
variadic tuples   265
Fold expressions   265
How to do it...   267
How it works...   268
There's more...   269

Manage allocated memory with
std::unique_ptr   270
How to do it...   271
How it works...   274

Share objects with std::shared_
ptr   275
How to do it...   276
How it works...   279

Use weak pointers with shared
objects   280
How to do it...   280
How it works...   282
There's more...   283

Share members of a managed
object   284
How to do it...   284
How it works...   286

Compare random number
engines   287
How to do it...   287
How it works...   291
There's more...   291

Compare random number
distribution generators   292
How to do it...   292
How it works...   295

9

Concurrency and Parallelism

Technical requirements	298	
Sleep for a specific amount of time	298	
How to do it...	298	
How it works...	299	
There's more...	300	
Use std::thread for concurrency	300	
How to do it...	300	
How it works...	304	
There's more...	305	
Use std::async for concurrency	306	
How to do it...	306	
How it works...	310	
Run STL algorithms in parallel with execution policies	312	
How to do it...	312	
How it works...	314	
Share data safely with mutex and locks	315	
How to do it...	315	

How it works...	323	
There's more...	323	
Share flags and values with std::atomic	324	
How to do it...	324	
How it works...	326	
There's more...	330	
Initialize threads with std::call_once	331	
How to do it...	331	
How it works...	332	
Use std::condition_variable to resolve the producer-consumer problem	333	
How to do it...	333	
How it works...	335	
Implement multiple producers and consumers	337	
How to do it...	337	
How it works...	340	

10

Using the File System

Technical requirements	344	
Specialize std::formatter for the path class	344	
How to do it...	344	
How it works...	346	
Use manipulation functions with path	347	

How to do it...	347	
How it works...	350	
List files in a directory	351	
How to do it...	351	
How it works...	360	
There's more...	360	

Search directories and files with
a grep utility   361
How to do it...   362
How it works...   368
See also...   368

Rename files with regex and
directory_iterator   368

How to do it...   368
How it works...   372
See also...   373

Create a disk usage counter   373
How to do it...   373
How it works...   378

11
A Few More Ideas

Technical requirement   379
Create a trie class for search
suggestions   380
How to do it...   380
How it works...   387

Calculate the error sum of two
vectors   388
How to do it...   388
How it works...   390
There's more...   390

Build your own algorithm: split 391
How to do it...   392
How it works...   395

Leverage existing algorithms:
gather   395
How to do it...   396
How it works...   399

Remove consecutive
whitespace   399
How to do it...   399
How it works...   400

Convert numbers to words   401
How to do it...   402
How it works...   410
There's more...   410

Index

Other Books You May Enjoy

Preface

About this book

The *C++20 STL Cookbook* provides recipes to help you get the most out of the C++ STL (Standard Template Library), including new features introduced with C++20.

C++ is a rich and powerful language. Built upon C, with syntactic extensions for type safety, generic programming, and object-oriented programming, C++ is essentially a low-level language. The STL provides a broad set of higher-level classes, functions, and algorithms to make your programming job easier, more effective, and less prone to error.

I've often said that C++ is five languages cobbled into one. The formal specification includes 1) the entire *C language*, 2) C's cryptic-yet-powerful *macro preprocessor*, 3) a feature-rich *class/object* model, 4) a *generic programming* model called *templates*, and finally, built upon C++ classes and templates, 5) the *STL*.

Prerequisite knowledge

This book presumes that you have a basic understanding of C++, including syntax, structure, data types, classes and objects, templates, and the STL.

The recipes and examples in this book presume that you understand the need to #include certain headers to use library functions. The recipes don't usually list all the necessary headers, preferring to focus on the techniques at hand. You're encouraged to download the example code, which has all the necessary #include directives and other front matter.

You may download the example code from GitHub: https://github.com/PacktPublishing/CPP-20-STL-Cookbook.

These assumptions mean that when you see a piece of code like this:

```
cout << "hello, world\n";
```

You should already know that you'll need to put this code in a `main()` function, you'll need to #include the `<iostream>` header, and `cout` is an object in the `std::` namespace:

```
#include <iostream>
int main() {
    std::cout << "hello, world\n";
}
```

The STL's power is derived from templates *(a brief primer)*

Templates are how C++ does *generic programming*, code that's independent of type while retaining type safety. C++ templates allow you to use tokens as placeholders for types and classes, like this:

```
template<typename T>
T add_em_up(T& lhs, T& rhs) {
    return lhs + rhs;
}
```

A template may be used for classes and/or functions. In this template function, the `T` represents a *generic type*, which allows this code to be used in the context of any compatible class or type:

```
int a{ 72 };  // see braced initialization below
int b{ 47 };
cout << add_em_up<int>(a, b) << "\n";
```

This invokes the template function with an `int` type. This same code can be used with any type or class that supports the + operator.

When the compiler sees a *template invocation*, like add_em_up<int>(a, b), it creates a *specialization*. This is what makes the code type safe. When you invoke add_em_up() with an `int` type, the specialization will look something like this:

```
int add_em_up(int& lhs, int& rhs) {
    return lhs + rhs;
}
```

The specialization takes the template and replaces all instances of the T placeholder with the type from the invocation, in this case, int. The compiler creates a separate specialization of the template each time it's invoked with a different type.

STL *containers*, like vector, stack, or map, along with their *iterators* and other supporting functions and algorithms, are built with templates so they can be used generically while maintaining type safety. This is what makes the STL so flexible. Templates are the *T* in the STL.

This book uses the C++20 standard

The C++ language is standardized by the International Organization for Standardization (ISO) on a roughly three-year cycle. The current standard is called C++20 (which was preceded by C++17, C++14, and C++11 before that). C++20 was approved in September 2020.

C++20 adds many important features to the language and the STL. New features like *format, modules, ranges*, and more will have significant impact on the way we use the STL.

There are also convenience changes. For example, if you want to remove every matching element of a vector, you may have been using the *erase-remove idiom* like this:

```
auto it = std::remove(vec1.begin(), vec1.end(), value);
vec1.erase(it, vec1.end());
```

Starting with C++20 you can use the new std::erase function and do all of that in one simple, optimized function call:

```
std::erase(vec1, value);
```

C++20 has many improvements, both subtle and substantial. In this book, we will cover much of it, especially what's relevant to the STL.

Braced initialization

You may notice that the recipes in this book often use *braced initialization* in place of the more familiar *copy initialization*.

```
std::string name{ "Jimi Hendrix" };   // braced initialization
std::string name = "Jimi Hendrix";    // copy initialization
```

The = operator pulls double-duty as both an assignment and a copy operator. It's common, familiar, and it works, so we've all been using it forever.

The downside of the = operator is that it's also a copy constructor, which often means *implicit narrowing conversion*. This is both inefficient and can lead to unintended type conversions, which can be difficult to debug.

Braced initialization uses the list initialization operator { } (introduced in C++11) to avoid those side effects. It's a good habit to get into and you'll see it a lot in this book.

It's also worth noting that the special case of T{ } is guaranteed to be zero-initialized.

```
int x;        // uninitialized            bad   :(
int x = 0;    // zero (copy constructed)  good  :)
int x{};      // zero (zero-initialized)   best :D
```

The empty brace zero initialization offers a useful shortcut for initializing new variables.

Hiding the std:: namespace

In most instances, the exercises in this book will hide the std:: namespace. This is mostly for page space and readability considerations. We all know that most STL identifiers are in the std:: namespace. I will normally use some form of the using declaration to avoid cluttering the examples with repetitive prefixes. For example, when using cout you can presume I've included a using declaration like this:

```
using std::cout;    // cout is now sans prefix
cout << "Hello, Jimi!\n";
```

I usually *will not show* the using declaration in the recipe listings. This allows us to focus on the purpose of the example.

It is poor practice to import the entire std:: namespace in your code. You should *avoid* a using namespace declaration like this:

```
using namespace std;    // bad. don't do that.
cout << "Hello, Jimi!\n";
```

The std:: namespace includes thousands of identifiers and there's no good reason to clutter your namespace with them. The potential for collisions is not trivial, and can be hard to track down. When you want to use a name without the std:: prefix, the preferred method is to import a single name at a time, as above.

To further avoid namespace collisions, I often use a separate namespace for classes that will be re-used. I tend to use namespace bw for my personal namespace. You may use something else that works for you.

Type aliases with using

This book uses the `using` directive for type aliases instead of `typedef`.

STL classes and types can be verbose at times. A templated iterator class, for example, may look like this:

```
std::vector<std::pair<int,std::string>>::iterator
```

Long type names are not just hard to type, they are prone to error.

One common technique is to abbreviate long type names with `typedef`:

```
typedef std::vector<std::pair<int,std::string>>::iterator
vecit_t
```

This declares an alias for our unwieldy iterator type. `typedef` is inherited from C and its syntax reflects that.

Beginning with C+11, the `using` keyword may be used to create a type alias:

```
using vecit_t =
std::vector<std::pair<int,std::string>>::iterator;
```

In most circumstances, a `using` alias is equivalent to `typedef`. The most significant difference is that a `using` alias may be templated:

```
template<typename T>
using v = std::vector<T>;
v<int> x{};
```

For these reasons, and for the sake of clarity, this book prefers the `using` directive for type aliases.

Abbreviated function templates

Beginning with C++20, an *abbreviated function template* may be specified without the template header. For example:

```
void printc(const auto& c) {
    for (auto i : c) {
        std::cout << i << '\n';
    }
}
```

The auto type in a parameter list works like an anonymous template typename. It is equivalent to:

```
template<typename C>
void printc(const C& c) {
    for (auto i : c) {
        std::cout << i << '\n';
    }
}
```

Though new in C++20, abbreviated function templates have been supported by the major compilers for some time already. This book will use abbreviated function templates in many of the examples.

The C++20 format() function

Until C++20 we've had a choice of using legacy printf() or the STL cout for formatting text. Both have serious flaws but we've used them because they work. Beginning with C++20, the format() function provides text formatting inspired by Python 3's formatter.

This course uses the new STL format() function liberally. Please see *Chapter 1, New C++20 Features*, for a more comprehensive description.

Use the STL to solve real-world problems

The recipes in this book use the STL to provide real-world solutions to real-world problems. They have been designed to rely exclusively on the STL and C++ standard libraries, with no external libraries. This should make it easy for you to experiment and learn without the distractions of installing and configuring third-party code.

Now, let's go have some fun with the STL. *Happy learning!*

Who this book is for

This book is for *intermediate to advanced* C++ programmers who want to get more out of the C++20 Standard Template Library. Basic knowledge of coding and C++ concepts are necessary to get the most out of this book.

What this book covers

Chapter 1, New C++20 Features, introduces the new STL features in C++20. It aims to familiarize you with the new language features so you may use them with the STL.

Chapter 2, General STL Features, discusses modern STL features added in recent C++ versions.

Chapter 3, STL Containers, covers the STL's comprehensive library of containers.

Chapter 4, Compatible Iterators, shows how to use and create STL-compatible iterators.

Chapter 5, Lambda Expressions, covers the use of lambdas with STL functions and algorithms.

Chapter 6, STL Algorithms, provides recipes for using and creating STL-compatible algorithms.

Chapter 7, Strings, Stream, and Formatting, describes the STL string and formatter classes.

Chapter 8, Utility Classes, covers STL utilities for date-and-time, smart pointers, optionals, and more.

Chapter 9, Concurrency and Parallelism, describes support for concurrency, including threads, async, atomic types, and more.

Chapter 10, Using the File System, covers the `std::filesystem` classes and how to put them to use with the latest advancements that came out with C++20.

Chapter 11, A Few More Ideas, provides a few more solutions, including a trie class, string split, and more. This provides advanced examples on how to put the STL to use for real-world problems.

The recipes in this book use the GCC compiler

Unless otherwise noted, most of the recipes in this book have been developed and tested using the GCC compiler, version 11.2, the latest stable version as of this writing.

As I write this, C++20 is still new and is not fully implemented on any available compiler. Of the three major compilers, *GCC* (GNU), *MSVC* (Microsoft), and *Clang* (Apple), the MSVC compiler is furthest along in implementing the new standard. Occasionally, we may run into a feature that is implemented on MSVC or another compiler, but not on GCC, in which case I will note which compiler I used. If a feature is not yet implemented on any available compiler, I will explain that I was unable to test it.

Where possible, code has been tested on one or more of these compilers	
GCC 11.2	Debian Linux 5.16.11
LLVM/Clang 13.1.6	macOS 12.13/Darwin 21.4
Microsoft C++ 19.32.31302	Windows 10

I strongly recommend that you install GCC to follow along with the recipes in this book. GCC is freely available under the GNU General Public License (GPL). The easiest way to get the latest version of GCC is to install *Debian Linux* (also GPL) and use `apt` with the `testing` repository.

If you are using the digital version of this book, we suggest you type the code yourself or download the code from the GitHub repository (link in the next section). This will avoid errors due to copying and pasting formatted code from the e-book.

Download the example code files

You can download the example code files for this book from GitHub at `https://github.com/PacktPublishing/CPP-20-STL-Cookbook`. In the event of updates and errata, code will be updated on the GitHub repository.

We also have other code bundles from our rich catalog of books and videos available at `https://github.com/PacktPublishing/`. Check them out!

Conventions used

There are a number of text conventions used throughout this book.

`Code in text`: Indicates code words in text, database table names, folder names, file names, file extensions, path names, dummy URLs, user input, and Twitter handles. Here is an example: "The `insert()` method takes an `initializer_list` and calls the private function `_insert()`:"

A block of code is set as follows:

```
int main() {
    Frac f{ 5, 3 };
    cout << format("Frac: {}\n", f);
}
```

When we wish to draw your attention to a particular part of a code block, the relevant lines or items are set in bold:

```
for(uint64_t i{ 2 }; i < n / 2; ++i) {
    if(n % i == 0) return false;
}
```

Any command-line input or output is written as follows:

```
$ ./producer-consumer
Got 0 from the queue
Got 1 from the queue
Got 2 from the queue
finished!
```

Bold: Indicates a new term, an important word, or words that you see onscreen. For example, words in menus or dialog boxes appear in the text like this. Here is an example: "Select **System info** from the **Administration** panel."

> **Tips or important notes**
> Appear like this.

Sections

In this book, you will find several headings that appear frequently (*How to do it...*, *How it works...*, *There's more...*, and *See also...*).

To give clear instructions on how to complete a recipe, use these sections as follows:

How to do it...

This section contains the steps required to follow the recipe.

How it works...

This section usually consists of a detailed explanation of what happened in the previous section.

There's more...

This section consists of additional information about the recipe in order to make you more knowledgeable about the recipe.

See also...

This section provides helpful links to other useful information for the recipe.

Get in touch

Feedback from our readers is always welcome.

General feedback: If you have questions about any aspect of this book, mention the book title in the subject of your message and email us at customercare@packtpub.com.

Errata: Although we have taken every care to ensure the accuracy of our content, mistakes do happen. If you have found a mistake in this book, we would be grateful if you would report this to us. Please visit www.packtpub.com/support/errata, selecting your book, clicking on the Errata Submission Form link, and entering the details.

Piracy: If you come across any illegal copies of our works in any form on the Internet, we would be grateful if you would provide us with the location address or website name. Please contact us at copyright@packt.com with a link to the material.

If you are interested in becoming an author: If there is a topic that you have expertise in and you are interested in either writing or contributing to a book, please visit authors.packtpub.com.

Share Your Thoughts

Once you've read *C++20 STL Cookbook*, we'd love to hear your thoughts! Scan the QR code below to go straight to the Amazon review page for this book and share your feedback.

https://packt.link/r/1803248718

Your review is important to us and the tech community and will help us make sure we're delivering excellent quality content.

1
New C++20 Features

This chapter concentrates on some of the more compelling features that C++20 adds to the STL. You can use some of these right away. Others may need to wait for implementation in your favorite compiler. But in the long run, I expect you'll want to know about most of these features.

There are a lot of new additions to the C++20 standard, far more than we could cover here. These are a few that I think will have long-term impact.

In this chapter we will cover the following recipes:

- Format text with the new `format` library
- Use compile-time vectors and strings with `constexpr`
- Safely compare integers of different types
- Use the "spaceship" operator `<=>` for three-way comparisons
- Easily find feature test macros with the `<version>` header
- Create safer templates with concepts and constraints
- Avoid re-compiling template libraries with modules
- Create views into containers with ranges

This chapter aims to familiarize you with these new features in C++20, so you may use them in your own projects and understand them when you encounter them.

Technical requirements

The code files for this chapter can be found on GitHub at `https://github.com/PacktPublishing/CPP-20-STL-Cookbook/tree/main/chap01`.

Format text with the new format library

Until now, if you wanted to format text, you could use either the legacy `printf` functions or the STL `iostream` library. Both have their strengths and flaws.

The `printf`-based functions are inherited from C and have proven efficient, flexible, and convenient for over 50 years. The formatting syntax can look a bit cryptic, but it's simple enough once you get used to it.

```
printf("Hello, %s\n", c_string);
```

The main weakness in `printf` is its lack of type safety. The common `printf()` function (and its relatives) use C's *variadic arguments* model to pass parameters to a formatter. This works great when it works, but it can cause serious problems when a parameter type doesn't match its corresponding format specifier. Modern compilers do as much type-checking as they can, but the model is inherently flawed and the protection can only go so far.

The STL `iostream` library brings type safety at the expense of readability and run-time performance. The `iostream` syntax is unusual, yet familiar. It overloads the *bitwise left-shift operator* (`<<`) to allow a chain of objects, operands, and *formatting manipulators*, which produce the formatted output.

```
cout << "Hello, " << str << endl;
```

The weakness of `iostream` is its complexity, in both syntax and implementation. Building a formatted string can be verbose and obscure. Many of the formatting manipulators must be reset after use, or they create cascading formatting errors that can be difficult to debug. The library itself is vast and complex, resulting in code significantly larger and slower than its `printf` equivalent.

This dismal situation has left C++ programmers with little option but to choose between two flawed systems, until now.

How to do it...

The new `format` library is in the `<format>` header. As of this writing, `format` is implemented only in the *MSVC* (Microsoft) compiler. By the time you read this, it should be available on more systems. Otherwise, you may use its reference implementation as a third-party library from `fmt.dev` (`j.bw.org/fmt`).

The `format` library is modeled on the `str.format()` method from Python 3. *Format strings* are substantially the same as those in Python and, for most purposes, they should be interchangeable. Let's examine some simple examples:

- In its simplest form, the `format()` function takes a `string_view` format string and a *variadic parameter pack* of arguments. It returns a `string`. Its function signature looks like this:

  ```
  template<typename... Args>
  string format(string_view fmt, const Args&... args);
  ```

- The `format()` function returns a `string` representation of virtually any type or value. For example:

  ```
  string who{ "everyone" };
  int ival{ 42 };
  double pi{ std::numbers::pi };

  format("Hello, {}!\n ", who);    // Hello, everyone!
  format("Integer: {}\n ", ival);  // Integer: 42
  format("π: {}\n", pi);           // π: 3.141592653589793
  ```

  The *format string* uses braces { } as a placeholder. With no *format specifiers*, the braces are effectively a type-safe *placeholder* which will convert a value of any compatible type to a reasonable string representation.

- You can include multiple placeholders in your format string, like this:

  ```
  format("Hello {} {}", ival, who);   // Hello 42
                                      // everyone
  ```

- You can specify the order of the replacement values. This could be useful for internationalization:

  ```
  format("Hello {1} {0}", ival, who); // Hello everyone 42
  format("Hola {0} {1}", ival, who);  // Hola 42 everyone
  ```

- You can align values, left (<), right (>), or center (^), with or without a fill character:

```
format("{:.<10}", ival);   // 42........
format("{:.>10}", ival);   // ........42
format("{:.^10}", ival);   // ....42....
```

- You can set the decimal precision of values:

```
format("π: {:.5}", pi);   // π: 3.1416
```

- And much, much more.

It's a rich and complete formatting specification that provides the type-safety of iostream with the performance and simplicity of printf, for the best of both worlds.

How it works...

The format library does not yet include a print() function, which is planned for C++23. The format() function itself returns a string object. So, if you want to print the string, you'll need to use either iostream or cstdio. (Sad face.)

You can print the string using iostream:

```
cout << format("Hello, {}", who) << "\n";
```

Or you may use cstdio:

```
puts(format("Hello, {}", who).c_str());
```

Neither is ideal, but it's not very hard to write a simple print() function. And we can use this process to understand a bit of the format library's inner workings.

Here's a simple implementation of a print() function using the format library:

```
#include <format>
#include <string_view>
#include <cstdio>
```

```
template<typename... Args>
void print(const string_view fmt_str, Args&&... args) {
    auto fmt_args{ make_format_args(args...) };
    string outstr{ vformat(fmt_str, fmt_args) };
    fputs(outstr.c_str(), stdout);
}
```

This uses the same arguments as the format() function. The first argument is a string_view object for the format string. This is followed by a variadic parameter pack for the arguments.

The make_format_args() function takes the parameter pack and returns an object that contains *type-erased values* suitable for formatting. This object is then passed to vformat(), which returns a string suitable for printing. We use fputs() to print the value to the console because it's far more efficient than cout.

We can now use this print() function in place of the cout << format() combination:

```
print("Hello, {}!\n", who);
print("π: {}\n", pi);
print("Hello {1} {0}\n", ival, who);
print("{:.^10}\n", ival);
print("{:.5}\n", pi);
```

Output:

```
Hello, everyone!
π: 3.141592653589793
Hello everyone 42
....42....
3.1416
```

When you eventually get a C++23 complier with print() support, you should be able to simply replace the above print() template function definition with using std::print; and all the print() calls should continue to work.

There's more...

It's nice to have the ability to format strings and primitives, but for the `format` library to be fully functional, it needs customization to work with your own classes.

For example, here's a simple `struct` with two members: a *numerator* and *denominator*. We would like this to print as a fraction:

```
struct Frac {
    long n;
    long d;
};

int main() {
    Frac f{ 5, 3 };
    print("Frac: {}\n", f);
}
```

When I compile this, it leads to a cascade of errors to the effect of, "No user-defined conversion operator...". Cool. So, let's fix it!

When the `format` system encounters an object for *conversion*, it looks for a *specialization* of a `formatter` object with the corresponding type. Standard specializations are included for common objects such as strings and numbers and such.

It's quite simple to create a specialization for our `Frac` type:

```
template<>
struct std::formatter<Frac>
{
    template<typename ParseContext>
    constexpr auto parse(ParseContext& ctx) {
        return ctx.begin();
    }

    template<typename FormatContext>
    auto format(const Frac& f, FormatContext& ctx) {
        return format_to(ctx.out(), "{0:d}/{1:d}",
            f.n, f.d);
    }
};
```

This `formatter` specialization is a class with two short template functions:

- The `parse()` function parses the *format string* from after the colon (or, if there is no colon, after the opening brace) up to but not including the closing brace. (In other words, the part that specifies the type of the object.) It takes a `ParseContext` object and returns an iterator. For our purposes, we can just return the `begin()` iterator because we don't need any new syntax for our *type*. You will rarely need to put anything else here.

- The `format()` function takes a `Frac` object and a `FormatContext` object. It returns an *end iterator*. The `format_to()` function makes this easy. It takes an iterator, a format string, and a parameter pack. In this case, the parameter pack is the two properties of our `Frac` class, the numerator and denominator.

  All we need to do here is provide a simple format string `"{0}/{1}"` and the numerator and denominator values. (The 0 and 1 indicate the position of the parameters. They're not strictly necessary but they could come in handy later.)

Now that we have a specialization for `Frac`, we can pass our object to `print()` to get a readable result:

```
int main() {
    Frac f{ 5, 3 };
    print("Frac: {}\n", f);
}
```

Output:

```
Frac: 5/3
```

The C++20 `format` library solves a long-standing problem by providing a type-safe text formatting library that is both efficient and convenient.

Use compile-time vectors and strings with constexpr

C++20 allows the use of `constexpr` in several new contexts. This provides improved efficiency, in that these things may be evaluated at compile time, instead of run time.

How to do it...

The specification includes the ability to use `string` and `vector` objects in `constexpr` context. It's important to note that these objects may not themselves be declared `constexpr`, but they may be used in a compile-time context:

```
constexpr auto use_string() {
    string str{"string"};
    return str.size();
}
```

You can also use algorithms in `constexpr` context:

```
constexpr auto use_vector() {
    vector<int> vec{ 1, 2, 3, 4, 5};
    return accumulate(begin(vec), end(vec), 0);
}
```

The result of the `accumulate` algorithm is available at compile time and in `constexpr` context.

How it works...

The `constexpr` specifier declares a variable or function that may be *evaluated at compile time*. Before C++20, this was limited to objects initialized with a literal value, or a function within limited constraints. C++17 allowed a somewhat expanded use and C++20 expands it further.

As of C++20, the STL `string` and `vector` classes now have `constexpr`-qualified constructors and destructors, which allow them to be invoked at compile time. This also means that the memory allocated for the `string` or `vector` object *must be freed at compile time*.

For example, this `constexpr` function, which returns a `vector`, will compile without error:

```
constexpr auto use_vector() {
    vector<int> vec{ 1, 2, 3, 4, 5};
    return vec;
}
```

But if you try to use the result in a run-time context, you will get an error about memory that was allocated during constant evaluation:

```
int main() {
    constexpr auto vec = use_vector();
    return vec[0];
}
```

This is because the `vector` object was allocated *and freed* during compilation. So, the object is no longer available at run time.

On the other hand, you can use some `constexpr`-qualified methods from the `vector` object, such as `size()`, at run time:

```
int main() {
    constexpr auto value = use_vector().size();
    return value;
}
```

Because the `size()` method is `constexpr`-qualified, the expression can be evaluated at compile time.

Safely compare integers of different types

Comparing different types of integers may not always produce the expected results. For example:

```
int x{ -3 };
unsigned y{ 7 };
if(x < y) puts("true");
else puts("false");
```

You may expect this code to print `true`, and that's understandable. -3 is usually less than 7. But it will print `false`.

The problem is that x is signed and y is unsigned. The standardized behavior is to convert the signed type to unsigned for the comparison. That seems counterintuitive, doesn't it? Indeed, you cannot reliably convert an unsigned value to a signed value of the same size, because a signed integer uses *two's complement* representation (which uses the most significant bit as a sign). Given the same sized integer, the maximum signed value is half that of an unsigned value. Using this example, if your integers are 32-bits, -3 (signed) becomes FFFF FFFD (hexadecimal), or 4,294,967,293 (unsigned decimal), which is *not less than 7.*

Some compilers may issue a warning when you try to compare signed with unsigned integer values, but most do not.

The C++20 standard includes a set of integer-safe comparison functions in the <utility> header.

How to do it...

The new integer comparison functions are found in the <utility> header. They each take two arguments, which correspond with the left- and right-hand sides of the operator.

```
#include <utility>
int main() {
    int x{ -3 };
    unsigned y{ 7 };
    if(cmp_less(x, y)) puts("true");
    else puts("false");
}
```

The cmp_less() function gives us the result we expect. -3 is less than 7 and the program now prints true.

The <utility> header provides a full complement of integer comparison functions. Assuming our values for x and y, we get these comparisons:

```
cmp_equal(x, y)          // x == y is false
cmp_not_equal(x, y)      // x != y is true
cmp_less(x, y)           // x < y is true
cmp_less_equal(x, y)     // x <= y is true
cmp_greater(x, y)        // x > y is false
cmp_greater_equal(x, y)  // x >= y is false
```

How it works...

Here's the sample implementation of the cmp_less() function from the C++20 standard, to give you a more complete picture of how it works:

```
template< class T, class U >
constexpr bool cmp_less( T t, U u ) noexcept
{
    using UT = make_unsigned_t<T>;
```

```
using UU = make_unsigned_t<U>;
if constexpr (is_signed_v<T> == is_signed_v<U>)
    return t < u;
else if constexpr (is_signed_v<T>)
    return t < 0 ? true : UT(t) < u;
else
    return u < 0 ? false : t < UU(u);
}
```

The UT and UU aliases are declared as make_unsigned_t, a useful helper type introduced with C++17. This allows safe conversions of signed to unsigned types.

The function first tests if both arguments are either signed or unsigned. If so, it returns a simple comparison.

It then tests if either side is signed. If that signed value is less than zero, it can return true or false without performing a comparison. Otherwise, it converts the signed value to unsigned and returns the comparison.

Similar logic is applied to each of the other comparison functions.

Use the "spaceship" operator <=> for three-way comparisons

The *three-way comparison* operator (<=>), commonly called the *spaceship* operator because it looks like a flying saucer in profile, is new in C++20. You may wonder, what's wrong with the existing six comparison operators? Nothing at all, and you will continue using them. The purpose of the spaceship is to provide a unified comparison operator for objects.

The common two-way comparison operators return one of two states, true or false, according to the result of the comparison. For example:

```
const int a = 7;
const int b = 42;
static_assert(a < b);
```

The a < b expression uses the *less-than comparison* operator (<) to test if a is less than b. The comparison operator returns true if the condition is satisfied, or false if not. In this case it returns true because 7 is less than 42.

The three-way comparison works differently. It returns one of three states. The spaceship operator will return a value equal to 0 if the operands are equal, *negative* if the left-hand operand is less than the right-hand operand, or *positive* if the left-hand operand is greater than the right-hand operator.

```
const int a = 7;
const int b = 42;
static_assert((a <=> b) < 0);
```

The returned value is *not an integer*. It's an object from the <compare> header that compares with 0.

If the operands have an integral type, the operator returns a strong_ordering object from the <compare> library.

```
strong_ordering::equal      // operands are equal
strong_ordering::less       // lhs is less than rhs
strong_ordering::greater    // lhs is greater than rhs
```

If the operands have a floating-point type, the operator returns a partial_ordering object:

```
partial_ordering::equivalent  // operands are equivelant
partial_ordering::less        // lhs is less than rhs
partial_ordering::greater     // lhs is greater than rhs
partial_ordering::unordered   // if an operand is unordered
```

These objects are designed to compare against a literal zero (0) with conventional comparison operators (for example, (a <=> b) < 0). This allows the results of the three-way comparison to be more precise than conventional comparisons.

If all of that seems a bit complicated, that's okay. For most applications you will never use the spaceship operator directly. Its real power is in its application as a unified comparison operator for objects. Let's dig a bit deeper.

How to do it...

Let's look at a simple class that encapsulates an integer and provides comparison operators:

```
struct Num {
    int a;
    constexpr bool operator==(const Num& rhs) const
```

```
        { return a == rhs.a; }
    constexpr bool operator!=(const Num& rhs) const
        { return !(a == rhs.a); }
    constexpr bool operator<(const Num& rhs) const
        { return a < rhs.a; }
    constexpr bool operator>(const Num& rhs) const
        { return rhs.a < a; }
    constexpr bool operator<=(const Num& rhs) const
        { return !(rhs.a < a); }
    constexpr bool operator>=(const Num& rhs) const
        { return !(a < rhs.a); }
};
```

It's not uncommon to see a list of comparison operator overloads like this. In fact, it should be even more complicated with *non-member friends* that work with objects on either side of the operator.

With the new spaceship operator, all of this can be accomplished with one overload:

```
#include <compare>
struct Num {
    int a;
    constexpr Num(int a) : a{a} {}
    auto operator<=>(const Num&) const = default;
};
```

Notice that we need to include the <compare> header for the three-way operator return types. Now we can declare some variables and test them with comparisons:

```
constexpr Num a{ 7 };
constexpr Num b{ 7 };
constexpr Num c{ 42 };

int main() {
    static_assert(a < c);
    static_assert(c > a);
    static_assert(a == b);
    static_assert(a <= b);
    static_assert(a <= c);
```

```
        static_assert(c >= a);
        static_assert(a != c);
        puts("done.");
}
```

The compiler will automatically favor the <=> operator for each of the comparisons.

Because the default <=> operator is already constexpr safe, we don't need to declare it as such in our member function.

How it works...

The operator<=> overload takes advantage of a new C++20 concept, *rewritten expressions*. During overload resolution, the compiler rewrites the expression according to a set of rules. For example, if we write a < b, the compiler will rewrite it to (a <=> b < 0) so that it works with our member operator. The compiler will rewrite every relevant comparison expression for the <=> operator, where we haven't included a more specific operator.

In fact, we no longer need a non-member function to handle comparisons with a compatible type on the left-hand side. The compiler will *synthesize* an expression that works with the member operator. For example, if we write 42 > a, the compiler will synthesize an expression with the operators reversed (a <=> 42 < 0) so that it works with our member operator.

> **Note**
>
> The <=> operator has *higher precedence* than the other comparison operators so it will always evaluate first. All comparison operators evaluate left-to-right.

There's more...

The default operator will work just fine with a wide variety of classes, including classes with multiple numeric members of different types:

```
struct Nums {
    int i;
    char c;
    float f;
    double d;
    auto operator<=>(const Nums&) const = default;
};
```

But what if you have a more complex type? Here's an example of a simple fraction class:

```
struct Frac {
    long n;
    long d;
    constexpr Frac(int a, int b) : n{a}, d{b} {}
    constexpr double dbl() const {
        return static_cast<double>(n) /
            static_cast<double>(d);
    }
    constexpr auto operator<=>(const Frac& rhs) const {
        return dbl() <=> rhs.dbl();
    };
    constexpr auto operator==(const Frac& rhs) const {
        return dbl() <=> rhs.dbl() == 0;
    };
};
```

In this case we need to define the operator<=> overload because our data members are not stand-alone scalar values. It's still quite simple and it works just as well.

Notice that we also needed an operator== overload. This is because the expression rewrite rules will not rewrite == and != with a custom operator<=> overload. You only need to define operator==. The compiler will rewrite the != expression as needed.

Now we can define some objects:

```
constexpr Frac a(10,15);    // compares equal with 2/3
constexpr Frac b(2,3);
constexpr Frac c(5,3);
```

And we can test them with normal comparison operators, as expected:

```
int main() {
    static_assert(a < c);
    static_assert(c > a);
    static_assert(a == b);
    static_assert(a <= b);
    static_assert(a <= c);
```

```
        static_assert(c >= a);
        static_assert(a != c);
}
```

The power of the spaceship operator is in its ability to streamline comparison overloads in your classes. It improves both simplicity and efficiency when compared to overloading each operator independently.

Easily find feature test macros with the <version> header

C++ has provided some form of feature test macros for as long as new features have been added. Beginning with C++20, the process is standardized, and all *library feature* test macros have been added to the <version> header. This will make it much easier to test for a new feature in your code.

This is a useful feature and it's very simple to use.

How to do it...

All feature test macros begin with the prefix __cpp_. Library features begin with __cpp_ lib_. Language feature test macros are typically defined by the compiler. Library feature test macros are defined in the new <version> header. Use them as you would any other preprocessor macro:

```
#include <version>
#ifdef __cpp_lib_three_way_comparison
#    include <compare>
#else
#    error Spaceship has not yet landed
#endif
```

In some cases, you can use the __has_include preprocessor operator (introduced in C++17) to test for the existence of an include file.

```
#if __has_include(<compare>)
#    include <compare>
#else
#    error Spaceship has not yet landed
#endif
```

You can use __has_include to test for the existence of any header file. Because it's a preprocessor directive, it doesn't require a header of its own to work.

How it works...

Generally, you can use the feature test macros by testing for a non-zero value using #ifdef or #if defined. Each of the feature test macros has a non-zero value that corresponds to the year and month it was accepted by the standards committee. For example, the __cpp_lib_three_way_comparison macro has a value of 201907. This means that it was accepted in July 2019.

```
#include <version>
#ifdef __cpp_lib_three_way_comparison
    cout << "value is " << __cpp_lib_three_way_comparison
        << "\n"
#endif
```

Output:

```
$ ./working
value is 201907
```

The value of the macro may be useful in some obscure cases where a feature has changed and you're dependent upon the changes. For most purposes, you can safely ignore the value and just test for non-zero with #ifdef.

Several websites maintain a complete list of feature test macros. I tend to use *cppreference* (https://j.bw.org/cppfeature) but there are others.

Create safer templates with concepts and constraints

Templates are great for writing code that works with different types. For example, this function will work with any numeric type:

```
template <typename T>
T arg42(const T & arg) {
    return arg + 42;
}
```

But what happens when you try to call it with a non-numeric type?

```
const char * n = "7";
cout << "result is " << arg42(n) << "\n";
```

Output:

```
Result is ion
```

This compiles and runs without error, but the result is unpredictable. In fact, the call is dangerous and it could easily crash or become a vulnerability. I would much prefer the compiler generate an error message so I can fix the code.

Now, with concepts, I can write it like this:

```
template <typename T>
requires Numeric<T>
T arg42(const T & arg) {
    return arg + 42;
}
```

The `requires` keyword is new for C++20. It applies constraints to a template. `Numeric` is the name of a *concept* that only accepts integer and floating-point types. Now, when I compile this code with a non-numeric parameter, I get a reasonable compiler error:

```
error: 'arg42': no matching overloaded function found
error: 'arg42': the associated constraints are not satisfied
```

Error messages like this are far more useful than most compiler errors.

Let's take a closer look at how to use concepts and constraints in your code.

How to do it...

A concept is simply a named constraint. The `Numeric` concept from above looks like this:

```
#include <concepts>
template <typename T>
concept Numeric = integral<T> || floating_point<T>;
```

This *concept* requires a type T, which satisfies either the `std::integral` or `std::floating_point` predefined concepts. These concepts are included in the `<concepts>` header.

Concepts and constraints may be used in class templates, function templates, or variable templates. We've seen a constrained function template, now here's a simple constrained class template example:

```
template<typename T>
requires Numeric<T>
struct Num {
    T n;
    Num(T n) : n{n} {}
};
```

And here's a simple variable template example:

```
template<typename T>
requires floating_point<T>
T pi{3.1415926535897932385L};
```

You can use concepts and constraints on any template. Let's consider some further examples. We'll be using function templates in these examples for simplicity.

- A constraint may use concepts or *type traits* to evaluate the characteristics of a type. You may use any of the type traits found in the <type_traits> header, so long as it returns a bool.

  For example:

  ```
  template<typename T>
  requires is_integral<T>::value  // value is bool
  constexpr double avg(vector<T> const& vec) {
      double sum{ accumulate(vec.begin(), vec.end(),
        0.0)
      };
      return sum / vec.size();
  }
  ```

- The requires keyword is new in C++20. It introduces a constraint for the template arguments. In this example, the constraint expression tests the template argument against the type trait is_integral.

- You can use one of the pre-defined traits found in the `<type_traits>` header, or you can define your own, just as you would a template variable. For use in constraints, the variable must return `constexpr bool`. For example:

```
template<typename T>
constexpr bool is_gt_byte{ sizeof(T) > 1 };
```

This defines a type trait called `is_gt_byte`. This trait uses the `sizeof` operator to test if the type `T` is larger than 1 byte.

- A *concept* is simply a named set of constraints. For example:

```
template<typename T>
concept Numeric = is_gt_byte<T> &&
    (integral<T> || floating_point<T>);
```

This defines a concept named `Numeric`. It uses our `is_gt_byte` constraint, along with the `floating_point` and `integral` concepts from the `<concepts>` header. We can use it to constrain a template to only accept numeric types that are greater than 1 byte in size.

```
template<Numeric T>
T arg42(const T & arg) {
    return arg + 42;
}
```

You'll notice that I've applied the constraint in the template declaration, rather than on a separate line in a `requires` expression. There are a few ways to apply a concept. Let's look at how this works.

How it works...

There are several different ways you can apply a concept or constraint:

- You can apply a concept or constraint with the `requires` keyword:

```
template<typename T>
requires Numeric<T>
T arg42(const T & arg) {
    return arg + 42;
}
```

- You can apply a concept in the template declaration:

```
template<Numeric T>
T arg42(const T & arg) {
    return arg + 42;
}
```

- You can use the `requires` keyword in a function signature:

```
template<typename T>
T arg42(const T & arg) requires Numeric<T> {
    return arg + 42;
}
```

- Or you can use a concept in a parameter list for an abbreviated function template:

```
auto arg42(Numeric auto & arg) {
    return arg + 42;
}
```

For many purposes, choosing one of these strategies may be a matter of style. And there are circumstances where one may be a better option than another.

There's more...

The standard uses the terms *conjunction*, *disjunction*, and *atomic*, to describe types of expressions that can be used to construct a constraint. Let's define these terms.

You can combine concepts and constraints using the && and || operators. These combinations are called *conjunctions* and *disjunctions*, respectively. You can think of them as logical *AND* and *OR*.

A *constraint conjunction* is formed by using the && operator with two constraints:

```
Template <typename T>
concept Integral_s = Integral<T> && is_signed<T>::value;
```

A conjunction is satisfied only if both sides of the && operator are satisfied. It is evaluated left-to-right. The operands of a conjunction are short-circuited, that is, if the left side constraint is not satisfied the right side will not be evaluated.

A *constraint disjunction* is formed by using the || operator with two constraints:

```
Template <typename T>
concept Numeric = integral<T> || floating_point<T>;
```

A disjunction is satisfied if either side of the || operator is satisfied. It is evaluated left-to-right. The operands of a conjunction are short-circuited, that is, if the left side constraint is satisfied the right side will not be evaluated.

An *atomic constraint* is an expression that returns a bool type, which cannot be further decomposed. In other words, it is not a conjunction or a disjunction.

```
template<typename T>
concept is_gt_byte = sizeof(T) > 1;
```

You can also use the logical ! (*NOT*) operator in an atomic constraint:

```
template<typename T>
concept is_byte = !is_gt_byte<T>;
```

As expected, the ! operator inverts the value of the bool expression to the right of the !.

Of course, we can combine all these expression types into a larger expression. We see examples of each of these constraint expressions in the following example:

```
template<typename T>
concept Numeric = is_gt_byte<T> &&
    (integral<T> || floating_point<T>);
```

Let's break this down. The sub-expression, (integral<T> || floating_point<T>) is a *disjunction*. The sub-expression, is_gt_byte<T> && (...) is a *conjunction*. And each of the sub-expressions integral<T>, floating_point<T>, and is_gt_byte<T>, are *atomic*.

These distinctions are mostly for descriptive purposes. While it's good to understand the details, as you write your code, it's safe to think of them as simple logical ||, &&, and ! operators.

Concepts and constraints are a welcome addition to the C++ standard and I'm looking forward to using them in my future projects.

Avoid re-compiling template libraries with modules

Header files have been around since the very beginning of the C language. Originally, they were mainly used for *text substitution macros* and linking *external symbols* between translation units. With the introduction of templates, C++ leveraged header files to carry actual code. Because templates need to be recompiled for changes in specializations, we've been carrying them around in header files for many years. As the STL continues to grow over the years, these header files have grown as well. The situation has become unwieldy and is no longer scalable for the future.

Header files typically contain a lot more than templates. They often contain configuration macros and other symbols that are required for system purposes, but not useful for the application. As the number of headers grows, the number of opportunities for symbol collisions grows as well. This is even more problematic when you consider the abundance of macros, which are not subject to namespace restrictions nor any form of type safety.

C++20 addresses this problem with *modules*.

How to do it...

You may be used to creating header files like this:

```
#ifndef BW_MATH
#define BW_MATH
namespace bw {
    template<typename T>
    T add(T lhs, T rhs) {
        return lhs + rhs;
    }
}
#endif // BW_MATH
```

This minimalist example illustrates several of the problems that modules address. The BW_MATH symbol is used as an *include guard*. Its only purpose is to prevent the header file from being included more than once, yet its symbol is carried throughout the translation unit. When you include this header in your source file, it may look like this:

```
#include "bw-math.h"
#include <format>
#include <string>
#include <iostream>
```

Now that BW_MATH symbol is available to every other header you've included, and every header included by the other headers, and on and on. That's a lot of opportunities for collision. And keep in mind, the compiler cannot check for these collisions. They're macros. That means they're translated by the preprocessor before the compiler ever has a chance to see them.

Now we get to the actual point of the header, the template function:

```
template<typename T>
T add(T lhs, T rhs) {
    return lhs + rhs;
}
```

Because it's a template, every time you use the add() function the compiler must create a separate specialization. This means that the template function must be parsed and specialized each time it's invoked. That's why templates go in header files; the source must be available at compile time. As the STL grows and evolves, with its many large template classes and functions, this becomes a significant scalability problem.

Modules solve these problems and more.

As a module, bw-math.h becomes bw-math.ixx (in the MSVC naming convention) and it looks like this:

```
export module bw_math;
export template<typename T>
T add(T lhs, T rhs) {
    return lhs + rhs;
}
```

Notice that the only symbols exported are the name of the module, bw_math, and the name of the function, add(). This keeps the namespace clean.

The usage is cleaner as well. When we use it in module-test.cpp, it looks like this:

```
import bw_math;
import std.core;

int main() {
    double f = add(1.23, 4.56);
    int i = add(7, 42);
    string s = add<string>("one ", "two");
```

```
cout <<
    "double: " << f << "\n" <<
    "int: " << i << "\n" <<
    "string: " << s << "\n";
}
```

The `import` declarations are used where we might otherwise use `#include` preprocessor directives. These import the symbol tables from the modules for linkage.

The output of our example looks like this:

```
$ ./module-test
double: 5.79
int: 49
string: one two
```

The module version works exactly as it did in a header file, only cleaner and more efficiently.

> **Note**
>
> The compiled module includes a separate *metadata file* (*module-name* . `ifc` in the MSVC naming convention), which describes the module interface. This allows the module to support templates. The metadata includes sufficient information for the compiler to create template specializations.

How it works...

The `import` and `export` declarations are at the core of the *Modules* implementation. Let's take another look at the `bw-math.ixx` module:

```
export module bw_math;
export template<typename T>
T add(T lhs, T rhs) {
    return lhs + rhs;
}
```

Notice the two `export` declarations. The first exports the module itself with `export module bw_math`. This declares the translation unit as a module. There must be a module declaration at the top of every module file, and before any other statements. The second `export` makes the function name `add()` available to the *module consumer*.

If your module requires #include directives, or other global fragments, you will need to first declare your module with a simple module declaration like this:

```
module;
#define SOME_MACRO 42
#include <stdlib.h>
export module bw_math;
...
```

The module; declaration, on a line by itself at the top of the file, introduces a *global module fragment*. Only preprocessor directives may appear in the global module fragment. This must be immediately followed by a standard module declaration (export module bw_math;) and the rest of the module content. Let's look closer at how this works:

- An export declaration makes a symbol visible to the *module consumer*, that is, the code that imports the module. Symbols default to private.

    ```
    export int a{7};   // visible to consumer
    int b{42};         // not visible
    ```

- You can export a block, like this:

    ```
    export {
        int a() { return 7; };    // visible
        int b() { return 42; };   // also visible
    }
    ```

- You can export a namespace:

    ```
    export namespace bw {  // all of the bw namespace is
    visible
        template<typename T>
        T add(T lhs, T rhs) {  // visible as bw::add()
            return lhs + rhs;
        }
    }
    ```

- Or, you can export individual symbols from a namespace:

```
namespace bw {   // all of the bw namespace is visible
    export template<typename T>
    T add(T lhs, T rhs) {   // visible as bw::add()
        return lhs + rhs;
    }
}
```

- An `import` declaration imports a module in the *consumer*:

```
import bw_math;
int main() {
    double f = bw::add(1.23, 4.56);
    int i = bw::add(7, 42);
    string s = bw::add<string>("one ", "two");
}
```

- You can even import a module and export it to the consumer to pass it along:

```
export module bw_math;
export import std.core;
```

The export keyword must precede the `import` keyword.

The `std.core` module is now available for the consumer:

```
import bw_math;
using std::cout, std::string, std::format;

int main() {
    double f = bw::add(1.23, 4.56);
    int i = bw::add(7, 42);
    string s = bw::add<string>("one ", "two");

    cout <<
        format("double {} \n", f) <<
        format("int {} \n", i) <<
        format("string {} \n", s);
}
```

As you can see, modules are a simple, straightforward alternative to header files. I know a lot of us are looking forward to the broad availability of modules. I can see this greatly reducing our dependency on header files.

> **Note**
>
> At the time of writing, the only complete implementation of modules is in a *preview release* of MSVC. The module filename extension (`.ixx`) may be different for other compilers. Also, the amalgamated `std.core` module is part of how MSVC implements the STL as modules in this release. Other compilers may not use this convention. Some details may change when fully compliant implementations are released.

In the example files, I've included a module version of my `format`-based `print()` function. This works on the current preview release of MSVC. It may require some small modifications to make it work on other systems, once they support enough of the modules specification.

Create views into containers with ranges

The new `ranges` library is one of the more significant additions to C++20. It provides a new paradigm for filtering and processing containers. Ranges provide clean and intuitive building blocks for more effective and readable code.

Let's start by defining a few terms:

- A **Range** is a collection of objects which can be iterated. In other words, any structure that supports the `begin()` and `end()` iterators is a range. This includes most STL containers.

- A **View** is a range that transforms another underlying range. Views are lazy, meaning they only operate as the range iterates. A view returns data from the underlying range and does not own any data itself. Views operate in *O(1)* constant time.

- A **View Adapter** is an object that takes a range and returns a view object. A view adapter may be chained with other view adapters using the | operator.

> **Note**
>
> The `<ranges>` library uses the `std::ranges` and the
> `std::ranges::view` namespaces. Recognizing that this is cumbersome,
> the standard includes an alias for `std::ranges::view` as the simply,
> `std::view`. I still find that cumbersome. For this recipe I will use the
> following aliases, to save space and because I find it more elegant:
>
> ```
> namespace ranges = std::ranges;   // save the
> fingers!
>
> namespace views = std::ranges::views;
> ```
>
> This applies to all the code in this recipe.

How to do it...

The `ranges` and `views` classes are in the `<ranges>` header. Let's look at how you can use them:

- A *View* is applied to a *Range*, like this:

  ```
  const vector<int> nums{ 1, 2, 3, 4, 5, 6, 7, 8, 9, 10 };
  auto result = ranges::take_view(nums, 5);
  for (auto v: result) cout << v << " ";
  ```

Output:

```
1 2 3 4 5
```

`ranges::take_view(range, n)` is a view that returns the first *n* elements.

You may also use the *view adapter* version of `take_view()`:

```
auto result = nums | views::take(5);
for (auto v: result) cout << v << " ";
```

Output:

```
1 2 3 4 5
```

View adapters are in the `std::ranges::views` namespace. A *view adapter*
takes the *range operand* from the left-hand side of the `|` operator, much like the
`iostreams` usage of the `<<` operator. The `|` operands are evaluated left-to-right.

- Because a view adapter is *iterable*, it also qualifies as a range. This allows them to be applied serially, like this:

```
const vector<int> nums{ 1, 2, 3, 4, 5, 6, 7, 8, 9, 10 };
auto result = nums | views::take(5) |
    views::reverse;
```

Output:

```
5 4 3 2 1
```

- The `filter()` view uses a predicate function:

```
auto result = nums |
    views::filter([](int i){ return 0 == i % 2; });
```

Output:

```
2 4 6 8 10
```

- The `transform()` view uses a transformation function:

```
auto result = nums |
    views::transform([](int i){ return i * i; });
```

Output:

```
1 4 9 16 25 36 49 64 81 100
```

- Of course, these views and adapters work on ranges of any type:

```
cosnt vector<string>
words{ "one", "two", "three", "four", "five" };
auto result = words | views::reverse;
```

Output:

```
five four three two one
```

- The ranges library also includes a few *range factories*. The `iota` factory will generate an incrementing series of values:

```
auto rnums = views::iota(1, 10);
```

Output:

```
1 2 3 4 5 6 7 8 9
```

The iota(value, bound) function generates a sequence starting with value and ending *before* bound. If bound is omitted, the sequence is infinite:

```
auto rnums = views::iota(1) | views::take(200);
```

Output:

```
1 2 3 4 5 6 7 8 9 10 11 12 [...] 196 197 198 199 200
```

Ranges, *Views*, and *View Adapters* are incredibly flexible and useful. Let's take a deeper look for a better understanding.

How it works...

To satisfy the basic requirements for a *Range*, an object must have at least two iterators, begin() and end(), where the end() iterator is a sentinel, used to determine the end point of a range. Most STL containers qualify as ranges, including string, vector, array, map, and others, with the notable exception of container-adapters, like stack and queue, which don't have begin and end iterators.

A *View* is an object which operates on a range and returns a modified range. A view operates lazily, and contains no data of its own. Instead of keeping a copy of the underlying data, it simply returns iterators to underlying elements as needed. Let's examine this code snippet:

```
vector<int> vi { 0, 1, 2, 3, 4, 5 };
ranges::take_view tv{vi, 2};
for(int i : tv) {
    cout << i << " ";
}
cout << "\n";
```

Output:

```
0 1
```

In this example, the take_view object takes two parameters, a *range* (in this case, a vector<int> object), and a *count*. The result is a *view* with the first *count* objects from the vector. At evaluation time, during the iteration of the for loop, the take_view object simply returns iterators that point to elements of the vector object, as needed. The vector object is not modified in this process.

Many of the views in the `ranges` namespace have corresponding *range adapters* in the `views` namespace. These adapters may be used with the *bitwise or* (`|`) operator, as a pipe, like this:

```
vector<int> vi { 0, 1, 2, 3, 4, 5 };
auto tview = vi | views::take(2);
for(int i : tview) {
    cout << i << " ";
}
cout << "\n";
```

Output:

```
0 1
```

As expected, the `|` operator evaluates left to right. And because the result of the range adapter is another range, these adapter expressions may be chained:

```
vector<int> vi { 0, 1, 2, 3, 4, 5, 6, 7, 8, 9 };
auto tview = vi | views::reverse | views::take(5);
for(int i : tview) {
    cout << i << " ";
}
cout << "\n";
```

Output:

```
9 8 7 6 5
```

The library includes a `filter` view that is used with a *predicate*, for defining simple filters:

```
vector<int> vi { 0, 1, 2, 3, 4, 5, 6, 7, 8, 9 };
auto even = [](long i) { return 0 == i % 2; };
auto tview = vi | views::filter(even);
```

Output:

```
0 2 4 6 8
```

Also included, is a `transform` view that is used with a *transform function* for transforming results:

```
vector<int> vi { 0, 1, 2, 3, 4, 5, 6, 7, 8, 9 };
auto even = [](int i) { return 0 == i % 2; };
auto x2 = [](auto i) { return i * 2; };
auto tview = vi | views::filter(even) | views::transform(x2);
```

Output:

```
0 4 8 12 16
```

There are quite a few useful views and view adapters in the library. Please check your favorite reference site, or (`https://j.bw.org/ranges`) for a complete list.

There's more...

Beginning with C++20, most of the algorithms in the `<algorithm>` header include versions for use with `ranges`. These versions are still in the `<algorithm>` header, but in the `std::ranges` namespace. This distinguishes them from the legacy algorithms.

This means that, instead of calling an algorithm with two iterators:

```
sort(v.begin(), v.end());
```

You can now call it with just a range, like this:

```
ranges::sort(v);
```

That's certainly more convenient, but how does it really help?

Consider the case where you want to sort part of a vector, you could do that the old way, like this:

```
sort(v.begin() + 5, v.end());
```

This would sort the elements of the vector after the first 5. With the `ranges` version, you can use a view to skip the first 5 elements:

```
ranges::sort(views::drop(v, 5));
```

You can even combine views:

```
ranges::sort(views::drop(views::reverse(v), 5));
```

In fact, you can even use range adapters as the argument to `ranges::sort`:

```
ranges::sort(v | views::reverse | views::drop(5));
```

In contrast, if you wanted to do this with the traditional `sort` algorithm and vector iterators, it would look something like this:

```
sort(v.rbegin() + 5, v.rend());
```

While that's certainly shorter, and not impossible to understand, I find the range adapters version far more intuitive.

You can find a complete list of algorithms that have been constrained to work with ranges on the *cppreference* site (`https://j.bw.org/algoranges`).

In this recipe, we've only scratched the surface of *Ranges* and *Views*. This feature is the culmination of over a decade of work by many different teams, and I expect it to fundamentally change the way we use containers in the STL.

2
General STL Features

This chapter is a general potpourri of STL features and techniques. These are mostly new features introduced over the past few years, which may not yet be widely used. These are useful techniques that will improve the simplicity and readability of your code.

In this chapter we will cover the following recipes:

- Use the new `span` class to make your C-arrays safer
- Use structured binding to return multiple values
- Initialize variables within `if` and `switch` statements
- Use template argument deduction for simplicity and clarity
- Use `if constexpr` to simplify compile-time decisions

Technical requirements

You can find the code for this chapter on GitHub at `https://github.com/PacktPublishing/CPP-20-STL-Cookbook/tree/main/chap02`.

Use the new span class to make your C-arrays safer

New for C++20, the `std::span` class is a simple wrapper that creates a view over a contiguous sequence of objects. The `span` doesn't own any of its own data, it refers to the data in the underlying structure. Think of it as `string_view` for C-arrays. The underlying structure may be a *C-array*, a `vector`, or an STL `array`.

How to do it...

You can create a span from any compatible contiguous-storage structure. The most common use case will involve a C-array. For example, if you try to pass a C-array directly to a function, the array is demoted to a pointer and the function has no easy way to know the size of the array:

```
void parray(int * a);   // loses size information
```

If you define your function with a `span` parameter, you can pass it a C-array and it will be promoted to `span`. Here's a template function that takes a `span` and prints out the size in elements and in bytes:

```
template<typename T>
void pspan(span<T> s) {
    cout << format("number of elements: {}\n", s.size());
    cout << format("size of span: {}\n", s.size_bytes());
    for(auto e : s) cout << format("{} ", e);
    cout << "\n";
}
```

You can pass a C-array to this function and it's automatically promoted to `span`:

```
int main() {
    int carray[] { 1, 2, 3, 4, 5, 6, 7, 8, 9, 10 };
    pspan<int>(carray);
}
```

Output:

```
number of elements: 10
number of bytes: 40
1 2 3 4 5 6 7 8 9 10
```

The purpose of span is to encapsulate the raw data to provide a measure of safety and utility, with a minimum of overhead.

How it works...

The span class itself doesn't own any data. The data belongs to the underlying data structure. The span is essentially a view over the underlying data. It also provides some useful member functions.

Defined in the <span> header, the span class looks something like:

```
template<typename T, size_t Extent = std::dynamic_extent>
class span {
    T * data;
    size_t count;
public:
    ...
};
```

The Extent parameter is a constant of type constexpr size_t, which is computed at compile time. It's either the number of elements in the underlying data or the std::dynamic_extent constant, which indicates that the size is variable. This allows span to use an underlying structure like a vector, which may not always be the same size.

All member functions are `constexpr` and `const` qualified. Member functions include:

Public member function	Return value
`T& front()`	The first element
`T& back()`	The last element
`T& operator[]`	An indexed element
`T* data()`	A pointer to the beginning of the sequence
`iterator begin()`	An iterator to the first element
`iterator end()`	An iterator following the last element
`iterator rbegin()`	A reverse iterator to the first element
`iterator rend()`	A reverse iterator following the last element
`size_t size()`	The number of elements in the sequence
`size_t size_bytes()`	The number of bytes in the sequence
`bool empty()`	True if empty
`span<T> first<count>()` `span<T> first(count)`	A sub-span consisting of the first count elements of the sequence
`span<T> last<count>()` `span<T> last(count)`	Returns a sub-span of the last count elements
`span<T> subspan(offset, count)`	Returns a sub-span consisting of count elements beginning at offset

> **Important Note**
>
> The `span` class is but a simple wrapper that performs no bounds checking. So, if you try to access element $n+1$ in a `span` of n elements, the result is *undefined*, which is tech for, "Bad. Don't do that."

Use structured binding to return multiple values

Structured binding makes it easy to unpack the values of a structure into separate variables, improving the readability of your code.

With structured binding you can directly assign the member values to variables like this:

```
things_pair<int,int> { 47, 9 };
auto [this, that] = things_pair;
cout << format("{} {}\n", this, that);
```

Output:

```
47 9
```

How to do it...

- *Structured binding* works with `pair`, `tuple`, `array`, and `struct`. Beginning with C++20, this includes bit-fields. This example uses a C-array:

```
int nums[] { 1, 2, 3, 4, 5 };
auto [ a, b, c, d, e ] = nums;
cout << format("{} {} {} {} {}\n", a, b, c, d, e);
```

Output:

```
1 2 3 4 5
```

Because the structured binding uses *automatic type deduction*, its type must be `auto`. The names of the individual variables are within the square brackets, `[ a, b, c, d, e ]`.

In this example the `int` C-array nums holds five values. These five values are assigned to the variables (a, b, c, d, and e) using *structured binding*.

- This also works with an STL `array` object:

```
array<int,5> nums { 1, 2, 3, 4, 5 };
auto [ a, b, c, d, e ] = nums;
cout << format("{} {} {} {} {}\n", a, b, c, d, e);
```

Output:

```
1 2 3 4 5
```

- Or you can use it with a `tuple`:

```
tuple<int, double, string> nums{ 1, 2.7, "three" };
auto [ a, b, c ] = nums;
cout << format("{} {} {}\n", a, b, c);
```

Output:

```
1 2.7 three
```

- When you use it with a `struct` it will take the variables in the order they're defined:

```
struct Things { int i{}; double d{}; string s{}; };
Things nums{ 1, 2.7, "three" };
auto [ a, b, c ] = nums;
cout << format ("{} {} {}\n", a, b, c);
```

Output:

```
1 2.7 three
```

- You can use a reference with a structured binding, which allows you to modify the values in the bound container, while avoiding duplication of the data:

```
array<int,5> nums { 1, 2, 3, 4, 5 };
auto& [ a, b, c, d, e ] = nums;
cout << format ("{} {}\n", nums[2], c);
c = 47;
cout << format ("{} {}\n", nums[2], c);
```

Output:

```
3 3
47 47
```

Because the variables are bound as a reference, you can assign a value to `c` and it will change the value in the array as well (nums [2]).

- You can declare the array `const` to prevent values from being changed:

```
const array<int,5> nums { 1, 2, 3, 4, 5 };
auto& [ a, b, c, d, e ] = nums;
c = 47;    // this is now an error
```

Or you can declare the binding `const` for the same effect, while allowing the array to be changed elsewhere and still avoid copying data:

```
array<int,5> nums { 1, 2, 3, 4, 5 };
const auto& [ a, b, c, d, e ] = nums;
c = 47;    // this is also an error
```

How it works...

Structured binding uses *automatic type deduction* to unpack the structure into your variables. It determines the type of each value independently, and assigns a corresponding type to each variable.

- Because structured binding uses automatic type deduction, you cannot specify a type for the binding. You must use `auto`. You should get a reasonable error message if you try to use a type for the binding:

```
array<int,5> nums { 1, 2, 3, 4, 5 };
int [ a, b, c, d, e ] = nums;
```

Output:

```
error: structured binding declaration cannot have type
'int'
note: type must be cv-qualified 'auto' or reference to
cv-qualified 'auto'
```

Above is the error from GCC when I try to use `int` with the structured binding declaration.

- It's common to use structured binding for a return type from a function:

```
struct div_result {
    long quo;
    long rem;
};

div_result int_div(const long & num, const long & denom)
{
    struct div_result r{};
    r.quo = num / denom;
    r.rem = num % denom;
    return r;
}

int main() {
    auto [quo, rem] = int_div(47, 5);
    cout << format("quotient: {}, remainder {}\n",
        quo, rem);
}
```

Output:

```
quotient: 9, remainder 2
```

• Because the map container classes return a pair for each element, it can be convenient to use structured binding to retrieve key/value pairs:

```
map<string, uint64_t> inhabitants {
    { "humans",   7000000000 },
    { "pokemon", 17863376 },
    { "klingons",   24246291 },
    { "cats",    1086881528 }
};

// I like commas
string make_commas(const uint64_t num) {
    string s{ std::to_string(num) };
    for(int l = s.length() - 3; l > 0; l -= 3) {
        s.insert(l, ",");
    }
    return s;
}

int main() {
    for(const auto & [creature, pop] : inhabitants) {
        cout << format("there are {} {}\n",
            make_commas(pop), creature);
    }
}
```

Output:

```
there are 1,086,881,528 cats
there are 7,000,000,000 humans
there are 24,246,291 klingons
there are 17,863,376 pokemon
```

Using structured binding to unpack structures should make your code clearer and easier to maintain.

Initialize variables within if and switch statements

Beginning with C++17, if and switch now have initialization syntax, much like the for loop has had since C99. This allows you to limit the scope of variables used within the condition.

How to do it...

You may be accustomed to code like this:

```
const string artist{ "Jimi Hendrix" };
size_t pos{ artist.find("Jimi") };
if(pos != string::npos) {
    cout << "found\n";
} else {
    cout << "not found\n";
}
```

This leaves the variable pos exposed outside the scope of the conditional statement, where it needs to be managed, or it can collide with other attempts to use the same symbol.

Now you can put the initialization expression inside the if condition:

```
if(size_t pos{ artist.find("Jimi") }; pos != string::npos) {
    cout << "found\n";
} else {
    cout << "not found\n";
}
```

Now the scope of the pos variable is confined to the scope of the conditional. This keeps your namespace clean and manageable.

How it works...

The initializer expression can be used in either `if` or `switch` statements. Here are some examples of each.

- Use an initializer expression with an `if` statement:

```
if(auto var{ init_value }; condition) {
    // var is visible
} else {
    // var is visible
}
// var is NOT visible
```

The variable defined in the initializer expression is visible within the scope of the entire `if` statement, including the `else` clause. Once control flows out of the `if` statement scope, the variable will no longer be visible, and any relevant destructors will be called.

- Use an initializer expression with a `switch` statement:

```
switch(auto var{ init_value }; var) {
case 1: ...
case 2: ...
case 3: ...

...
Default: ...
}
// var is NOT visible
```

The variable defined in the initializer expression is visible within the scope of the entire `switch` statement, including all the `case` clauses and the `default` clause, if included. Once control flows out of the `switch` statement scope, the variable will no longer be visible, and any relevant destructors will be called.

There's more...

One interesting use case is to limit the scope of a `lock_guard` that's locking a mutex. This becomes simple with an initializer expression:

```
if (lock_guard<mutex> lg{ my_mutex }; condition) {
    // interesting things happen here
}
```

The `lock_guard` locks the mutex in its constructor and unlocks it in its destructor. Now the `lock_guard` will be automatically destroyed when it runs out of the scope of the `if` statement. In the past you would have had to delete it or enclose the whole `if` statement in an extra block of braces.

Another use case could be using a legacy interface that uses output parameters, like this one from SQLite:

```
if(
    sqlite3_stmt** stmt,
    auto rc = sqlite3_prepare_v2(db, sql, -1, &_stmt,
        nullptr);
    !rc) {
            // do SQL things
} else {   // handle the error
    // use the error code
    return 0;
}
```

Here I can keep the statement handle and the error code localized to the scope of the `if` statement. Otherwise, I would need to manage those objects globally.

Using initializer expressions will help keep your code tight and uncluttered, more compact, and easier to read. Refactoring and managing your code will also become easier.

Use template argument deduction for simplicity and clarity

Template argument deduction occurs when the *types* of the arguments to a template function, or class template constructor (beginning with C++17), are clear enough to be understood by the compiler without the use of template arguments. There are certain rules to this feature, but it's mostly intuitive.

How to do it...

In general, template argument deduction happens automatically when you use a template with clearly compatible arguments. Let's consider some examples.

- In a function template, argument deduction usually looks something like this:

```
template<typename T>
const char * f(const T a) {
    return typeid(T).name();
}
int main() {
    cout << format("T is {}\n", f(47));
    cout << format("T is {}\n", f(47L));
    cout << format("T is {}\n", f(47.0));
    cout << format("T is {}\n", f("47"));
    cout << format("T is {}\n", f("47"s));
}
```

Output:

```
T is int
T is long
T is double
T is char const *
T is class std::basic_string<char...
```

Because the types are easily discernable there is no reason to specify a template parameter like f<int>(47) in the function call. The compiler can deduce the <int> type from the argument.

> **Note**
>
> The above output shows meaningful type names where most compilers will use shorthand, like i for int and PKc for const char *, and so on.

- This works just as well for multiple template parameters:

```
template<typename T1, typename T2>
string f(const T1 a, const T2 b) {
    return format("{} {}", typeid(T1).name(),
        typeid(T2).name());
}

int main() {
    cout << format("T1 T2: {}\n", f(47, 47L));
    cout << format("T1 T2: {}\n", f(47L, 47.0));
    cout << format("T1 T2: {}\n", f(47.0, "47"));
}
```

Output:

```
T1 T2: int long
T1 T2: long double
T1 T2: double char const *
```

Here the compiler is deducing types for both T1 and T2.

- Notice that the types must be compatible with the template. For example, you cannot take a reference from a literal:

```
template<typename T>
const char * f(const T& a) {
    return typeid(T).name();
}

int main() {
    int x{47};
```

```
    f(47);   // this will not compile
    f(x);    // but this will
}
```

- Beginning with C++17 you can also use template parameter deduction with classes. So now this will work:

```
pair p(47, 47.0);      // deduces to pair<int, double>
tuple t(9, 17, 2.5);   // deduces to tuple<int, int,
double>
```

This eliminates the need for `std::make_pair()` and `std::make_tuple()` as you can now initialize these classes directly without the explicit template parameters. The `std::make_*` helper functions will remain available for backward compatibility.

How it works...

Let's define a class so we can see how this works:

```
template<typename T1, typename T2, typename T3>
class Thing {
    T1 v1{};
    T2 v2{};
    T3 v3{};
public:
    explicit Thing(T1 p1, T2 p2, T3 p3)
    : v1{p1}, v2{p2}, v3{p3} {}

    string print() {
        return format("{}, {}, {}\n",
            typeid(v1).name(),
            typeid(v2).name(),
            typeid(v3).name()
        );
    }
};
```

This is a template class with three types and three corresponding data members. It has a `print()` function, which returns a formatted string with the three type names.

Without template parameter deduction, I would have to instantiate an object of this type like this:

```
Things<int, double, string> thing1{1, 47.0, "three" }
```

Now I can do it like this:

```
Things thing1{1, 47.0, "three" }
```

This is both simpler and less error prone.

When I call the `print()` function on the `thing1` object, I get this result:

```
cout << thing1.print();
```

Output:

```
int, double, char const *
```

Of course, your compiler may report something effectively similar.

Before C++17, template parameter deduction didn't apply to classes, so you needed a helper function, which may have looked like this:

```
template<typename T1, typename T2, typename T3>
Things<T1, T2, T3> make_things(T1 p1, T2 p2, T3 p3) {
    return Things<T1, T2, T3>(p1, p2, p3);
}
...
auto thing1(make_things(1, 47.0, "three"));
cout << thing1.print();
```

Output:

```
int, double, char const *
```

The STL includes a few of these helper functions, like `make_pair()` and `make_tuple()`, etc. These are now obsolescent, but will be maintained for compatibility with older code.

There's more...

Consider the case of a constructor with a parameter pack:

```
template <typename T>
class Sum {
    T v{};
public:
    template <typename... Ts>
    Sum(Ts&& ... values) : v{ (values + ...) } {}
    const T& value() const { return v; }
};
```

Notice the *fold expression* in the constructor (`values + ...`). This is a C++17 feature that applies an operator to all the members of a parameter pack. In this case, it initializes v to the sum of the parameter pack.

The constructor for this class accepts an arbitrary number of parameters, where each parameter may be a different class. For example, I could call it like this:

```
Sum s1 { 1u, 2.0, 3, 4.0f };   // unsigned, double, int,
                               // float
Sum s2 { "abc"s, "def" };      // std::sring, c-string
```

This, of course, doesn't compile. The template argument deduction fails to find a common type for all those different parameters. We get an error message to the effect of:

```
cannot deduce template arguments for 'Sum'
```

We can fix this with a *template deduction guide*. A deduction guide is a helper pattern to assist the compiler with a complex deduction. Here's a guide for our constructor:

```
template <typename... Ts>
Sum(Ts&& ... ts) -> Sum<std::common_type_t<Ts...>>;
```

This tells the compiler to use the `std::common_type_t` trait, which attempts to find a common type for all the parameters in the pack. Now our argument deduction works and we can see what types it settled on:

```
Sum s1 { 1u, 2.0, 3, 4.0f };   // unsigned, double, int,
                               // float
Sum s2 { "abc"s, "def" };      // std::sring, c-string
```

```
auto v1 = s1.value();
auto v2 = s2.value();
cout << format("s1 is {} {}, s2 is {} {}",
        typeid(v1).name(), v1, typeid(v2).name(), v2);
```

Output:

```
s1 is double 10, s2 is class std::string abcdef
```

Use if constexpr to simplify compile-time decisions

An if constexpr (*condition*) statement is used where code needs to be executed based on a compile-time condition. The *condition* may be any constexpr expression of type bool.

How to do it...

Consider the case where you have a template function that needs to operate differently depending upon the type of the template parameter.

```
template<typename T>
auto value_of(const T v) {
    if constexpr (std::is_pointer_v<T>) {
        return *v;   // dereference the pointer
    } else {
        return v;    // return the value
    }
}

int main() {
    int x{47};
    int* y{&x};
    cout << format("value is {}\n", value_of(x));   // value
    cout << format("value is {}\n", value_of(y));
                                                // pointer
    return 0;
}
```

Output:

```
value is 47
value is 47
```

The type of the template parameter T is available at compile time. The constexpr if statement allows the code to easily distinguish between a pointer and a value.

How it works...

The constexpr if statement works like a normal if statement except it's evaluated at *compile time*. The *runtime code* will not contain any branch statements from a constexpr if statement. Consider our branch statement from above:

```
if constexpr (std::is_pointer_v<T>) {
    return *v;  // dereference the pointer
} else {
        return v;   // return the value
    }
```

The condition is_pointer_v<T> tests a template parameter, which is not available at runtime. The constexpr keyword tells the compiler that this if statement needs to evaluate at compile time, while the template parameter <T> is available.

This should make a lot of meta programming situations much easier. The if constexpr statement is available in C++17 and later.

3
STL Containers

In this chapter, we will focus on the container classes in the STL. In short, a *container* is an object that contains a collection of other objects, or *elements*. The STL provides a complete suite of container types that form the foundation of the STL itself.

A quick overview of the STL container types

The STL provides a comprehensive set of container types, including *sequential containers*, *associative containers*, and *container adapters*. Here's a brief overview:

Sequential containers

The sequential containers provide an interface where the elements are arranged in sequence. While you may use the elements sequentially, some of these containers use contiguous storage, and others do not. The STL includes these sequential containers:

- The `array` is a fixed-size sequence that holds a specific number of elements in contiguous storage. Once allocated, it cannot change size. This is the simplest and fastest contiguous storage container.

- The `vector` is like an array that can shrink and grow. Its elements are stored contiguously, so changing size may involve the expense of allocating memory and moving data. A `vector` may keep extra space in reserve to mitigate that cost. Inserting and deleting elements from anywhere other than the *back* of a `vector` will trigger realignment of the elements to maintain contiguous storage.

- The `list` is a doubly-linked list structure that allows elements to be inserted and deleted in constant (*O(1)*) time. Traversing the list happens in linear *O(n)* time. A single-linked variant is available as `forward_list`, which only iterates forward. A `forward_list` uses less space and is somewhat more efficient than a doubly-linked `list`, but lacks some capability.

- The `deque` (commonly pronounced, *deck*) is a **d**ouble-**e**nded **que**ue. It's a sequential container that can be expanded or contracted on both ends. A `deque` allows random access to its elements, much like a `vector`, but does not guarantee contiguous storage.

Associative containers

An associative container associates a key with each element. Elements are referenced by their key, rather than their position in the container. STL associative containers include these containers:

- The `set` is an associative container where each element is also its own key. Elements are ordered, usually by some sort of binary tree. Elements in a `set` are immutable and cannot be modified, but they can be inserted and removed. Elements in a `set` are *unique*, duplicates are not allowed. A `set` iterates in order according to its sorting operators.

- The `multiset` is like a `set` with non-unique keys, where duplicates are allowed.

- The `unordered_set` is like a `set` that does not iterate in order. Elements are not sorted in any specific order, but are organized according to their hash values for fast access.

- The `unordered_multiset` is like an `unordered_set` with non-unique keys, where duplicates are allowed.

- The `map` is an associative container for key-value pairs, where each *key* is mapped to a specific *value* (or *payload*). The types of the key and value may be different. Keys are unique but values are not. A `map` iterates in order of its keys, according to its sorting operators.

- The `multimap` is like a `map` with non-unique keys, where duplicate keys are allowed.

- The `unordered_map` is like a `map` that does not iterate in order.

- The `unordered_multimap` is like an `unordered_map` with non-unique keys, where duplicates are allowed.

Container adapters

A container adapter is a class which encapsulates an underlying container. The container class provides a specific set of member functions to access the underlying container elements. The STL provides these container adapters:

- The `stack` provides a **LIFO** (last-in, first-out) interface where elements may be added and extracted from only one end of the container. The underlying container may be one of `vector`, `deque`, or `list`. If no underlying container is specified, the default is `deque`.

- The `queue` provides a **FIFO** (first-in, first-out) interface where elements may be added at one end of the container and extracted from the other end. The underlying container may be one of `deque` or `list`. If no underlying container is specified, the default is `deque`.

- The `priority_queue` keeps the greatest value element at the top, according to a *strict weak ordering*. It provides a constant time lookup of the greatest value element, at the expense of logarithmic time insertion and extraction. The underlying container may be one of `vector` or `deque`. If no underlying container is specified, the default is `vector`.

In this chapter we will cover the following recipes:

- Use uniform erasure functions to delete items from a container
- Delete items from an unsorted vector in constant time
- Access vector elements directly and safely
- Keep vector elements sorted
- Efficiently insert elements into a map
- Efficiently modify the keys of map items
- Use `unordered_map` with custom keys
- Use set to sort and filter user input
- A simple RPN calculator with deque
- A word frequency counter with map
- Find long sentences with a vector of vectors
- A ToDo list using multimap

Technical requirements

You can find the code for this chapter on GitHub at https://github.com/
PacktPublishing/CPP-20-STL-Cookbook/tree/main/chap03.

Use uniform erasure functions to delete items from a container

Before C++20, the *erase-remove idiom* was commonly used to efficiently delete elements
from an STL container. This was a little cumbersome, but not a great burden. It was
common to use a function like this for the task:

```
template<typename Tc, typename Tv>
void remove_value(Tc & c, const Tv v) {
    auto remove_it = std::remove(c.begin(), c.end(), v);
    c.erase(remove_it, c.end());
}
```

The std::remove() function is from the <algorithms> header. std::remove()
searches for the specified value and removes it by shifting elements forward from the end
of the container. It does not change the size of the container. It returns an iterator past
the end of the shifted range. We then call the container's erase() function to delete the
remaining elements.

This two-step process is now reduced to one step with the new uniform erasure function:

```
std::erase(c, 5);    // same as remove_value() function
```

This one function call does the same thing as the remove_value() function we
wrote above.

There's also a version that uses a predicate function. For example, to remove all even
numbered values from a numeric container:

```
std::erase_if(c, [](auto x) { return x % 2 == 0; });
```

Let's look at the uniform erasure functions in a bit more detail.

How to do it...

There are two forms of the uniform erasure functions. The first form, called `erase()`, takes two parameters, a container and a value:

```
erase(container, value);
```

The container may be any of the sequential containers (`vector`, `list`, `forward_list`, `deque`), except `array`, which cannot change size.

The second form, called `erase_if()`, takes a container and a predicate function:

```
erase_if(container, predicate);
```

This form works with any of the containers that work with `erase()`, plus the associative containers, `set`, `map`, and their multi-key and unordered variants.

The functions `erase()` and `erase_if()` are defined, as non-member functions, in the header for the corresponding container. There is no need to include another header.

Let's look at some examples:

- First, let's define a simple function to print the size and elements of a sequential container:

```
void printc(auto & r) {
    cout << format("size({}) ", r.size());
    for( auto & e : r ) cout << format("{} ", e);
    cout << "\n";
}
```

    The `printc()` function uses the C++20 `format()` function to format a string for `cout`.

- Here's a `vector` with 10 integer elements, printed with our `printc()` function:

```
vector v{ 1, 2, 3, 4, 5, 6, 7, 8, 9 };
printc(v);
```

    Output:

```
size: 10: 0 1 2 3 4 5 6 7 8 9
```

We see that the vector has 10 elements. Now we can use `erase()` to remove all elements with the value 5:

```
erase(v, 5);
printc(v);
```

Output:

```
size: 9: 0 1 2 3 4 6 7 8 9
```

The `vector` version of the `std::erase()` function is defined in the `<vector>` header. After the `erase()` call, the element with the value 5 has been removed and the vector has 9 elements.

- This works just as well with a `list` container:

```
list l{ 0, 1, 2, 3, 4, 5, 6, 7, 8, 9 };
printc(l);
erase(l, 5);
printc(l);
```

Output:

```
size: 10: 0 1 2 3 4 5 6 7 8 9
size: 9: 0 1 2 3 4 6 7 8 9
```

The `list` version of the `std::erase()` function is defined in the `<list>` header. After the `erase()` call, the element with the value 5 has been removed and the `list` has 9 elements.

- We can use `erase_if()` to remove all the even numbered elements with a simple predicate function:

```
vector v{ 0, 1, 2, 3, 4, 5, 6, 7, 8, 9 };
printc(v);
erase_if(v, [](auto x) { return x % 2 == 0; });
printc(v);
```

Output:

```
size: 10: 0 1 2 3 4 5 6 7 8 9
size: 5: 1 3 5 7 9
```

- The `erase_if()` function also works with associative containers, like map:

```
void print_assoc(auto& r) {
    cout << format("size: {}: ", r.size());
    for( auto& [k, v] : r ) cout << format("{}:{} ",
        k, v);
    cout << "\n";
}

int main() {
    map<int, string> m{ {1, "uno"}, {2, "dos"},
        {3, "tres"}, {4, "quatro"}, {5, "cinco"} };
    print_assoc(m);
    erase_if(m,
        [] (auto& p) { auto& [k, v] = p;
        return k % 2 == 0; }
    );
    print_assoc(m);
}
```

Output:

```
size: 5: 1:uno 2:dos 3:tres 4:quatro 5:cinco
size: 3: 1:uno 3:tres 5:cinco
```

Because each element of a map is returned as a `pair`, we need a different function to print them. The `print_assoc()` function unpacks the `pair` elements with a *structured binding* in the `for` loop. We also use a structured binding in the predicate function of `erase_if()` to isolate the key for filtering the even numbered elements.

How it works...

The `erase()` and `erase_if()` functions are simply wrappers that perform the *erase-remove idiom* in one step. They perform the same operations as a function, like this:

```
template<typename Tc, typename Tv>
void remove_value(Tc & c, const Tv v) {
    auto remove_it = std::remove(c.begin(), c.end(), v);
    c.erase(remove_it, c.end());
}
```

If we consider a simple `vector` of `int`, called `vec`, with the following values:

```
vector vec{ 0, 1, 2, 3, 4, 5, 6, 7, 8, 9 };
```

We can visualize `vec` as a one-row table of `int` values:

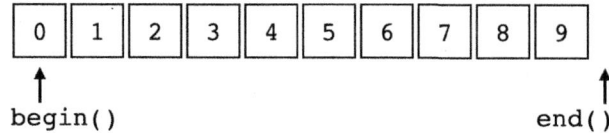

Figure 3.1 – begin() and end() iterators

The `begin()` iterator points at the first element, and the `end()` iterator points *past* the last element. This configuration is standard for all STL sequential containers.

When we call `remove(c.begin(), c.end(), 5)`, the algorithm searches for matching elements, starting at the `begin()` iterator. For each matching element that it finds, it shifts the next element into its place. It continues searching and shifting until it reaches the `end()` iterator. The result is a container where all the remaining elements are at the beginning, without the deleted elements, and in their original order. The `end()` iterator is unchanged and the remaining elements are *undefined*. We can visualize the operation like this:

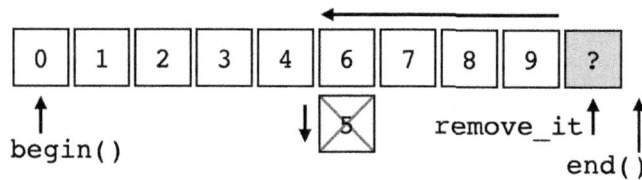

Figure 3.2 – Removing an element

The `remove()` function returns an iterator (`remove_it`) that points to the first element *past* the elements that were shifted. The `end()` iterator remains as it was before the `remove()` operation. To further illustrate, if we were to remove all even-numbered elements using `remove_if()`, our result would look like this:

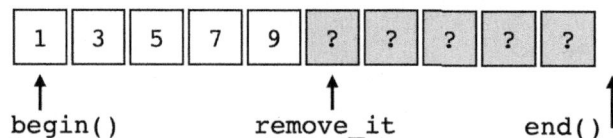

Figure 3.3 – After removing even-numbered elements

In this case, all that remains is the five odd-numbered elements followed by five elements of *undefined* value.

The container's erase() function is then called to erase the remaining elements:

```
c.erase(remove_it, c.end());
```

The container's erase() function is called with the remove_it and end() iterators to delete all the undefined elements.

The erase() and erase_if() functions call both the remove() function and the container's erase() function, in order to perform the *erase-remove idiom* in one step.

Delete items from an unsorted vector in constant time

Using the uniform erasure functions (or the *erase-remove idiom*) to delete items from the middle of a vector takes *O(n)* (*linear*) time. This is because elements must be shifted from the end of the vector to close the gap of the deleted items. If the order of items in the vector is not important, we can optimize this process to take *O(1)* (*constant*) time. Here's how.

How to do it...

This recipe takes advantage of the fact that removing an element from the end of a vector is quick and easy.

- Let's start by defining a function to print out a vector:

```
void printc(auto & r) {
    cout << format("size({}) ", r.size());
    for( auto & e : r ) cout << format("{} ", e);
    cout << '\n';
}
```

- In our main() function we define a vector of int and print it using printc():

```
int main() {
    vector v{ 0, 1, 2, 3, 4, 5, 6, 7, 8, 9 };
    printc(v);
}
```

Output:

```
size(10) 0 1 2 3 4 5 6 7 8 9
```

- Now we'll write the function that will delete an element from the vector:

```
template<typename T>
void quick_delete(T& v, size_t idx) {
    if (idx < v.size()) {
        v[idx] = move(v.back());
        v.pop_back();
    }
}
```

The quick_delete() function takes two arguments, a vector v and an index idx. We first check to make sure our index is within boundaries. Then we call the move() function from the <algorithms> header to move the last element of the vector to the position of our index. Finally, the v.pop_back() function is called to shorten the vector from the back.

- Let's also include a version of quick_delete() for use with an iterator instead of an index.

```
template<typename T>
void quick_delete(T& v, typename T::iterator it) {
    if (it < v.end()) {
        *it = move(v.back());
        v.pop_back();
    }
}
```

This version of quick_delete() operates from an iterator instead of an index. Otherwise, it works the same as the indexed version.

- Now we can call it from our main() function:

```
int main() {
    vector v{ 12, 196, 47, 38, 19 };
    printc(v);
    auto it = std::ranges::find(v, 47);
    quick_delete(v, it);
    printc(v);
    quick_delete(v, 1);
    printc(v);
}
```

And the output will look like this:

```
size(5)  12 196 47 38 19
size(4)  12 196 19 38
size(3)  12 38 19
```

The first call to quick_delete() uses an iterator from the std::ranges::find() algorithm. This deletes the value 47 from the vector. Notice the value from the back of the vector (19) takes its place. The second call to quick_delete() uses an index (1) to delete the second element from the vector (196). Again, the value from the back of the vector takes its place.

How it works...

The quick_delete() function uses a simple trick to delete elements from a vector quickly and efficiently. The element at the back of the vector is moved (*not copied*) into the position of the element to be deleted. The deleted element is discarded in the process. Then, the pop_back() function shortens the vector by one element from the end.

This takes advantage of the fact that deleting the element at the back of the vector is especially cheap. The pop_back() function operates at constant complexity, as it only needs to change the end() iterator.

This diagram shows the state of the vector before and after the quick_delete() operation:

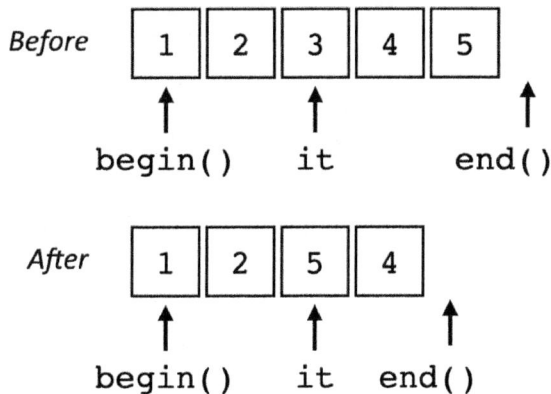

Figure 3.4 – Before and after quick_delete()

The quick_remove() operation simply *moves* the element from the back of the vector into the position of the iterator (it), then shortens the vector by one element. It's important to use std::move() instead of an assignment to move the element. The move operation is much faster than a copy-assignment, especially for large objects.

If you don't require ordered elements, this is an extremely efficient technique. It happens in constant (*O(1)*) time and without touching any other elements.

Access vector elements directly and safely

The vector is one of the most widely used containers in the STL, and for good reason. It's just as convenient as an array but far more powerful and flexible. It's common practice to use the [] operator to access elements in a vector like this:

```
vector v{ 19, 71, 47, 192, 4004 };
auto & i = v[2];
```

The vector class also provides a member function for the same purpose:

```
auto & i = v.at(2);
```

The result is the same but there is an important difference. The at() function does bounds checking and the [] operator does not. This is intentional, as it allows the [] operator to maintain compatibility with the original C-array. Let's examine this in a bit more detail.

How to do it...

There are two ways to access an element with an index in a vector. The at() member function does bounds checking, and the [] operator does not.

- Here's a simple main() function that initializes a vector and accesses an element:

```
int main() {
    vector v{ 19, 71, 47, 192, 4004 };
    auto & i = v[2];
    cout << format("element is {}\n", i);
}
```

Output:

```
element is 47
```

Here, I used the [] operator to directly access the third element in the vector. As with most sequential objects in C++, the index starts at 0 so the third element is number 2.

- The vector has five elements, numbered 0 through 4. If I were to try to access element number 5 that would be beyond the boundary of the vector:

```
vector v{ 19, 71, 47, 192, 4004 };
auto & i = v[5];
cout << format("element is {}\n", i);
element is 0
```

This result is extremely deceiving. It's a common error, since humans tend to count from 1, not 0. But there is no guarantee that an element past the end of the vector has any particular value.

- Even worse, the [] operator will silently allow you to *write* to a position beyond the end of the vector:

```
vector v{ 19, 71, 47, 192, 4004 };
v[5] = 2001;
auto & i = v[5];
cout << format("element is {}\n", i);
element is 2001
```

I have now written to memory that is not under my control and the compiler has *silently* allowed it, with no error messages or crashes. But do not be fooled—this is extremely dangerous code, and it *will* cause problems at some point in the future. Out of bounds memory access is one of the primary causes of security breaches.

- The solution is to use the at() member function wherever possible, instead of the [] operator:

```
vector v{ 19, 71, 47, 192, 4004 };
auto & i = v.at(5);
cout << format("element is {}\n", i);
```

Now we get a run-time exception:

```
terminate called after throwing an instance of 'std::out_
of_range'
  what():  vector::_M_range_check: __n (which is 5) >=
this->size() (which is 5)
Aborted
```

The code compiles without error, but the at () function checks the boundaries of the container and throws a *run-time exception* when you try to access memory outside of those boundaries. This is the exception message from code compiled with the GCC compiler. The message will be different in different environments.

How it works...

The [] operator and the at () member function do the same job; they provide direct access to container elements based on their indexed position. The [] operator does it without any bounds checking, so it may be a tiny bit faster in some intensely iterative applications.

That said, the at () function *should be your default choice*. While the bounds checking may take a few CPU cycles, it's cheap insurance. For most applications the benefit is well worth the cost.

While the vector class is commonly used as a direct-access container, the array and deque containers also support both the [] operator and the at () member function. These caveats apply there as well.

There's more...

In some applications you may not want your application to just *crash* when an out-of-bounds condition is encountered. In this case, you can *catch* the exception, like this:

```
int main() {
    vector v{ 19, 71, 47, 192, 4004 };
    try {
        v.at(5) = 2001;
    } catch (const std::out_of_range & e) {
        std::cout <<
            format("Ouch!\n{}\n", e.what());
    }
    cout << format("end element is {}\n", v.back());
}
```

Output:

```
Ouch!
vector::_M_range_check: __n (which is 5) >= this->size() (which
is 5)
end element is 4004
```

The `try` block catches the exception specified in the `catch` clause, in this case the exception is `std::out_of_range`. The `e.what()` function returns a C-string with the error message from the STL library. Each library will have different messages.

Keep in mind that this also applies to `array` and `deque` containers.

Keep vector elements sorted

The `vector` is a sequential container that keeps elements in the order in which they were inserted. It does not sort elements, nor change their order in any way. Other containers, such as `set` and `map`, keep elements sorted, but those containers are not random-access and may not have the features you need. You can, however, keep your vector sorted. It just requires a little bit of management.

How to do it...

The idea with this recipe is to create a simple function, `insert_sorted()`, that inserts an element into the correct position in a vector to keep the vector sorted.

- For convenience, we'll start with a *type alias* for a vector of strings:

    ```
    using Vstr = std::vector<std::string>;
    ```

    I like a type alias here because the exact details of the vector are not so important as its application.

- Then we can define a couple of support functions:

    ```
    // print a vector
    void printv(const auto& v) {
        for(const auto& e : v) {
            cout << format("{} ", e);
        }
        cout << "\n";
    }

    // is it sorted?
    void psorted(const Vstr& v) {
        if(std::ranges::is_sorted(v)) cout<< "sorted: ";
        else cout << "unsorted: ";
        printv(v);
    }
    ```

The `printv()` function is simple enough; it prints the elements of the vector on one line.

The `psorted()` function uses the *ranges* version of the `is_sorted()` algorithm to tell us if the vector is sorted. Then it calls `printv()` to print the vector.

- Now we can initialize a `Vstr` vector in our `main()` function:

```
int main() {
    Vstr v{
        "Miles",
        "Hendrix",
        "Beatles",
        "Zappa",
        "Shostakovich"
    };
    psorted(v);
}
```

Output:

unsorted: Miles Hendrix Beatles Zappa Shostakovich

At this point we have a `Vstr` vector with the names of some interesting musicians, in no particular order.

- Let's sort our vector using the `ranges` version of the `sort()` algorithm.

```
std::ranges::sort(v);
psorted(v);
```

Output:

sorted: Beatles Hendrix Miles Shostakovich Zappa

- At this point, we want to be able to insert items into the vector so that they're already in sorted order. The `insert_sorted()` function does this for us:

```
void insert_sorted(Vstr& v, const string& s) {
    const auto pos{ std::ranges::lower_bound(v, s) };
    v.insert(pos, s);
}
```

The `insert_sorted()` function uses the *ranges* version of the `lower_bound()` algorithm to get an iterator for the `insert()` function that keeps the vector sorted.

- Now we can use the `insert_sorted()` function to insert more musicians into the vector:

```
insert_sorted(v, "Ella");
insert_sorted(v, "Stones");
```

Output:

```
sorted: Beatles Ella Hendrix Miles Shostakovich Stones
Zappa
```

How it works...

The `insert_sorted()` function is used to insert elements into a sorted vector while maintaining its order:

```
void insert_sorted(Vstr& v, const string& s) {
    const auto pos{ std::ranges::lower_bound(v, s) };
    v.insert(pos, s);
}
```

The `lower_bound()` algorithm finds the first element *not less than* the argument. We then use the iterator returned by `lower_bound()` to insert an element at the correct position.

In this case we're using the ranges version of `lower_bound()`, but either version will work.

There's more...

The `insert_sorted()` function can be made more generic by using a template. This version will work with other container types, such as `set`, `deque`, and `list`.

```
template<typename C, typename E>
void insert_sorted(C& c, const E& e) {
    const auto pos{ std::ranges::lower_bound(c, e) };
    c.insert(pos, e);
}
```

Keep in mind that the `std::sort()` algorithm (and its derivatives) requires a container that supports random access. Not all STL containers fulfill this requirement. Notably, `std::list` does not.

Efficiently insert elements into a map

The map class is an associative container that holds *key-value pairs*, where keys must be unique within the container.

There are a number of ways to populate a map container. Consider a map defined like this:

```
map<string, string> m;
```

You can add an element with the [] operator:

```
m["Miles"] = "Trumpet"
```

You can use the insert() member function:

```
m.insert(pair<string,string>("Hendrix", "Guitar"));
```

Or, you can use the emplace() member function:

```
m.emplace("Krupa", "Drums");
```

I tend to gravitate toward the emplace() function. Introduced with C++11, emplace() uses *perfect forwarding* to **emplace** (create in place) the new element for the container. The parameters are forwarded directly to the element constructors. This is quick, efficient, and easy to code.

Though it's certainly an improvement over the other options, the problem with emplace() is that it constructs an object even when it's not needed. This involves calling the constructors, allocating memory, and moving data around, and then discarding that temporary object.

To solve this problem, C++17 provides the new try_emplace() function which only constructs the *value object* if it's needed. This is especially important with large objects or many emplacements.

> **Note**
>
> Each element of a *map* is a key-value *pair*. Within the pair structure, the elements are named, first and second, but their purpose in the map is *key* and *value*. I tend to think of the value object as the *payload*, as this is usually the point of the map. To search for an existing key, the try_emplace() function must construct the key object; this cannot be avoided. But it need not construct the payload object unless and until it's needed for insertion into the map.

How to do it...

The new `try_emplace()` function avoids the overhead of constructing the *payload object* unless and until it is needed. This creates a valuable efficiency in the case of key collisions, especially with large payloads. Let's take a look:

- First, we create a payload class. For demonstration purposes, this class has a simple `std::string` payload and displays a message when constructed:

```
struct BigThing {
    string v_;
    BigThing(const char * v) : v_(v) {
        cout << format("BigThing constructed {}\n", v_);
    }
};
using Mymap = map<string, BigThing>;
```

This `BigThing` class has only one member function, a constructor that displays a message when the object is constructed. We'll use this to keep track of how often a `BigThing` object is constructed. In practice, of course, this class would be bigger, and use more resources.

Each map element will consist of a pair of objects, a `std::string` for the key and a `BigThing` object for the payload. `Mymap` is just a convenience alias. This allows us to focus on function rather than form.

- We'll also create a `printm()` function to print the contents of the map:

```
void printm(Mymap& m) {
    for(auto& [k, v] : m) {
        cout << format("[{}:{}] ", k, v.v_);
    }
    cout << "\n";
}
```

This uses the C++20 `format()` function to print out the map, so we can keep track of the elements as we insert them.

- In our `main()` function we create the map object and insert some elements:

```cpp
int main() {
    Mymap m;
    m.emplace("Miles", "Trumpet");
    m.emplace("Hendrix", "Guitar");
    m.emplace("Krupa", "Drums");
    m.emplace("Zappa", "Guitar");
    m.emplace("Liszt", "Piano");
    printm(m);
}
```

Output:

```
BigThing constructed Trumpet
BigThing constructed Guitar
BigThing constructed Drums
BigThing constructed Guitar
BigThing constructed Piano
[Hendrix:Guitar]  [Krupa:Drums]  [Liszt:Piano]
[Miles:Trumpet]  [Zappa:Guitar]
```

Our output shows the construction of each of the payload objects, and then the output from the `printm()` function call.

- I used the `emplace()` function to add the elements to the map, and each payload element was constructed just once. We can use the `try_emplace()` function and the result will be the same:

```cpp
Mymap m;
m.try_emplace("Miles", "Trumpet");
m.try_emplace("Hendrix", "Guitar");
m.try_emplace("Krupa", "Drums");
m.try_emplace("Zappa", "Guitar");
m.try_emplace("Liszt", "Piano");
printm(m);
```

Output:

```
BigThing constructed Trumpet
BigThing constructed Guitar
BigThing constructed Drums
```

```
BigThing constructed Guitar
BigThing constructed Piano
[Hendrix:Guitar] [Krupa:Drums] [Liszt:Piano]
[Miles:Trumpet] [Zappa:Guitar]
```

- The difference between `emplace()` and `try_emplace()` shows up when we try to insert new elements with duplicate keys:

```
cout << "emplace(Hendrix)\n";
m.emplace("Hendrix", "Singer");
cout << "try_emplace(Zappa)\n";
m.try_emplace("Zappa", "Composer");
printm(m);
```

Output:

```
emplace(Hendrix)
BigThing constructed Singer
try_emplace(Zappa)
[Hendrix:Guitar] [Krupa:Drums] [Liszt:Piano]
[Miles:Trumpet] [Zappa:Guitar]
```

The `emplace()` function tried to add an element with a duplicate key (`"Hendrix"`). It failed but *still constructed* the payload object (`"Singer"`). The `try_emplace()` function also tried to add an element with a duplicate key (`"Zappa"`). It failed and *did not* construct the payload object.

This example demonstrates the distinction between `emplace()` and `try_emplace()`.

How it works...

The `try_emplace()` function signature is similar to that of `emplace()`, so it should be easy to retrofit legacy code. Here's the `try_emplace()` function signature:

```
pair<iterator, bool> try_emplace( const Key& k,
Args&&... args );
```

At first glance, this looks different from the `emplace()` signature:

```
pair<iterator,bool> emplace( Args&&... args );
```

The distinction is that try_emplace() uses a separate parameter for the *key* argument, which allows it to be isolated for construction. Functionally, if you're using *template argument deduction*, try_emplace() can be a drop-in replacement:

```
m.emplace("Miles", "Trumpet");
m.try_emplace("Miles", "Trumpet");
```

The return value of try_emplace() is the same as that of emplace(), a pair representing an iterator and a bool:

```
const char * key{"Zappa"};
const char * payload{"Composer"};
if(auto [it, success] = m.try_emplace(key, payload);
        !success) {
    cout << "update\n";
    it->second = payload;
}
printm(m);
```

Output:

```
update
BigThing constructed Composer
[Hendrix:Guitar] [Krupa:Drums] [Liszt:Piano] [Miles:Trumpet]
[Zappa:Composer]
```

Here I used *structured binding* (auto [it, success] =) with an if *initializer statement* to test the return value and conditionally update the payload. Notice that it still just constructs the payload object once.

It's worth noting that the try_emplace() function also works with unordered_map. We change our alias and everything works the same except unordered:

```
using Mymap = unordered_map<string, BigThing>;
```

The advantage of try_emplace() is that it only constructs the payload object *if and when* it's ready to store it in the map. In practice, this should save significant resources at run-time. You should always favor try_emplace() over emplace().

Efficiently modify the keys of map items

A map is an associative container that stores key-value pairs. The container is ordered by the keys. The keys must be unique and they are const-qualified, so they cannot be changed.

For example, if I populate a map and attempt to change the key, I'll get an error at compilation time:

```
map<int, string> mymap {
    {1, "foo"}, {2, "bar"}, {3, "baz"}
};
auto it = mymap.begin();
it->first = 47;
```

Output:

```
error: assignment of read-only member ...
    5 |        it->first = 47;
      |        ~~~~~~~~~~^~~~
```

If you need to re-order a map container, you may do so by swapping keys using the extract() method.

New with C++17, extract() is a member function in the map class and its derivatives. It allows elements of a map to be extracted from the sequence without touching the payload. Once extracted, the key is no longer const-qualified and may be modified.

Let's look at an example.

How to do it...

In this example we'll define a map that represents contestants in a race. At some point during the race, the order changes and we need to modify the keys of the map.

- We'll start by defining an alias for the map type:

    ```
    using Racermap = map<unsigned int, string>;
    ```

    This allows us to use the type consistently throughout our code.

- We'll write a function for printing out the map:

```
void printm(const Racermap &m)
{
    cout << "Rank:\n";
    for (const auto& [rank, racer] : m) {
        cout << format("{}:{}\n", rank, racer);
    }
}
```

We can pass the map to this function at any time to print out the current rankings of our contestants.

- In our main() function we define a map with the initial state of our racers:

```
int main() {
    Racermap racers {
        {1, "Mario"}, {2, "Luigi"}, {3, "Bowser"},
        {4, "Peach"}, {5, "Donkey Kong Jr"}
    };
    printm(racers);
    node_swap(racers, 3, 5);
    printm(racers);
}
```

The key is an int indicating the rank of the racer. The value is a string with the name of the racer.

We then call printm() to print the current rank. The call to node_swap() will swap the keys of two racers, then we print gain.

- At some point, one of the racers falls behind and another racer takes the opportunity to move up in the rankings. The node_swap() function will swap the ranking of two racers:

```
template<typename M, typename K>
bool node_swap(M & m, K k1, K k2) {
    auto node1{ m.extract(k1) };
    auto node2{ m.extract(k2) };
    if(node1.empty() || node2.empty()) {
        return false;
    }
```

```
swap(node1.key(), node2.key());
m.insert(move(node1));
m.insert(move(node2));
return true;
}
```

This function uses the `map.extract()` method to extract the specified elements from the map. These extracted elements are called *nodes*.

A *node* is a new concept beginning with C++17. This allows an element to be extracted from a map-type structure without touching the element itself. The node is unlinked, and a *node handle* is returned. Once extracted, the node handle provides *writable* access to the key via the node's `key()` function. We can then swap the keys and insert them back into the map, without ever having to copy or manipulate the payload.

- When we run this code we get a printout of the map, before and after the node swap:

Output:

```
Rank:
1:Mario
2:Luigi
3:Bowser
4:Peach
5:Donkey Kong Jr
Rank:
1:Mario
2:Luigi
3:Donkey Kong Jr
4:Peach
5:Bowser
```

This is all made possible by the `extract()` method and the new `node_handle` class. Let's take a closer look at how this works.

How it works...

This technique uses the new `extract()` function, which returns a `node_handle` object. As the name suggests, a `node_handle` is a handle to a *node*, which consists of an associative element and its related structures. The extract function *disassociates* the node while leaving it in place, and returns a `node_handle` object. This has the effect of removing the node from the associative container without touching the data itself. The `node_handle` allows you to access the disassociated node.

The `node_handle` has a member function, `key()`, which returns a *writable* reference to the node key. This allows you to change the key, while it's disassociated from the container.

There's more...

There are a few things to keep in mind when using `extract()` and a `node_handle`:

- If the key is not found, the `extract()` function returns an *empty* node handle. You can test if a node handle is empty with the `empty()` function:

  ```
  auto node{ mapthing.extract(key) };
  if(node.empty()) {
      // node handle is empty
  }
  ```

- There are two overloads of the `exract()` function:

  ```
  node_type extract(const key_type& x);
  node_type extract(const_iterator position);
  ```

  We used the first form, by passing a key. You may also use an iterator, which should not require a lookup.

- Keep in mind that you cannot make a reference from a literal, so a call like `extract(1)` will usually crash with a segmentation fault.

- Keys must remain unique when inserted into a `map`.

  For example, if I try to change a key to a value already in the map:

  ```
  auto node_x{ racers.extract(racers.begin()) };
  node_x.key() = 5;  // 5 is Donkey Kong Jr
  auto status = racers.insert(move(node_x));
  if(!status.inserted) {
      cout << format("insert failed, dup key: {}",
  ```

```
            status.position->second);
        exit(1);
    }
```

The insert fails and we get our error message:

```
insert failed, dup key: Donkey Kong Jr
```

In this example I've passed the `begin()` iterator to `extract()`. I then assigned the key a value that's already in use (5, *Donkey Kong Jr*). The insert failed and the resulting `status.inserted` is false. `status.position` is an iterator to the found key. In the `if()` block, I used `format()` to print the value the found key.

Use unordered_map with custom keys

With an ordered `map`, the type of the key must be sortable, which means it must at least support the less-than < comparison operator. Suppose you want to use an associative container with a custom type that is not sortable. For example, a vector where `(0, 1)` is not smaller or larger than `(1, 0)`, it simply points in a different direction. In such cases, you may still use the `unordered_map` type. Let's look at how to do this.

How to do it...

For this recipe we'll create an `unordered_map` object that uses *x/y* coordinates for the key. We will need a few support functions for this.

- First, we'll define a structure for the coordinates:

```
struct Coord {
    int x{};
    int y{};
};
```

This is a simple structure with two members, x and y, for the coordinates.

- Our map will use the `Coord` structure for the key, and an `int` for the value:

```
using Coordmap = unordered_map<Coord, int>;
```

We use a `using` alias to make it convenient to use our map.

- To use the `Coord` struct as a key, we need a couple of overloads. These are required for use with an `unordered_map`. First, we'll define an equality comparison operator:

```
bool operator==(const Coord& lhs, const Coord& rhs) {
    return lhs.x == rhs.x && lhs.y == rhs.y;
}
```

It's a simple function that compares the x members with each other, and the y members with each other.

- We also need a `std::hash` class specialization. This makes it possible to retrieve map elements with the key:

```
namespace std {
    template<>
    struct hash<Coord> {
        size_t operator()(const Coord& c) const {
            return static_cast<size_t>(c.x)
                + static_cast<size_t>(c.y);
        }
    };
}
```

This provides a specialization for the default `hash` class used by the `std::unordered_map` class. It must be in the `std` namespace.

- We'll also write a print function to print a `Coordmap` object:

```
void print_Coordmap(const Coordmap& m) {
    for (const auto& [key, value] : m) {
        cout << format("{{ ({}, {}): {} }} ",
            key.x, key.y, value);
    }
    cout << '\n';
}
```

This uses the C++20 `format()` function to print the *x/y* key and the value. Notice the use of the double braces, { { and } }, to print single braces.

- Now that we have all our support functions, we can write the `main()` function.

```
int main() {
    Coordmap m {
        { {0, 0}, 1 },
        { {0, 1}, 2 },
        { {2, 1}, 3 }
    };
    print_Coordmap(m);
}
```

Output:

```
{ (2, 1): 3 } { (0, 1): 2 } { (0, 0): 1 }
```

At this point, we've defined a `Coordmap` object that accepts `Coord` objects for the keys and maps them to arbitrary values.

- We can also access individual members based on the `Coord` keys:

```
Coord k{ 0, 1 };
cout << format("{{ ({}, {}): {} }}\n", k.x, k.y,
m.at(k));
```

Output:

```
{ (0, 1): 2 }
```

Here we define a `Coord` object named k, and we use that with the `at()` function to retrieve a value from the `unordered_map`.

How it works...

The `unordered_map` class relies on a hash class to lookup elements from the key. We normally instantiate an object like this:

```
std::unordered_map<key_type, value_type> my_map;
```

What's not obvious here is that, because we haven't one, it's using a *default hash class*. The full template type definition of the `unordered_map` class looks like this:

```
template<
    class Key,
    class T,
    class Hash = std::hash<Key>,
```

```
    class KeyEqual = std::equal_to<Key>,
    class Allocator = std::allocator< std::pair<const Key,
      T> >
> class unordered_map;
```

The template provides default values for `Hash`, `KeyEqual`, and `Allocator`, so we don't normally include them in our definitions. In our example, we've provided a specialization for the default `std::hash` class.

The STL contains specializations of `std::hash` for most of the standard types, like `string`, `int`, and so on. For it to work with our class, it needs a specialization.

We could have passed a function to the template parameter, like this:

```
std::unordered_map<coord, value_type, my_hash_type> my_map;
```

That certainly would work. In my view, the specialization is more general.

Use set to sort and filter user input

The `set` container is an associative container where each element is a *single value*, which is used as the key. Elements in a `set` are maintained in sorted order and duplicate keys are not allowed.

The `set` container is often misunderstood, and it does have fewer and more specific uses than more general containers such as `vector` and `map`. One common use for a `set` is to filter duplicates from a set of values.

How to do it...

In this recipe we will read words from the *standard input* and filter out the duplicates.

- We'll start by defining an alias for an `istream` iterator. We'll use this to get input from the command line.

  ```
  using input_it = istream_iterator<string>;
  ```

- In the `main()` function, we'll define a `set` for our words:

  ```
  int main() {
      set<string> words;
  ```

  The `set` is defined as a set of `string` elements.

- We define a pair of iterators for use with the `inserter()` function:

```
input_it it{ cin };
input_it end{};
```

The end iterator is initialized with its default constructor. This is known as the *end-of-stream* iterator. When our input ends, this iterator will compare equal with the `cin` iterator.

- The `inserter()` function is used to insert elements into the `set` container:

```
copy(it, end, inserter(words, words.end()));
```

We use `std::copy()` to conveniently copy words from the input stream.

- Now we can print out our `set` to see the results:

```
for(const string & w : words) {
    cout << format("{} ", w);
}
cout << '\n';
```

- We can run the program by piping a bunch of words to its input:

```
$ echo "a a a b c this that this foo foo foo" | ./
set-words
a b c foo that this
```

The `set` has eliminated the duplicates and retained a sorted list of the words that were inserted.

How it works...

The `set` container is the heart of this recipe. It only holds unique elements. When you insert a duplicate, that insert will fail. So, you end up with a sorted list of each unique element.

But that's not the only interesting part of this recipe.

The `istream_iterator` is an input iterator that reads objects from a stream. We instantiated the input iterator like this:

```
istream_iterator<string> it{ cin };
```

Now we have an input iterator of type `string` from the `cin` stream. Every time we dereference this iterator, it will return one word from the input stream.

We also instantiated another `istream_iterator`:

```
istream_iterator<string> end{};
```

This calls the default constructor, which gives us a special *end-of-stream* iterator. When the input iterator reaches the end of the stream, it will become equal to the *end-of-stream* iterator. This is convenient for ending loops, such as the one created by the `copy()` algorithm.

The `copy()` algorithm takes three iterators, the beginning and end of the range to copy, and a destination iterator:

```
copy(it, end, inserter(words, words.end()));
```

The `inserter()` function takes a container and an iterator for the insertion point, and returns an `insert_iterator` of the appropriate type for the container and its elements.

This combination of `copy()` and `inserter()` makes it easy to copy elements from a stream into the `set` container.

A simple RPN calculator with deque

An **RPN (Reverse Polish Notation)** calculator is a stack-based calculator that uses postfix notation, where the operator follows the operands. It's commonly used in printing calculators and, notably, the HP 12C, the most popular electronic calculator of all time.

After becoming familiar with its operational modality, many people prefer an RPN calculator. (I've been using the HP 12C and 16C since they were first introduced in the early 1980s.) For example, using conventional algebraic notation, to add 1 and 2 you would type `1 + 2`. Using RPN, you would type `1 2 +`. The operator comes *after* the operands.

Using an algebraic calculator, you would need to press an = key to indicate that you want a result. With an RPN calculator this is unnecessary because the operator processes immediately, serving a double purpose. On the other hand, an RPN calculator often requires an *Enter* keypress to push an operand onto the stack.

We can easily implement an RPN calculator using a stack-based data structure. For example, consider an RPN calculator with a four-position stack:

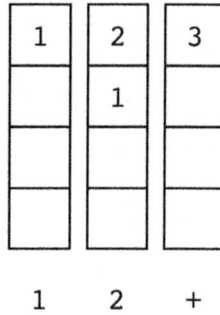

1   2   +

Figure 3.5 – RPN addition operation

Each operand is pushed onto the stack as they are entered. When the operator is entered, the operands are popped off, operated upon, and the result is pushed back onto the stack. The result may then be used in the next operation. For example, consider the case of (3+2)×3:

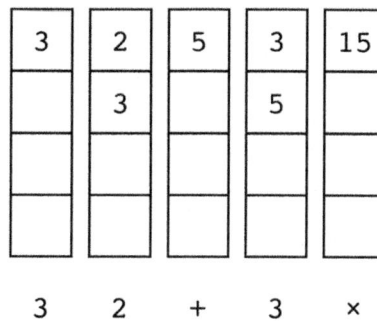

3   2   +   3   ×

Figure 3.6 – RPN stack operations

One advantage of RPN is that you can leave operands on the stack for future calculations, reducing the need for separate memory registers. Consider the case of (9×6) + (2×3):

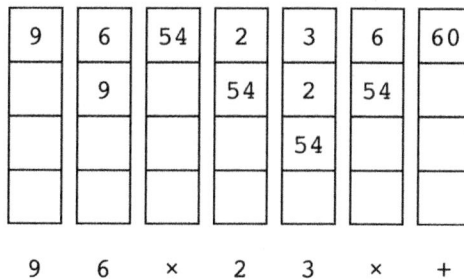

9   6   ×   2   3   ×   +

Figure 3.7 – RPN multiple stack operations

Notice that we first perform the operations within the parentheses, then the final operation on the intermediate results. This may seem more complex at first, but it makes a lot of sense once you get used to it.

Now, let's build a simple RPN calculator using the STL deque container.

How to do it...

For this implementation, we'll use a deque container for our stack. Why not use a stack container? The stack class is a container-adapter, which uses another container (usually a deque) for its storage. For our purposes, stack doesn't provide any tangible advantage over deque. And deque allows us to iterate over and display the RPN stack, like a paper tape calculator.

- We'll encapsulate our RPN calculator in a class. There are a few advantages to using a class here. *Encapsulation* provides *safety*, *reusability*, *extensibility*, and a *clean interface*. We'll call our class RPN:

```
class RPN {
    deque<double> deq_{};
    constexpr static double zero_{0.0};
    constexpr static double inf_
        { std::numeric_limits<double>::infinity() };
    ...  // public and private members go here
};
```

The deque data store, named deq_, is in the private area of the class to protect it. This is where we store the RPN stack.

The zero_ constant is used throughout the class, both as a return value and as a comparison operand. The inf_ constant is used for a divide-by-zero error. These constants are declared constexpr static so they don't take up space in every instance.

I like to name private data members with a trailing underscore to remind me that they're private.

- We don't need an explicit constructor or destructor because the deque class manages its own resources. So, our public interface consists of just three functions:

```
public:
    // process an operand/operator
    double op(const string & s) {
        if(is_numeric(s)) {
            double v{stod(s, nullptr)};
            deq_.push_front(v);
            return v;
        }
        else return optor(s);
    }

    // empty the stack
    void clear() {
        deq_.clear();
    }

    // print the stack
    string get_stack_string() const {
        string s{};
        for(auto v : deq_) {
            s += format("{} ", v);
        }
        return s;
    }
```

The double op() function is the main entry point for the RPN class. It takes a string, with either a number or an operator. If it's a number, it's converted into a double and pushed onto the stack. If it's an operator, we call optor() to perform the operation. This is the main logic of the class.

The void clear() function simply calls clear() on the deque to empty the stack.

And finally, the string get_stack_string() function returns the contents of the stack in a string.

- In the `private` section, we have the supporting utilities that make the interface work. The `pop_get2()` function pops two operands from the stack and returns them as a pair. We use this as operands for the operators:

```
pair<double, double> pop_get2() {
    if(deq_.size() < 2) return {zero_, zero_};
    double v1{deq_.front()};
    deq_.pop_front();
    double v2{deq_.front()};
    deq_.pop_front();
    return {v2, v1};
}
```

- The `is_numeric()` function checks to see if the string is entirely numeric. We also allow the decimal . character.

```
bool is_numeric(const string& s) {
    for(const char c : s) {
        if(c != '.' && !std::isdigit(c)) return
            false;
    }
    return true;
}
```

- The `optor()` function performs the operators. We use a `map` container to map an operator to a corresponding lambda function.

```
double optor(const string& op) {
    map<string, double (*)(double, double)> opmap {
        {"+", [](double l, double r){ return l + r; }},
        {"-", [](double l, double r){ return l - r; }},
        {"*", [](double l, double r){ return l * r; }},
        {"/", [](double l, double r){ return l / r; }},
        {"^", [](double l, double r)
            { return pow(l, r); }},
        {"%", [](double l, double r)
            { return fmod(l, r); }}
    };
    if(opmap.find(op) == m.end()) return zero_;
```

```
        auto [l, r] = pop_get2();
        // don't divide by zero
        if(op == "/" && r == zero_) deq_.push_front(inf_);
        else deq_.push_front(opmap.at(op)(l, r));
        return deq_.front();
    }
```

The map container with lambda functions makes a quick and easy jump table.

We use the `find()` function in map to test if we have a valid operator.

After a test for divide-by-zero, the map is dereferenced, and the operator is called.

The result of the operation is pushed onto the stack and returned.

- Those are all the function members of the RPN class. Now we can use it in our `main()` function:

```
int main() {
    RPN rpn;

    for(string o{}; cin >> o; ) {
        rpn.op(o);
        auto stack_str{rpn.get_stack_string()};
        cout << format("{}: {}\n", o, stack_str);
    }
}
```

We'll test this is by piping a string into the program from the command line. We use a `for` loop to fetch each word from the `cin` stream and pass it to `rpn.op()`. I like the `for` loop here, as it's easy to contain the scope of the `o` variable. We then print the stack using the `get_stack_string()` function after each command line item.

- We can run the program by piping in an expression like this:

```
$ echo "9 6 * 2 3 * +" | ./rpn
9: 9
6: 6 9
*: 54
2: 2 54
3: 3 2 54
*: 6 54
+: 60
```

This looks like a lot of coding but it's actually quite simple. With the comments, the RPN class is less than 70 lines of code. The full `rpn.cpp` source code is in the GitHub repository.

How it works...

The RPN class operates by first determining the nature of each chunk of input. If it's a number, we push it onto the stack. If it's an operator, we pop two operands off the top of the stack, apply the operation, and push the result back on the stack. If we don't recognize the input, we just ignore it.

The `deque` class is a double-ended queue. To use it as a stack, we pick an end and both push and pop from that same end. I chose the `front` end of the deque, but it would work just as well from the `back`. We just need to do everything from the same end.

If we determine that an input is numeric, we convert it to a `double` and push it onto the front of the deque using `push_front()`.

```
if(is_numeric(s)) {
    double v{stod(s, nullptr)};
    deq_.push_front(v);
    return v;
}
```

When we need to use values from the stack, we pop them off the front of the deque. We use `front()` to get the value, and then `pop_front()` to pop it off the stack.

```
pair<double, double> pop_get2() {
    if(deq_.size() < 2) return {zero_, zero_};
    double v1{deq_.front()};
    deq_.pop_front();
    double v2{deq_.front()};
    deq_.pop_front();
    return {v2, v1};
}
```

Using a map for our operators makes it easy to both check if an operator is valid, and to execute the operation.

```
map<string, double (*)(double, double)> opmap {
    {"+", [](double l, double r){ return l + r; }},
    {"-", [](double l, double r){ return l - r; }},
    {"*", [](double l, double r){ return l * r; }},
    {"/", [](double l, double r){ return l / r; }},
    {"^", [](double l, double r){ return pow(l, r); }},
    {"%", [](double l, double r){ return fmod(l, r); }}
};
```

We can test for the validity of an operator by using the `find()` function:

```
if(opmap.find(op) == opmap.end()) return zero_;
```

And we can call the operator by dereferencing the map with the `at ()` function:

```
opmap.at(op)(l, r)
```

We both call the operator lambda and push the result onto the deque in one statement:

```
deq_.push_front(opmap.at(op)(l, r));
```

There's more...

In this recipe, we use the `cin` stream to feed operations to the RPN calculator. It would be just as easy to do this with an STL container.

```
int main() {
    RPN rpn;
    vector<string> opv{ "9", "6", "*", "2", "3", "*", "+"
        };
    for(auto o : opv) {
        rpn.op(o);
        auto stack_str{rpn.get_stack_string()};
        cout << format("{}: {}\n", o, stack_str);
    }
}
```

Output:

```
9: 9
6: 6 9
*: 54
2: 2 54
3: 3 2 54
*: 6 54
+: 60
```

By putting the RPN calculator in a class with a clean interface, we've created a flexible tool that can be used in many different contexts.

A word frequency counter with map

This recipe uses the unique key property of the map container to count duplicate words from a stream of text.

The STL map container is an *associative* container. It consists of elements organized in *key-value pairs*. The keys are used for lookup and must be unique.

In this recipe, we will leverage the unique key requirement of the STL map container to count the number of occurrences of each word in a text file.

How to do it...

There are a few parts to this task that we can solve separately:

1. We need to get the text from a file. We'll use the cin stream for this.

2. We need to separate words from punctuation and other non-word content. We'll use the regex (Regular Expression) library for this.

3. We need to count the frequency of each word. This is the main objective of the recipe. We'll use the STL map container for this.

4. Finally, we need to sort the results, first by frequency and then alphabetically by word within frequency. For this we'll use a the STL sort algorithm with a vector container.

Even with all those tasks, the resulting code is relatively short, just about 70 lines with headers and all. Let's dive in:

- We'll start with some aliases for convenience:

```
namespace ranges = std::ranges;
namespace regex_constants = std::regex_constants;
```

  For namespaces within the `std::` space, I like to make aliases that are shorter, but still let me know that I'm using a token in a particular namespace. Especially with the `ranges` namespace, which often re-uses the names of existing algorithms.

- We store the regular expression in a constant. I don't like to clutter up the global namespace because that can lead to collisions. I tend to use a namespace based on my initials for things like this:

```
namespace bw {
    constexpr const char * re{"(\\w+)"};
}
```

  It's easy enough to get it later using `bw::re`, and that tells me exactly what it is.

- At the top of `main()`, we define our data structures:

```
int main() {
    map<string, int> wordmap{};
    vector<pair<string, int>> wordvec{};
    regex word_re(bw::re);
    size_t total_words{};
```

  Our main map is called `wordmap`. We have a `vector` named `wordvec` that we'll use as a sorting container. And finally, our `regex` class, `word_re`.

- The `for` loop is where most of the work happens. We read text from the `cin` stream, apply the `regex`, and store words in the `map`:

```
for(string s{}; cin >> s; ) {
    auto words_begin{
        sregex_iterator(s.begin(), s.end(), word_re) };
    auto words_end{ sregex_iterator() };

    for(auto r_it{words_begin}; r_it != words_end;
      ++r_it) {
        smatch match{ *r_it };
```

```
auto word_str{match.str()};
ranges::transform(word_str, word_str.begin(),
    [](unsigned char c){ return tolower(c); });
auto [map_it, result] =
    wordmap.try_emplace(word_str, 0);
auto & [w, count] = *map_it;
++total_words;
++count;
    }
}
```

I like a `for` loop for this because it allows me to contain the scope of the `s` variable.

We start by defining iterators for the `regex` results. This allows us to distinguish multiple words even when surrounded only by punctuation. The `for(r_it...)` loop returns individual words from the `cin` string.

The `smatch` type is a specialization of a `regex` string match class. It gives us the next word from our `regex`.

We then use the `transform` algorithm to make the words lowercase – so we can count words regardless of case. (For example, "The" is the same word as "the".)

Next, we use `try_emplace()` to add the word to the map. If it's already there, it will not be replaced.

Finally, we increment the count for the word in the map with `++count`.

- Now we have the words and their frequency counts in our `map`. But they're in alphabetical order and we want them in descending order of frequency. For this, we put them in a vector and sort them:

```
auto unique_words = wordmap.size();
wordvec.reserve(unique_words);
ranges::move(wordmap, back_inserter(wordvec));
ranges::sort(wordvec, [](const auto& a, const
  auto& b) {
    if(a.second != b.second)
        return (a.second > b.second);
    return (a.first < b.first);
});
cout << format("unique word count: {}\n",
```

```
            total_words);
        cout << format("unique word count: {}\n",
            unique_words);
```

`wordvec` is a vector of pairs, with the word and the frequency count.
We use the `ranges::move()` algorithm to populate the `vector`, then the
`ranges::sort()` algorithm to sort the `vector`. Notice that the *predicate lambda
function* sorts first by the count (descending) and then by the word (ascending).

- Finally, we print the results:

```
        for(int limit{20}; auto& [w, count] : wordvec) {
            cout << format("{}: {}\n", count, w);
            if(--limit == 0) break;
        }
    }
```

I set a limit to print only the first 20 entries. You can comment out the `if(--
limit == 0) break;` line to print the whole list.

- In the example files, I've included a text file with a copy of *The Raven*, by Edgar
Allen Poe. The poem is in the public domain. We can use this to test the program:

```
$ ./word-count < the-raven.txt
total word count: 1098
unique word count: 439
56: the
38: and
32: i
24: my
21: of
17: that
17: this
15: a
14: door
11: chamber
11: is
11: nevermore
10: bird
10: on
```

```
10: raven
9: me
8: at
8: from
8: in
8: lenore
```

The poem has 1,098 words total, and 439 of them are unique.

How it works...

The core of the recipe is the use of a `map` object to count duplicate words. But there are other parts that merit consideration.

We use the `cin` stream to read text from the *standard input*. By default, `cin` will skip *whitespace* when reading into a `string` object. By putting a string object on the right-hand side of the `>>` operator (`cin >> s`) we get chunks of text separated by whitespace. This is a good enough definition of a word-at-a-time for many purposes, but we need linguistic words. And for that we will use a regular expression.

The `regex` class provides a choice of regular expression *grammars* and it defaults to *ECMA* grammar. In the ECMA grammar, the regular expression `"(\w+)"` is a shortcut for `"([A-Za-z0-9_]+)"`. This will select words that include these characters.

Regular expressions are a language unto themselves. To learn more about regular expressions, I recommend the book *Mastering Regular Expressions* by Jeffrey Friedl.

As we get each word from the `regex` engine, we use the map object's `try_emplace()` method to conditionally add the word to our `wordmap`. If the word is not in the map, we add it with a count of 0. If the word is already in the map, the count is untouched. We increment the count later in the loop, so it's always correct.

After the map is populated with all the unique words from the file, we transfer it to a vector using the `ranges::move()` algorithm. The `move()` algorithm makes this transfer quick and efficient. Then we can sort it in the vector using `ranges::sort()`. The *predicate lambda function* for sorting includes comparisons for both sides of the pair, so we end up with a result that's sorted by both word count (descending) and the word.

Find long sentences with a vector of vectors

It can be useful for a writer to make sure they are using variety of sentence lengths, or to ensure none of their sentences are too long. Let's build a tool that evaluates a text file for sentence length.

Choosing the appropriate container is key when using the STL. If you need something ordered, it's often best to use an associative container, such as map or multimap. In this case, however, since we need a custom sort, it's easier to sort a vector.

The vector is generally the most flexible of the STL containers. Whenever another container type seems appropriate, but is missing one important capability, the vector is often an effective solution. In this case, where we need a custom sort, the vector works great.

This recipe uses a *vector of vectors*. The inner vector stores the words of a sentence, and the outer vector stores the inner vectors. As you'll see, this affords a lot of flexibility while retaining all the relevant data.

How to do it...

This program needs to read in words, find the ends of sentences, store and sort the sentences, then print out the results.

- We'll start by writing a little function to tell us when we've hit the end of a sentence:

```
bool is_eos(const string_view & str) {
    constexpr const char * end_punct{ ".!?" };
    for(auto c : str) {
        if(strchr(end_punct, c) != nullptr) return
            true;
    }
    return false;
}
```

The is_eos() function uses string_view because it's efficient and we don't need anything more. Then we use the strchr() library function to check if a word contains one of the end-of-sentence punctuation characters (" . ! ? "). These are the three possible characters to end a sentence in the English language.

- In the `main()` function, we start by defining the *vector of vectors*:

  ```
  vector<vector<string>> vv_sentences{vector<string>{}};
  ```

  This defines a `vector` of elements typed `vector<string>` named `vv_sentences`. The `vv_sentences` object is initialized with one empty vector for the first sentence.

  This creates a vector that contains other vectors. The inner vectors will each hold a sentence of words.

- Now we can process the stream of words:

  ```
  for(string s{}; cin >> s; ) {
      vv_sentences.back().emplace_back(s);
      if(is_eos(s)) {
          vv_sentences.emplace_back(vector<string>{});
      }
  }
  ```

  The `for` loop returns one word at a time from the input stream. The `back()` method on the `vv_sentences` object is used to access the current vector of words, and the current word is added using `emplace_back()`. Then we call `is_eos()` to see if this was the end of a sentence. If so, we add a new empty vector to `vv_sentences` to start the next sentence.

- Because we always add a new empty vector to the end of `vv_sentences` after each end-of-sentence character, we will usually end up with an empty sentence vector at the end. Here we check for this, and delete it if necessary:

  ```
  // delete back if empty
  if(vv_sentences.back().empty())
      vv_sentences.pop_back();
  ```

- Now we can sort the `vv_sentences` vector by the size of the sentences:

  ```
  sort(vv_sentences, [](const auto& l,
      const auto& r) {
          return l.size() > r.size();
      });
  ```

  This is why the `vector` is so convenient for this project. It's quick and easy to sort using the `ranges::sort()` algorithm with a simple *predicate* for sorting by size in descending order.

- Now we can print our result:

```cpp
constexpr int WLIMIT{10};
for(auto& v : vv_sentences) {
    size_t size = v.size();
    size_t limit{WLIMIT};
    cout << format("{}: ", size);
    for(auto& s : v) {
        cout << format("{} ", s);
        if(--limit == 0) {
            if(size > WLIMIT) cout << "...";
            break;
        }
    }
    cout << '\n';
}
cout << '\n';
```

The outer loop and the inner loop correspond to the outer and inner vectors. We simply loop through the vectors and print out the size of the inner vector with `format("{}: ", size)` and then each word with `format("{} ", s)`. We don't want to print the very long sentences in their entirety, so we define a limit of 10 words and print an ellipsis if there's more.

- The output looks like this, using the first few paragraphs of this recipe for input:

```
$ ./sentences < sentences.txt
27: It can be useful for a writer to make sure ...
19: Whenever another container type seems appropriate,
but is missing one ...
18: If you need something ordered, it's often best to use
...
17: The inner vector stores the words of a sentence, and
...
16: In this case, however, since we need a descending
sort, ...
16: In this case, where we need our output sorted in ...
15: As you'll see, this affords a lot of flexibility
while ...
```

```
12: Let's build a tool that evaluates a text file for ...
11: The vector is generally the most flexible of the STL
...
9: Choosing the appropriate container key when using the
STL.
7: This recipe uses a vector of vectors.
```

How it works...

Finding punctuation is simple using the `strchr()` function from the C Standard Library. Remember, all of C and its Standard Library are included in the definition of the C++ language. There's no reason not to use it where appropriate.

```
bool is_eos(const string_view & str) {
    constexpr const char * end_punct{ ".!?" };
    for(auto c : str) {
        if(strchr(end_punct, c) != nullptr) return true;
    }
    return false;
}
```

This function will fail to properly separate sentences if there's punctuation in the middle of words. That may happen in some forms of poetry or in a badly formatted text file. I've seen this done with `std::string` iterators, and with regular expressions, but for our purposes this is quick and easy.

We read the text file one word at a time using `cin`:

```
for(string s{}; cin >> s; ) {
    ...
}
```

This avoids the overhead of reading a large file into memory all at once. The `vector` will already be large, containing all the words of the file. It's not necessary to also hold the entire text file in memory. In the rare case that a file is too large, it would be necessary to find another strategy, or use a database.

The *vector of vectors* may look complex at first glance, but it's no more complicated than using two separate vectors.

```
vector<vector<string>> vv_sentences{vector<string>{}};
```

This declares an *outer* vector, with *inner* elements of type vector<string>. The *outer* vector is named vv_sentences. The *inner* vectors are anonymous; they require no name. This definition initializes the vv_sentences object with one element, an empty vector<string> object.

The *current* inner vector will always be available as vv_senteces.back():

```
vv_sentences.back().emplace_back(s);
```

When we've completed one inner vector, we simply create a new one with:

```
vv_sentences.emplace_back(vector<string>{});
```

This creates a new anonymous vector<string> object and *emplaces* it at the back of the vv_sentences object.

A ToDo list using multimap

An ordered task list (or a *ToDo list*) is a common computing application. Formally stated, it's a list of tasks associated with a priority, sorted in reverse numerical order.

You may be tempted to use a priority_queue for this, because as the name implies, it's already sorted in priority (reverse numerical) order. The disadvantage of a priority_ queue is that it has no iterators, so it's difficult to operate on it without pushing and popping items to and from the queue.

For this recipe, we'll use a multimap for the ordered list. The multimap *associative container* keeps items in order, and it can be accessed using *reverse iterators* for the proper sort order.

How to do it...

This is a short and simple recipe that initializes a multimap and prints it in reverse order.

- We start with a type alias for our multimap:

    ```
    using todomap = multimap<int, string>;
    ```

    Our todomap is a multimap with an int key and a string payload.

- We have a small utility function for printing the todomap in reverse order:

```
void rprint(todomap& todo) {
    for(auto it = todo.rbegin(); it != todo.rend();
      ++it) {
        cout << format("{}: {}\n", it->first,
          it->second);
    }
    cout << '\n';
}
```

This uses reverse iterators to print the todomap.

- The main() function is short and sweet:

```
int main()
{
    todomap todo {
        {1, "wash dishes"},
        {0, "watch teevee"},
        {2, "do homework"},
        {0, "read comics"}
    };
    rprint(todo);
}
```

We initialize the todomap with tasks. Notice that the tasks are not in any particular order, but they do have priorities in the keys. The rprint() function will print them in priority order.

- The output looks like this:

```
$ ./todo
2: do homework
1: wash dishes
0: read comics
0: watch teevee
```

The ToDo list prints out in priority order, just as we need it.

How it works...

It's a short and simple recipe. It uses the `multimap` container to hold items for a prioritized list.

The only trick is in the `rprint()` function:

```cpp
void rprint(todomap& todo) {
    for(auto it = todo.rbegin(); it != todo.rend(); ++it) {
        cout << format("{}: {}\n", it->first, it->second);
    }
    cout << '\n';
}
```

Notice the reverse iterators, `rbegin()` and `rend()`. It's not possible to change the sort order of a `multimap`, but it does provide reverse iterators. This makes the `multimap` behave exactly as we need it for our prioritized list.

4

Compatible Iterators

Iterators are a fundamental concept in the STL. Iterators are implemented with the semantics of C pointers, using the same increment, decrement, and dereference operators. The pointer idiom is familiar to most C/C++ programmers, and it allows *algorithms* such as std::sort and std::transform to work on primitive memory buffers as well as STL containers.

Iterators are fundamental

The STL uses iterators to navigate the elements of its container classes. Most containers include begin() and end() iterators. These are usually implemented as member functions that return an iterator object. The begin() iterator points to the initial container element, and the end() iterator points *past* the final element:

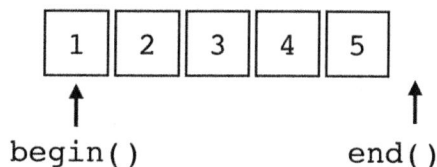

Figure 4.1 – The begin() and end() iterators

The end() iterator may function as a *sentinel* for containers of indeterminate length. We'll see some examples of that in this chapter.

Most STL containers define their own specific *iterator type*. For example, for a vector of int:

```
std::vector<int> v;
```

The iterator type would be defined as:

```
std::vector<int>::iterator v_it;
```

You can see how this could easily get out of hand. If we had a vector of vector of string:

```
std::vector<std::vector<int, std::string>> v;
```

Its iterator type would be:

```
std::vector<std::vector<int, std::string>>::iterator v_it;
```

Fortunately, C++11 gave us automatic type deduction and the auto type. By using auto, we rarely need to use the full iterator type definition. For example, if we need an iterator in a for loop, we can use the auto type:

```
for(auto v_it = v.begin(); v_it != v.end(); ++v_it) {
    cout << *v_it << '\n';
}
```

Notice the use of the dereference operator * to access the elements from the iterator. This is the same syntax you would use to dereference a pointer:

```
const int a[]{ 1, 2, 3, 4, 5 };
size_t count{ sizeof(a) / sizeof(int) };
for(const int* p = a; count > 0; ++p, --count) {
    cout << *p << '\n';
}
```

This also means that you can use a range-based for loop with either a primitive array:

```
const int a[]{ 1, 2, 3, 4, 5 };
for(auto e : a) {
    cout << e << '\n';
}
```

Or with an STL container:

```
std::vector<int> v{ 1, 2, 3, 4, 5 };
for(auto e : v) {
    cout << e << '\n';
}
```

The range-based `for` loop is just a shorthand for a `for` loop with iterators:

```
{
    auto begin_it{ std::begin(container) };
    auto end_it{ std::end(container) };
    for ( ; begin_it != end_it; ++begin_it) {
        auto e{ *begin_it };
        cout << e << '\n';
    }
}
```

Because iterators use the same syntax as a primitive pointer, the range-based `for` loop works the same with either container.

Notice that the range-based `for` loop calls `std::begin()` and `std::end()`, instead of directly calling the `begin()` and `end()` member functions. The `std::` functions call the member functions to get the iterators. So, why not just call the member functions? The `std::` non-member functions are designed to also work with primitive arrays. That's why a `for` loop works with an array:

```
const int arr[]{ 1, 2, 3, 4, 5 };
for(auto e : arr) {
    cout << format("{} ", e);
}
```

Output:

```
1 2 3 4 5
```

For most purposes, I tend to favor the member function `begin()` and `end()` because they are more explicit. Others favor the `std::` non-member functions because they are more general. Six or half-dozen; I suggest you pick a style and stick with it.

Iterator categories

Prior to C++20, iterators were divided into categories based on their capabilities:

Iterator Category					Iterator Capability
Contiguous Iterator	Random Access Iterator	Bidirectional Iterator	Forward Iterator	Input Iterator	• Read • Increment once
					• Increment multiple times
					• Decrement
					• Random access
					• Contiguous storage (such as an array)
When any of the above iterators can also write, they are called *mutable iterators*.					
Output Iterator					• Write • Increment once

These categories are hierarchical, where the more capable iterators inherit the capabilities of the less capable iterators. In other words, the *input iterator* can read and increment once. The *forward iterator* has the capabilities of the Input Iterator *plus* it can increment multiple times. The *bidirectional iterator* has those capabilities *plus* it can decrement. And on down the list.

The *output iterator* can write and increment once. If any of the other iterators can also write, it is considered a *mutable iterator*.

Iterator concepts

Concepts and *constraints* are new with C++20. A concept is simply a named constraint that restricts the types of arguments to a template function or class, and helps the compiler choose appropriate specializations.

Beginning with C++20, the STL defines iterators in terms of concepts instead of categories. Each of these concepts are in the `std::` namespace.

Concept	Description
`indirectly_readable`	An iterator can be read by the dereference operator, `*`. This includes pointers, smart pointers, and input iterators.
`indirectly_writable`	The object reference of the iterator is writable.
`weakly_incrementable`	This can be incremented with `++` but does not preserve equality. For example, where `a == b`, `++a` may not equal `++b`.
`incrementable`	This can be incremented with `++` and equality is preserved.
`input_or_output_iterator`	An iterator can be incremented and dereferenced. Every iterator must satisfy this concept.
`sentinel_for`	A sentinel iterator is used to find the end of an object of indeterminate size, such as an input stream.
`sized_sentinel_for`	A sentinel iterator may be used with another iterator and the `-` operator to determine its distance in constant time.
`input_iterator`	An iterator that may be read and incremented.
`output_iterator`	An iterator that may be written to and incremented.
`forward_iterator`	This modifies `input_iterator` to include `incrementable`.
`bidirectional_iterator`	This modifies `forward_iterator` by adding the ability to decrement with the `--` operator. It preserves equality.
`random_access_iterator`	This modifies `bidirectional_iterator` by adding support for the `+`, `+=`, `-`, `-=`, and `[]` operators.
`contiguous_iterator`	This modifies `random_access_iterator` to indicate contiguous storage.

You can use these concepts to constrain the arguments of a template:

```
template<typename T>
requires std::random_access_iterator<typename T::iterator>
void printc(const T & c) {
        for(auto e : c) {
        cout << format("{} ", e);
    }
    cout << '\n';
    cout << format("element 0: {}\n", c[0]);
}
```

This function requires a random_access_iterator. If I call it with a list, which is not a random-access container, the compiler will give me an error:

```
int main()
{
    list<int> c{ 1, 2, 3, 4, 5 };
    printc(c);
}
```

The list iterator type does not support the random_access_iterator concept. So, the compiler gives me an error:

```
error: no matching function for call to 'printc(std::__
cxx11::list<int>&)'
    27 |      printc(c);
       |      ~~~~~~^~~
note: candidate: 'template<class T>  requires  random_access_
iterator<typename T::iterator> void printc(const T&)'
    16 | void printc(const T & c) {
       |      ^~~~~~
note:    template argument deduction/substitution failed:
note: constraints not satisfied
```

This is the error output from GCC. Your errors may look different.

If I call it with a `vector`, which is a random-access container:

```
int main()
{
    vector<int> c{ 1, 2, 3, 4, 5 };
    printc(c);
}
```

Now it compiles and runs without error:

```
$ ./working
1 2 3 4 5
element 0: 1
```

While there are different types of iterators for different types of capabilities (and concepts), the complexity is there to support of ease of use.

With this introduction to iterators, let's now proceed with the following recipes in this chapter:

- Create an iterable range
- Make your iterators compatible with STL iterator traits
- Use iterator adapters to fill STL containers
- Create a generator as iterators
- Use reverse iterator adapters to iterate backward
- Iterate objects of unknown length with a sentinel
- Build a zip iterator adapter
- Create a random-access iterator

Technical requirements

You can find the code files for this chapter on GitHub at `https://github.com/PacktPublishing/CPP-20-STL-Cookbook/tree/main/chap04`.

Create an iterable range

This recipe describes a simple class that generates an iterable range, suitable for use with the range-based `for` loop. The idea is to create a *sequence generator* that iterates from a beginning value to an ending value.

To accomplish this task, we need an iterator class, along with the object interface class.

How to do it...

There's two major parts to this recipe, the main interface, Seq, and the `iterator` class.

- First, we'll define the Seq class. It only needs to implement the `begin()` and `end()` member functions:

```cpp
template<typename T>
class Seq {
    T start_{};
    T end_{};
public:
    Seq(T start, T end) : start_{start}, end_{end} {}
    iterator<T> begin() const {
        return iterator{start_};
    }
    iterator<T> end() const { return iterator{end_}; }
};
```

  The constructor sets up the `start_` and `end_` variables. These are used to construct the `begin()` and `end()` iterators, respectively. The member functions `begin()` and `end()` return `iterator` objects.

- The `iterator` class is normally defined inside the public section of the container class. This is called a *member class* or a *nested class*. We'll insert it right after the Seq constructor:

```cpp
public:
    Seq(T start, T end) : start_{ start }, end_{ end } {}
    class iterator {
        T value_{};
    public:
        explicit iterator(T position = 0)
            : value_{position} {}
```

```
T operator*() const { return value_; }
iterator& operator++() {
    ++value_;
    return *this;
}
bool operator!=(const iterator& other) const {
    return value_ != other.value_;
}
};
```

It's traditional to name the iterator class `iterator`. This allows it to be referenced as Seq<*type*>::iterator.

The `iterator` constructor is qualified `explicit` to avoid implicit conversions.

The `value_` variable is maintained by the iterator. This is used to return a value from the pointer dereference.

The minimum requirement for supporting the range-based `for` loop is a dereference operator `*`, a pre-increment operator `++`, and the not-equal comparison operator `!=`.

- Now we can write a `main()` function to test our sequence generator:

```
int main()
{
    Seq<int> r{ 100, 110 };

    for (auto v : r) {
        cout << format("{} ", v);
    }
    cout << '\n';
}
```

This constructs a `Seq` object and prints out its sequence.

The output looks like this:

```
$ ./seq
100 101 102 103 104 105 106 107 108 109
```

How it works...

The point of this recipe is to make a sequence generator that works with a range-based `for` loop. Let's first consider the equivalent code for the range-based `for` loop:

```
{
    auto begin_it{ std::begin(container) };
    auto end_it{ std::end(container) };
    for ( ; begin_it != end_it; ++begin_it) {
        auto v{ *begin_it };
        cout << v << '\n';
    }
}
```

From this equivalent code, we can deduce the requirements for an object to work with the `for` loop:

- `begin()` and `end()` iterators
- Iterator support for the not-equal comparison `!=` operator
- Iterator support for the prefix increment `++` operator
- Iterator support for the dereference `*` operator

Our main `Seq` class interface only has three public member functions: the constructor, and the `begin()` and `end()` iterators:

```
Seq(T start, T end) : start_{ start }, end_{ end } {}
iterator begin() const { return iterator{start_}; }
iterator end() const { return iterator{end_}; }
```

The implementation of the `Seq::iterator` class carries the actual payload:

```
class iterator {
    T value_{};
```

This is the common configuration because the payload is only accessed through iterators.

We've implemented only the three operators we need:

```
T operator*() const { return value_; }
iterator& operator++() {
    ++value_;
```

```
        return *this;
    }
    bool operator!=(const iterator& other) const {
        return value_ != other.value_;
    }
```

This is all we need to support the range-based `for` loop:

```
Seq<int> r{ 100, 110 };
for (auto v : r) {
    cout << format("{} ", v);
}
```

There's more...

It's traditional, but not required, to define the iterator as a member class of the container. This allows the `iterator` type to be subordinate to the container type:

```
Seq<int>::iterator it = r.begin();
```

It's not as important post C++11 because of the `auto` type, but it's still considered best practice.

Make your iterators compatible with STL iterator traits

Many STL algorithms require iterators to conform to certain traits. Unfortunately, these requirements are inconsistent across compilers, systems, and C++ versions.

For our purposes, we'll use the class from the *Create an iterable range* recipe to illustrate the issue. You may find this makes more sense if you read that recipe before continuing.

In `main()`, if I add a call to the `minmax_element()` algorithm:

```
Seq<int> r{ 100, 110 };
auto [min_it, max_it] = minmax_element(r.begin(), r.end());
cout << format("{} - {}\n", *min_it, *max_it);
```

It does not compile. The error messages are vague, cryptic, and cascading, but if you look closely, you'll see that our iterator does not meet the requirements to be compatible with this algorithm.

Okay, let's fix that.

How to do it...

We need to make a few simple additions to our iterator to make it compatible with the algorithm. Our iterator needs to meet the minimum requirements for a *forward iterator*, so let's start there:

- We have almost all the operators necessary for a forward iterator. The only one we're missing is the equality comparison operator ==. We can easily add this to our iterator with an operator==() overload:

```
bool operator==(const iterator& other) const {
    return value_ == other.value_;
}
```

Interestingly, this makes the code compile and run on some systems, but not on *Clang*, where we get the error message:

No type named 'value_type' in 'std::iterator_traits<Seq<int>::iterator>'

This tells me that we need to set up the traits in the iterator.

- The iterator_traits class looks for a set of *type definitions* (implemented as using aliases) in the iterator class:

```
public:
    using iterator_concept  = std::forward_iterator_tag;
    using iterator_category =
      std::forward_iterator_tag;
    using value_type        = std::remove_cv_t<T>;
    using difference_type   = std::ptrdiff_t;
    using pointer           = const T*;
    using reference         = const T&;
```

I tend to put these at the top of the public: section of the iterator class, where they'll be easy to see.

Now we have a fully conforming *forward iterator* class, and the code runs on all the compilers I have.

How it works...

The `using` statements are traits that may be used to define what capabilities the iterator can perform. Let's look at each of them:

```
using iterator_concept  = std::forward_iterator_tag;
using iterator_category = std::forward_iterator_tag;
```

The first two are the *category* and the *concept*, and both are set to `forward_iterator_tag`. This value indicates that the iterator conforms to the forward iterator specification.

Some code doesn't look at those values, and instead looks for individual settings and capabilities:

```
using value_type       = std::remove_cv_t<T>;
using difference_type   = std::ptrdiff_t;
using pointer           = const T*;
using reference         = const T&;
```

The `value_type` alias is set to `std::remove_cv_t<T>`, which is the type of the value, with any `const` qualifier removed.

The `difference_type` alias is set to `std::ptrdiff_t`, as special type for pointer differences.

The `pointer` and `reference` aliases are set to `const`-qualified versions of the pointer and reference, respectively.

Defining these type aliases is a basic requirement for most iterators.

There's more...

It's worth noting that defining these traits allows us to use concept-restricted templates with our iterator. For example:

```
template<typename T>
requires std::forward_iterator<typename T::iterator>
void printc(const T & c) {
    for(auto v : c) {
        cout << format("{} ", v);
    }
    cout << '\n';
}
```

This function that prints our sequence is restricted by the `forward_iterator` concept. If our class did not qualify, it wouldn't compile.

We can also use the `ranges::` versions of the algorithms:

```
auto [min_it, max_it] = ranges::minmax_element(r);
```

This makes it more convenient to use our iterators.

We can test for `forward_range` compatibility with a static assertion:

```
static_assert(ranges::forward_range<Seq<int>>);
```

Use iterator adapters to fill STL containers

An iterator is essentially an abstraction. It has a specific interface and is used in specific ways. But beyond that, it's just code and it can be used for other purposes. An *iterator adapter* is a class that looks like an iterator but does something else.

The STL comes with an assortment of iterator adapters. Often used with the `algorithm` library, they are quite useful. The STL iterator adaptors generally fall into three categories:

- **Insert iterators**, or *inserters*, are used to insert elements into a container.
- **Stream iterators** read from and write to a stream.
- **Reverse iterators** reverse the direction of an iterator.

How to do it...

In this recipe, we'll look at a few examples of STL iterator adapters:

- We'll start with a simple function to print the contents of a container:

```
void printc(const auto & v, const string_view s = "") {
    if(s.size()) cout << format("{}: ", s);
    for(auto e : v) cout << format("{} ", e);
    cout << '\n';
}
```

The `printc()` function allows us to easily view the results of our algorithms. It includes an optional `string_view` argument for a description.

- In our `main()` function, we'll define a couple of `deque` containers. We're using `deque` containers so we can insert at both ends:

```
int main() {
    deque<int> d1{ 1, 2, 3, 4, 5 };
    deque<int> d2(d1.size());
    copy(d1.begin(), d1.end(), d2.begin());
    printc(d1);
    printc(d2, "d2 after copy");
}
```

Output:

```
1 2 3 4 5
d2 after copy: 1 2 3 4 5
```

We defined deque d1 with five `int` values, and d2 with space for the same number of elements. The `copy()` algorithm will not allocate space, so d2 must have room for the elements.

The `copy()` algorithm takes three iterators: the *begin* and *end* iterators indicate the range of elements to copy from, and the *begin* iterator of the destination range. It does not check the iterators to make sure they're valid. (Try this without allocating space in a `vector` and you'll get a *segmentation fault* error.)

We call `printc()` on both containers to show the results.

- The `copy()` algorithm is not always convenient for this. Sometimes you want to copy and add elements to the end of a container. It would be nice to have an algorithm that calls `push_back()` for each element. This is where an iterator adapter is useful. Let's add some code at the end of `main()`:

```
copy(d1.begin(), d1.end(), back_inserter(d2));
printc(d2, "d2 after back_inserter");
```

Output:

```
d2 after back_inserter: 1 2 3 4 5 1 2 3 4 5
```

`back_inserter()` is an *insert iterator adapter* that calls `push_back()` for each item assigned to it. You can use it anywhere an output iterator is expected.

- There's also a `front_inserter()` adapter for when you want to insert at the front of a container:

```
deque<int> d3{ 47, 73, 114, 138, 54 };
copy(d3.begin(), d3.end(), front_inserter(d2));
printc(d2, "d2 after front_inserter");
```

Output:

d2 after front_inserter: 54 138 114 73 47 1 2 3 4 5 1 2 3 4 5

The `front_inserter()` adapter inserts elements at the front using the container's `push_front()` method. Notice that the elements in the destination are reversed, because each element is inserted before the previous one.

- If we want to insert in the middle, we can use the `inserter()` adapter:

```
auto it2{ d2.begin() + 2};
copy(d1.begin(), d1.end(), inserter(d2, it2));
printc(d2, "d2 after middle insert");
```

Output:

d2 after middle insert: 54 138 1 2 3 4 5 114 73 47 ...

The `inserter()` adapter takes an iterator for the insertion begin point.

- *Stream iterators* are convenient for reading from and writing to `iostream` objects, this is `ostream_iterator()`:

```
cout << "ostream_iterator: ";
copy(d1.begin(), d1.end(), ostream_iterator<int>(cout));
cout << '\n';
```

Output:

ostream_iterator: 12345

- And here is `istream_iterator()`:

```
vector<string> vs{};
copy(istream_iterator<string>(cin),
    istream_iterator<string>(),
    back_inserter(vs));
printc(vs, "vs2");
```

Output:

```
$ ./working < five-words.txt
vs2: this is not a haiku
```

The `istream_iterator()` adapter will return an end iterator by default, if no stream is passed.

- *Reverse adapters* are included with most containers, as function members `rbegin()` and `rend()`:

```
for(auto it = d1.rbegin(); it != d1.rend(); ++it) {
    cout << format("{} ", *it);
}
cout << '\n';
```

Output:

```
5 4 3 2 1
```

How it works...

The iterator adapters work by wrapping around an existing container. When you call an adapter, like `back_inserter()` with a container object:

```
copy(d1.begin(), d1.end(), back_inserter(d2));
```

The adapter returns an object that *mimics* an iterator, in this case a `std::back_insert_iterator` object, which calls the `push_back()` method on the container object each time a value is assigned to the iterator. This allows the adapter to be used in place of an iterator, while performing its useful task.

The `istream_adapter()` also requires a *sentinel*. A sentinel signals the end of an iterator of indeterminate length. When you read from a stream, you don't know how many objects are in the stream until you hit the end. When the stream hits the end, the sentinel will compare equal with the iterator, signaling the end of the stream. The `istream_adapter()` will create a sentinel when it's called without a parameter:

```
auto it = istream_adapter<string>(cin);
auto it_end = istream_adapter<string>();  // creates sentinel
```

This allows you to test for the end of a stream, as you would with any container:

```
for(auto it = istream_iterator<string>(cin);
        it != istream_iterator<string>();
        ++it) {
    cout << format("{} ", *it);
}
cout << '\n';
```

Output:

```
$ ./working < five-words.txt
this is not a haiku
```

Create a generator as iterators

A *generator* is an iterator that generates its own sequence of values. It does not use a container. It creates values on the fly, returning one at a time as needed. A C++ generator stands on its own; it does not need to wrap around another object.

In this recipe, we'll build a generator for a *Fibonacci sequence*. This is a sequence where each number is the sum of the previous two numbers in the sequence, starting with 0 and 1:

$$F_0 = 0, \; F_1 = 1$$

and

$$F_n = F_{n-1} + F_{n-2}$$

for $n > 1$

Figure 4.2 – Definition of a Fibonacci sequence

The first ten values of the Fibonacci sequence, not counting zero, are: 1, 1, 2, 3, 5, 8, 13, 21, 34, 55. This is a close approximation of the *golden ratio* found in nature.

How to do it...

A Fibonacci sequence is often created with a *recursive loop*. Recursion in a generator can be difficult and resource-intensive, so instead we'll just save the previous two values in the sequence and add them together. This is more efficient.

- First let's define a function to print the sequence:

```
void printc(const auto & v, const string_view s = "") {
    if(s.size()) cout << format("{}: ", s);
    for(auto e : v) cout << format("{} ", e);
    cout << '\n';
}
```

We've used this `printc()` function before. It prints an iterable range, along with a description string, if provided.

- Our class begins with a *type alias*, and a few object variables, all in the `private` section.

```
class fib_generator {
    using fib_t = unsigned long;
    fib_t stop_{};
    fib_t count_ { 0 };
    fib_t a_ { 0 };
    fib_t b_ { 1 };
```

The `stop_` variable will be used later as a *sentinel*. It's set to the number of values to generate. `count_` is used to keep track of how many values we've generated. `a_` and `b_` are the previous two sequence values, used for calculating the next value.

- Still in the `private` section, we have a simple function for calculating the next value in the Fibonacci sequence.

```
constexpr void do_fib() {
    const fib_t old_b = b_;
    b_ += a_;
    a_ = old_b;
}
```

- Now in the `public` section, we have a simple constructor with a default value:

```
public:
    explicit fib_generator(fib_t stop = 0) : stop_{ stop
} {}
```

This constructor is used without an argument to create a sentinel. The `stop` argument initializes the `stop_` variable to represent how many values to generate.

- The rest of the public functions are the operator overloads expected of a *forward iterator*:

```
fib_t operator*() const { return b_; }
constexpr fib_generator& operator++() {
    do_fib();
    ++count_;
    return *this;
}
fib_generator operator++(int) {
    auto temp{ *this };
    ++*this;
    return temp;
}
bool operator!=(const fib_generator &o) const {
    return count_ != o.count_;
}
bool operator==(const fib_generator&o) const {
    return count_ == o.count_;
}
const fib_generator& begin() const { return *this; }
const fib_generator end() const {
    auto sentinel = fib_generator();
    sentinel.count_ = stop_;
    return sentinel;
}
fib_t size() { return stop_; }
};
```

There's also a simple `size()` function which can be useful if you need to initialize a target container for a copy operation.

- Now we can use the generator in our main function with a simple call to `printc()`:

```
int main() {
    printc(fib_generator(10));
}
```

This creates an anonymous `fib_generator` object to pass to the `printc()` function.

- We get this output with the first 10 Fibonacci numbers, not including zero:

```
1 1 2 3 5 8 13 21 34 55
```

How it works...

The `fib_generator` class operates as a forward iterator, simply because it provides all the necessary interface functions:

```
fib_generator {
public:
    fib_t operator*() const;
    constexpr fib_generator& operator++();
    fib_generator operator++(int);
    bool operator!=(const fib_generator &o) const;
    bool operator==(const fib_generator&o) const;
    const fib_generator& begin() const;
    const fib_generator end() const;
};
```

As far as the range-based `for` loop is concerned, this is an iterator because it looks like an iterator.

The value is calculated in the `do_fib()` function:

```
constexpr void do_fib() {
    const fib_t old_b = b_;
    b_ += a_;
    a_ = old_b;
}
```

This simply adds b_ += a_, stores the result in b_ and the old b_ in a_, setting it up for the next iteration.

The dereference operator * returns the value from b_, which is the next value in the sequence:

```
fib_t operator*() const { return b_; }
```

The end() function creates an object where the count_ variable is equal to the stop_ variable, creating a *sentinel*:

```
const fib_generator end() const {
    auto sentinel = fib_generator();
    sentinel.count_ = stop_;
    return sentinel;
}
```

Now the equality comparison operator can easily detect the end of the sequence:

```
bool operator==(const fib_generator&o) const {
    return count_ == o.count_;
}
```

There's more...

If we want to make our generator work with the algorithm library, we need to provide the traits aliases. These go at the top of the public section:

```
public:
    using iterator_concept  = std::forward_iterator_tag;
    using iterator_category = std::forward_iterator_tag;
    using value_type        = std::remove_cv_t<fib_t>;
    using difference_type   = std::ptrdiff_t;
    using pointer           = const fib_t*;
    using reference         = const fib_t&;
```

Now we can use our generator with algorithms:

```
fib_generator fib(10);
auto x = ranges::views::transform(fib,
    [](unsigned long x){ return x * x; });
printc(x, "squared:");
```

This uses the `ranges::views` version of the `transform()` algorithm to square every value. The resulting object can be used wherever you can use an iterator. We get this output from the `printc()` call:

```
squared:: 1 1 4 9 25 64 169 441 1156 3025
```

Use reverse iterator adapters to iterate backward

A *reverse iterator adapter* is an abstraction that reverses the direction of an iterator class. It requires a bidirectional iterator.

How to do it...

Most bidirectional containers in the STL include a reverse iterator adapter. Other containers, such as the primitive C-array, do not. Let's look at some examples:

- Let's start with the `printc()` function we've used throughout this chapter:

```cpp
void printc(const auto & c, const string_view s = "") {
    if(s.size()) cout << format("{}: ", s);
    for(auto e : c) cout << format("{} ", e);
    cout << '\n';
}
```

This uses a range-based `for` loop to print the elements of a container.

- The range-based `for` loop works even with primitive C-arrays, which have no iterator class. So, our `printc()` function already works with a C-array:

```cpp
int main() {
    int array[]{ 1, 2, 3, 4, 5 };
    printc(array, "c-array");
}
```

We get this output:

```
c-array: 1 2 3 4 5
```

- We can use the `begin()` and `end()` iterator adapters to create normal forward iterators for the C-array:

```
auto it = std::begin(array);
auto end_it = std::end(array);
while (it != end_it) {
    cout << format("{} ", *it++);
}
```

Output from the `for` loop:

```
1 2 3 4 5
```

- Or we can use the `rbegin()` and `rend()` reverse iterator adapters to create reverse iterators for the C-array:

```
auto it = std::rbegin(array);
auto end_it = std::rend(array);
while (it != end_it) {
    cout << format("{} ", *it++);
}
```

Now our output is reversed:

```
5 4 3 2 1
```

- We can even create a modified version of `printc()` that prints in reverse:

```
void printr(const auto & c, const string_view s = "") {
    if(s.size()) cout << format("{}: ", s);
    auto rbegin = std::rbegin(c);
    auto rend = std::rend(c);
    for(auto it = rbegin; it != rend; ++it) {
        cout << format("{} ", *it);
    }
    cout << '\n';
}
```

When we call it with the C-array:

```
printr(array, "rev c-array");
```

We get this output:

```
rev c-array: 5 4 3 2 1
```

- Of course, this works just as well with any bidirectional STL container:

```
vector<int> v{ 1, 2, 3, 4, 5 };
printc(v, "vector");
printr(v, "rev vector");
```

Output:

```
vector: 1 2 3 4 5
rev vector: 5 4 3 2 1
```

How it works...

A normal iterator class has a begin() iterator that points to the first element, and an end() iterator that points *past* the last element:

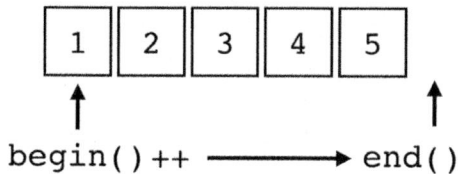

Figure 4.3 – Forward iterator

You iterate the container by incrementing the begin() iterator with the ++ operator, until it reaches the value of the end() iterator.

A reverse iterator adapter *intercepts the iterator interface* and turns it around so the begin() iterator points at to the last element, and end() iterator points *before* the first element. The ++ and -- operators are also inverted:

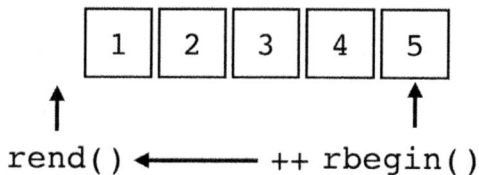

Figure 4.4 – Reverse iterator adapter

In the reversed iterator, the ++ operator decrements and the -- operator increments.

It's worth noting that most bidirectional STL containers already include a reverse iterator adapter, accessible by member functions `rbegin()` and `rend()`:

```
vector<int> v;
it = v.rbegin();
it_end = v.rend();
```

These iterators will operate in reverse and are suitable for many purposes.

Iterate objects of unknown length with a sentinel

Some objects don't have a specific length. To know their length, you need to iterate through all their elements. For example, elsewhere in this chapter we've seen a *generator* that doesn't have a specific length. A more common example would be a *C-string*.

A C-string is a primitive C-array of characters, terminated with a null `'\0'` value.

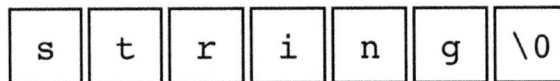

Figure 4.5 – A C-string with its null terminator

We use C-strings all the time, even if we don't realize it. Any *literal* string in C/C++ is a C-string:

```
std::string s = "string";
```

Here, the STL string `s` is initialized with a literal string. The literal string is a C-string. If we look at the individual characters in hexadecimal, we'll see the null terminator:

```
for (char c : "string") {
    std::cout << format("{:02x} ", c);
}
```

The word "string" has six letters. The output from our loop shows seven elements in the array:

```
73 74 72 69 6e 67 00
```

The seventh element is the null terminator.

The loop sees the primitive C-array of characters, with seven values. The fact that it's a string is an abstraction invisible to the loop. If we want the loop to treat it like a string, we'll need an *iterator* and a *sentinel*.

A *sentinel* is an object that signals the end of an iterator of indeterminate length. When the iterator hits the end of the data, the sentinel will compare equal with the iterator.

To see how this works, let's build an iterator for C-strings!

How to do it...

To use a sentinel with a C-string, we need to build a custom iterator. It doesn't need to be complicated, just the essentials for use with a range-based `for` loop.

- We'll start with a couple of convenience definitions:

```
using sentinel_t = const char;
constexpr sentinel_t nullchar = '\0';
```

The `using` alias for `sentinel_t` is `const char`. We'll use this for the sentinel in our class.

We also define the constant `nullchar` for the null character terminator.

- Now we can define our iterator type:

```
class cstr_it {
    const char *s{};
public:
    explicit cstr_it(const char *str) : s{str} {}
    char operator*() const { return *s; }
    cstr_it& operator++() {
        ++s;
        return *this;
    }
    bool operator!=(sentinel_t) const {
        return s != nullptr && *s != nullchar;
    }
    cstr_it begin() const { return *this; }
    sentinel_t end() const { return nullchar; }
};
```

This is short and simple. It's the minimum necessary for a range-based `for` loop. Notice the `end()` function returns a `nullchar` and the `operator!=()` overload compares against the `nullchar`. That's all we need for the sentinel.

- Now we can define a function for printing our C-string using the sentinel:

```
void print_cstr(const char * s) {
    cout << format("{}: ", s);
    for (char c : cstr_it(s)) {
        std::cout << format("{:02x} ", c);
    }
    std::cout << '\n';
}
```

In this function we first print the string. Then we use the `format()` function to print each individual character as a hexadecimal value.

- Now we can call `print_cstr()` from our `main()` function:

```
int main() {
    const char carray[]{"array"};
    print_cstr(carray);

    const char * cstr{"c-string"};
    print_cstr(cstr);
}
```

The output looks like this:

```
array: 61 72 72 61 79
c-string: 63 2d 73 74 72 69 6e 67
```

Notice that there are no extraneous characters and no null terminators. This is because our sentinel tells the for loop to stop when it sees the `nullchar`.

How it works...

The sentinel part of the iterator class is very simple. We can easily use the null terminator as the sentinel value by returning it in the `end()` function:

```
sentinel_t end() const { return nullchar; }
```

Then the not-equal comparison operator can test for it:

```
bool operator!=(sentinel_t) const {
    return s != nullptr && *s != nullchar;
}
```

Notice that the parameter is just a type (`sentinel_t`). A parameter type is necessary for the function signature, but we don't need the value. All that's necessary is to compare the current iterator with the sentinel.

This technique should be useful whenever you have a type or class that doesn't have a predetermined end point for comparison.

Build a zip iterator adapter

Many scripting languages include a function for *zipping* two sequences together. A typical zip operation will take two input sequences and return a pair of values for each position in both inputs:

Consider the case of two sequences – they can be containers, iterators, or initialization lists:

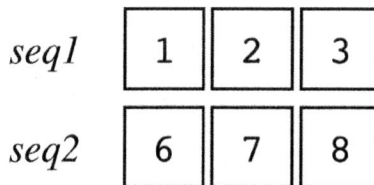

Figure 4.6 – Containers to be zipped

We want to *zip* them together to make a new sequence with pairs of elements from the first two sequences:

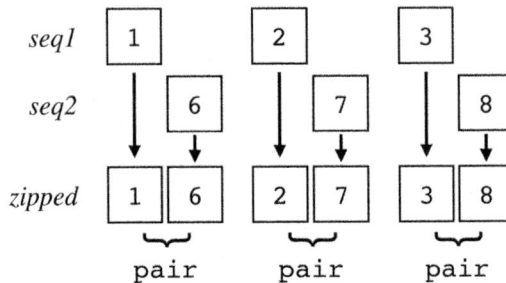

Figure 4.7 – Zip operation

In this recipe we will accomplish this task with an iterator adapter.

How to do it...

In this recipe we'll build a zip iterator adapter that takes two containers of the same type and zips the values into `std::pair` objects:

- In our `main()` function we want to call our adapter with two vectors:

```cpp
int main()
{
    vector<std::string> vec_a {"Bob", "John", "Joni"};
    vector<std::string> vec_b {"Dylan", "Williams",
        "Mitchell"};
    cout << "zipped: ";
    for(auto [a, b] : zip_iterator(vec_a, vec_b)) {
        cout << format("[{}, {}] ", a, b);
    }
    cout << '\n';
}
```

This allows us to use the `zip_iterator` in place of the individual `vector` iterators.

And we expect an output like this:

```
zipped: [Bob, Dylan] [John, Williams] [Joni, Mitchell]
```

- Our iterator adapter is in a class called `zip_iterator`. We'll start with some type aliases for convenience:

```
template<typename T>
class zip_iterator {
    using val_t = typename T::value_type;
    using ret_t = std::pair<val_t, val_t>;
    using it_t = typename T::iterator;
```

These allow us to conveniently define objects and functions.

- We don't store any data in our iterator. We only store copies of the target containers' `begin()` and `end()` iterators:

```
it_t ita_{};
it_t itb_{};
// for begin() and end() objects
it_t ita_begin_{};
it_t itb_begin_{};
it_t ita_end_{};
it_t itb_end_{};
```

`ita_` and `itb_` are iterators from the target containers. The other four iterators are used to generate the `begin()` and `end()` iterators for the `zip_iterator` adapter.

- We also have a private constructor:

```
// private constructor for begin() and end() objects
zip_iterator(it_t ita, it_t itb) : ita_{ita}, itb_{itb}
{}
```

This is used later to construct adapter objects specifically for `begin()` and `end()` iterators.

- In the `public` section, we start with the iterator *traits* type definitions:

```
public:
    using iterator_concept  =
        std::forward_iterator_tag;
    using iterator_category =
        std::forward_iterator_tag;
    using value_type        = std::pair<val_t, val_t>;
    using difference_type   = long int;
    using pointer           = const val_t*;
    using reference         = const val_t&;
```

- The constructor sets up all the private iterator variables:

```
zip_iterator(T& a, T& b)  :
    ita_{a.begin()},
    itb_{b.begin()},
    ita_begin_{ita_},
    itb_begin_{itb_},
    ita_end_{a.end()},
    itb_end_{b.end()}
{}
```

- We define the minimum operator overloads to work with a forward iterator:

```
zip_iterator& operator++() {
    ++ita_;
    ++itb_;
    return *this;
}
bool operator==(const zip_iterator& o) const {
    return ita_ == o.ita_ || itb_ == o.itb_;
}
bool operator!=(const zip_iterator& o) const {
    return !operator==(o);
}
ret_t operator*() const {
    return { *ita_, *itb_ };
}
```

- And finally, the begin() and end() functions return the respective iterators:

```
zip_iterator begin() const
    { return zip_iterator(ita_begin_, itb_begin_); }
zip_iterator end() const
    { return zip_iterator(ita_end_, itb_end_); }
```

These are made simple by the stored iterators and the private constructor.

- Now let's expand our main() function for testing:

```
int main()
{
    vector<std::string> vec_a {"Bob", "John", "Joni"};
    vector<std::string> vec_b {"Dylan", "Williams",
        "Mitchell"};

    cout << "vec_a: ";
    for(auto e : vec_a) cout << format("{} ", e);
    cout << '\n';

    cout << "vec_b: ";
    for(auto e : vec_b) cout << format("{} ", e);
    cout << '\n';

    cout << "zipped: ";
    for(auto [a, b] : zip_iterator(vec_a, vec_b)) {
        cout << format("[{}, {}] ", a, b);
    }
    cout << '\n';
}
```

- This gives us the output we're looking for:

```
vec_a: Bob John Joni
vec_b: Dylan Williams Mitchell
zipped: [Bob, Dylan] [John, Williams] [Joni, Mitchell]
```

How it works...

The *zipped iterator adapter* is an example of how flexible the iterator abstraction can be. We can take the iterators of two containers and use them in one aggregated iterator. Let's see how this works.

The main constructor for the `zip_iterator` class takes two container objects. For the purposes of this discussion, we'll refer to these objects as the *target* objects.

```
zip_iterator(T& a, T& b) :
    ita_{a.begin()},
    itb_{b.begin()},
    ita_begin_{ita_},
    itb_begin_{itb_},
    ita_end_{a.end()},
    itb_end_{b.end()}
{}
```

The constructor initializes the `ita_` and `itb_` variables from the target `begin()` iterators. These will be used to navigate the target objects. The target `begin()` and `end()` iterators are also saved for later use.

These variables are defined in the private section:

```
it_t ita_{};
it_t itb_{};
// for begin() and end() objects
it_t ita_begin_{};
it_t itb_begin_{};
it_t ita_end_{};
it_t itb_end_{};
```

The `it_t` type is defined as the type of the target iterator class:

```
using val_t = typename T::value_type;
using ret_t = std::pair<val_t, val_t>;
using it_t = typename T::iterator;
```

The other aliased types are `val_t` for the type of the target value, and `ret_t` for the return `pair`. These type definitions are used for convenience throughout the class.

The begin() and end() functions use a private constructor that only initializes the ita_ and itb_ values:

```
zip_iterator begin() const
    { return zip_iterator(ita_begin_, itb_begin_); }
zip_iterator end() const
    { return zip_iterator(ita_end_, itb_end_); }
```

The private constructor looks like this:

```
// private constructor for begin() and end() objects
zip_iterator(it_t ita, it_t itb) : ita_{ita}, itb_{itb} {}
```

This is a constructor that takes it_t iterators for parameters. It only initializes ita_ and itb_ so they can be used in the comparison operator overloads.

The rest of the class just acts like a normal iterator, but it's operating on iterators from the target class:

```
zip_iterator& operator++() {
    ++ita_;
    ++itb_;
    return *this;
}
bool operator==(const zip_iterator& o) const {
    return ita_ == o.ita_ || itb_ == o.itb_;
}
bool operator!=(const zip_iterator& o) const {
    return !operator==(o);
}
```

The dereference operator returns a std::pair object (ret_t is an alias for std::pair<val_t, val_t>). This is the interface for retrieving a value from the iterator.

```
ret_t operator*() const {
    return { *ita_, *itb_ };
}
```

There's more...

The `zip_iterator` adapter can be used to easily zip objects into a `map`:

```cpp
map<string, string> name_map{};

for(auto [a, b] : zip_iterator(vec_a, vec_b)) {
    name_map.try_emplace(a, b);
}


cout << "name_map: ";
for(auto [a, b] : name_map) {
    cout << format("[{}, {}] ", a, b);
}
cout << '\n';
```

If we add this code to `main()`, we get this output:

```
name_map: [Bob, Dylan] [John, Williams] [Joni, Mitchell]
```

Create a random-access iterator

This recipe is an example of a full-featured contiguous/random-access iterator. This is the most complete type of iterator for a container. A random-access iterator includes all the features of all the other types of container iterators, along with its random-access capabilities.

While I felt it important to include a complete iterator in this chapter, with over 700 lines of code this example is somewhat larger than the other examples in this book. I'll cover the essential components of the code here. Please see the full source at https://github.com/PacktPublishing/CPP-20-STL-Cookbook/blob/main/chap04/container-iterator.cpp.

How to do it...

We need a container for our iterator. We'll use a simple array for this, and we'll call it `Container`. The `iterator` class is nested within the `Container` class.

All of this is designed to be consistent with the STL container interfaces.

- `Container` is defined as a `template` class. Its `private` section has only two elements:

```
template<typename T>
class Container {
    std::unique_ptr<T[]> c_{};
    size_t n_elements_{};
```

We use a `unique_pointer` for the data. We let the *smart pointer* manage its own memory. This mitigates the need for a `~Container()` destructor. The n_elements_ variable keeps the size of our container.

- In the public section, we have our constructors:

```
Container(initializer_list<T> l) : n_elements_{l.size()}
{
    c_ = std::make_unique<T[]>(n_elements_);
    size_t index{0};
    for(T e : l) {
        c_[index++] = e;
    }
}
```

The first constructor uses an `initializer_list` to pass elements for the container. We call `make_unique` to allocate space and populate the container with a range-based `for` loop.

- We also have a constructor that allocates space without populating the elements:

```
Container(size_t sz) : n_elements_{sz} {
    c_ = std::make_unique<T[]>(n_elements_);
}
```

The `make_unique()` function constructs empty objects for element.

- The size() function returns the number of elements:

```
size_t size() const {
    return n_elements_;
}
```

- The operator[]() function returns an indexed element:

```
const T& operator[](const size_t index) const {
    return c_[index];
}
```

- The at() function returns an indexed element *with bounds checking*:

```
T& at(const size_t index) const {
    if(index > n_elements_ - 1) {
        throw std::out_of_range(
            "Container::at(): index out of range"
        );
    }
    return c_[index];
}
```

This is consistent with STL usage. The at() function is the preferred method.

- The begin() and end() functions call the iterator constructor with the address of the container data.

```
iterator begin() const { return iterator(c_.get()); }
iterator end() const {
    return iterator(c_.get() + n_elements_);
}
```

The unique_ptr::get() function returns the address from the smart pointer.

- The iterator class is nested within the Container class as a public member.

```
class iterator {
    T* ptr_;
```

The iterator class has one private member, a pointer that's initialized in the begin() and end() methods of the Container class.

- The iterator constructor takes a pointer to the container data.

```
iterator(T* ptr = nullptr) : ptr_{ptr} {}
```

We provide a default value because the standard requires a default constructor.

Operator overloads

This iterator provides operator overloads for the following operators: ++, *postfix ++*, --, *postfix --*, [], *default comparison* <=> *(C++20)*, ==, *, ->, +, *non-member +, numeric -, object -*, +=, and -=. We'll cover a few notable overloads here. See the source code for all of them.

- The C++20 default comparison operator <=> provides the functionality of the full suite of comparison operators, except the equality == operator:

```
const auto operator<=>(const iterator& o) const {
    return ptr_ <=> o.ptr_;
}
```

This is a C++20 feature, so it requires a compliant compiler and library.

- There are two + operator overloads. These support *it + n* and *n + it* operations.

```
iterator operator+(const size_t n) const {
    return iterator(ptr_ + n);
}
// non-member operator (n + it)
friend const iterator operator+(
        const size_t n, const iterator& o) {
    return iterator(o.ptr_ + n);
}
```

The friend declaration is a special case. When used in a template class member function, it's the equivalent of a non-member function. This allows a non-member function to be defined in the class context.

- The - operator also has two overloads. We need to support both a numeric operand and an iterator operand.

```
const iterator operator-(const size_t n) {
    return iterator(ptr_ - n);
}
const size_t operator-(const iterator& o) {
    return ptr_ - o.ptr_;
}
```

This allows both *it – n* and *it – it* operations. There's no need for a non-member function, as *n – it* is not a valid operation.

Validation code

The C++20 specification §23.3.4.13 requires a specific set of operations and results for a valid random-access iterator. I've included a `unit_tests()` function in the source code to validate those requirements.

The `main()` function creates a `Container` object and performs some simple validation functions.

- First, we create a `Container<string>` object x with ten values.

```
Container<string> x{"one", "two", "three", "four",
"five",
    "six", "seven", "eight", "nine", "ten" };
cout << format("Container x size: {}\n", x.size());
```

The output gives the number of elements:

```
Container x size: 10
```

- We display the elements of the container with a range-based `for` loop:

```
puts("Container x:");
for(auto e : x) {
    cout << format("{} ", e);
}
cout << '\n';
```

Output:

```
Container x:
one two three four five six seven eight nine ten
```

- Next, we test several direct access methods:

```
puts("direct access elements:");
cout << format("element at(5): {}\n", x.at(5));
cout << format("element [5]: {}\n", x[5]);
cout << format("element begin + 5: {}\n",
    *(x.begin() + 5));
cout << format("element 5 + begin: {}\n",
    *(5 + x.begin()));
cout << format("element begin += 5: {}\n",
    *(x.begin() += 5));
```

Output:

```
direct access elements:
element at(5): six
element [5]: six
element begin + 5: six
element 5 + begin: six
element begin += 5: six
```

- We test the container with a ranges::views pipe and views::reverse:

```
puts("views pipe reverse:");
auto result = x | views::reverse;
for(auto v : result) cout << format("{} ", v);
cout << '\n';
```

Output:

```
views pipe reverse:
ten nine eight seven six five four three two one
```

- Finally, we create a Container object y with 10 uninitialized elements:

```
Container<string> y(x.size());
cout << format("Container y size: {}\n", y.size());
for(auto e : y) {
    cout << format("[{}] ", e);
}
cout << '\n';
```

Output:

```
Container y size: 10
[] [] [] [] [] [] [] [] [] []
```

How it works...

Although it's a lot of code, this iterator is no more complicated than a smaller iterator. Most of the code is in the operator overloads, which are mostly one or two lines of code each.

The container itself is managed by a *smart pointer*. This is simplified by the fact that it's a flat array and doesn't require expansion or compression.

Of course, the STL provides a flat `std::array` class, as well as other more complex data structures. Still, you may find it valuable to demystify the workings of a complete iterator class.

5
Lambda Expressions

The C++11 standard introduced the *lambda expression* (sometimes called the *lambda function*, or just *lambda*). This feature allows an anonymous function to be used in the context of an expression. Lambdas may be used in function calls, containers, variables, and other expression contexts. It may sound innocuous, but it's remarkably useful.

Let's start with a brief review of lambda expressions.

Lambda expressions

A lambda is essentially an anonymous function as a literal expression:

```cpp
auto la = []{ return "Hello\n"; };
```

The variable `la` may now be used as if it were a function:

```cpp
cout << la();
```

It can be passed to another function:

```cpp
f(la);
```

It can be passed to another lambda:

```
const auto la = []{ return "Hello\n"; };
const auto lb = [](auto a){ return a(); };
cout << lb(la);
```

Output:

Hello

Or it can be passed anonymously (as a literal):

```
const auto lb = [](auto a){ return a(); };
cout << lb([]{ return "Hello\n"; });
```

Closures

The term *closure* is often applied to any anonymous function. Strictly speaking, a closure is a function that allows the use of symbols outside its own lexical scope.

You may have noticed the square brackets in the definition of a lambda:

```
auto la = []{ return "Hello\n"; };
```

The square brackets are used to specify a list of *captures*. Captures are outside variables that are accessible from within the scope of the lambda body. If I try to use an outside variable without listing it as a capture, I'll get a compilation error:

```
const char * greeting{ "Hello\n" };
const auto la = []{ return greeting; };
cout << la();
```

When I try to compile this with GCC, I get the following error:

In lambda function:

error: 'greeting' is not captured

This is because the body of the lambda has its own lexical scope and the greeting variable is outside of that scope.

I can specify the `greeting` variable in a capture. This allows the variable into the scope of the lambda:

```cpp
const char * greeting{ "Hello\n" };
const auto la = [greeting]{ return greeting; };
cout << la();
```

Now it compiles and runs as expected:

```
$ ./working
Hello
```

This ability to capture variables outside its own scope is what makes a lambda a *closure*. People use the term in different ways, and that's fine, so long as we can understand each other. Still, it's good to know what the term means.

Lambda expressions allow us to write good, clean generic code. They allow the use of *functional programming* patterns, where we can use lambdas as functional parameters to algorithms and even other lambdas.

In this chapter, we will cover the use of lambdas with the STL, in the following recipes:

- Use lambdas for scoped reusable code
- Use lambdas as predicates with the algorithm library
- Use `std::function` as a polymorphic wrapper
- Concatenate lambdas with recursion
- Combine predicates with logical conjunction
- Call multiple lambdas with the same input
- Use mapped lambdas for a jump table

Technical requirements

You can find the code for this chapter on GitHub at `https://github.com/ PacktPublishing/CPP-20-STL-Cookbook/tree/main/chap05`.

Use lambdas for scoped reusable code

Lambda expressions can be defined and stored for later use. They can be passed as parameters, stored in data structures, and called in different contexts with different parameters. They are as flexible as functions, but with the mobility of data.

How to do it...

Let's start with a simple program that we'll use to test various configurations of lambda expressions:

- We'll first define a `main()` function and use it to experiment with lambdas:

```
int main() {
    ... // code goes here
}
```

- Inside the `main()` function, we'll declare a couple of lambdas. The basic definition of a lambda requires a pair of square brackets and a block of code in curly brackets:

```
auto one = [](){ return "one"; };
auto two = []{ return "two"; };
```

Notice that the first example `one` includes parentheses after the square brackets, and the second example `two` does not. The empty parameter parentheses are commonly included, but are not always required. The return type is inferred by the compiler.

- I can call these functions with `cout`, or with `format`, or in any context that will take a C-string:

```
cout << one() << '\n';
cout << format("{}\n", two());
```

- In many cases, the compiler can determine the return type from *automatic type deduction*. Otherwise, you can specify the return type with the `->` operator:

```
auto one = []() -> const char * { return "one"; };
auto two = []() -> auto { return "two"; };
```

Lambdas use the *trailing return type* syntax. This consists of the `->` operator followed by the type specification. If the return type is not specified, it is considered `auto`. If you use a trailing return type, *the parameter parentheses are required*.

- Let's define a lambda to print out the values from our other lambdas:

```
auto p = [](auto v) { cout << v() << '\n'; };
```

The p() lambda expects a lambda (or function) as its parameter v, and calls it in its function body.

The auto type parameter makes this lambda an *abbreviated template*. Before C++20, this was the only way to template a lambda. Beginning with C++20, you may specify template parameters (without the template keyword) after the capture brackets. This is the equivalent with template parameters:

```
auto p = []<template T>(T v) { cout << v() << '\n'; };
```

The abbreviated auto version is simpler and more common. It works well for most purposes.

- Now we can pass an anonymous lambda in the function call:

```
p([]{ return "lambda call lambda"; });
```

The output is:

```
lambda call lambda
```

- If we need to pass parameters to an anonymous lambda, we can put them in parentheses after the lambda expression:

```
<< [](auto l, auto r){ return l + r; }(47, 73)
    << '\n';
```

The function parameters, 47 and 73, are passed to the anonymous lambda in the parentheses after the function body.

- You can access variables from the outside scope of the lambda by including them as *captures* in the square brackets:

```
int num{1};
p([num]{ return num; });
```

- Or you can capture them by reference:

```
int num{0};
auto inc = [&num]{ num++; };
for (size_t i{0}; i < 5; ++i) {
    inc();
```

```
    }
    cout << num << '\n';
```

The output is as follows:

```
    5
```

This allows you to modify a captured variable.

- You can also define a local capture variable that maintains its state:

```
    auto counter = [n = 0]() mutable { return ++n; };
    for (size_t i{0}; i < 5; ++i) {
        cout << format("{}, ", counter());
    }
    cout << '\n';
```

Output:

```
    1, 2, 3, 4, 5,
```

The mutable specifier allows the lambda to modify its captures. Lambdas default to const-qualified.

As with the trailing return type, any *specifier* requires the parameter parentheses.

- The lambda supports two types of *default capture*:

```
    int a = 47;
    int b = 73;
    auto l1 = []{ return a + b; };
```

If I try to compile this code, I get an error that includes:

```
    note: the lambda has no capture-default
```

One type of default capture is indicated by an equal sign:

```
    auto l1 = [=]{ return a + b; };
```

This will capture all the symbols in the lambda's scope. The equal sign performs *capture by copy*. It will capture a copy of the objects as if they were copied with an assignment operator.

The other default capture uses an ampersand for *capture by reference*:

```
    auto l1 = [&]{ return a + b; };
```

This is a default capture that captures by reference.

The default captures only use symbols when they are referenced, so they're not as messy as they may look. That said, I recommend explicit captures where possible as they generally improve readability.

How it works...

The syntax of a lambda expression is as follows:

```
[ capture-list ] ( parameters )
        mutable             (optional)
        constexpr           (optional)
        exception attr      (optional)
        -> return type      (optional)
    { body }
```

Figure 5.1 – Syntax of the lambda expression

The only required parts of a lambda expression are the capture list and the body, which may be empty:

```
[]{}
```

This is the minimal lambda expression. It captures nothing and does nothing.

Let's consider each of the parts.

Capture-list

The *capture-list* specifies what we capture, if anything. It cannot be omitted, but it may be empty. We can use [=] to capture all variables *by copy* or [&] to capture all variables *by reference*, within the scope of the lambda.

You may capture individual variables by listing them in the brackets:

```
[a, b]{ return a + b; }
```

The specified captures default to copy. You may capture by reference with the reference operator:

```
[&a, &b]{ return a + b; }
```

When you capture by reference, you may modify the referenced variable.

> **Note**
>
> You cannot capture object members directly. You may capture `this` or `*this` to dereference class members.

Parameters

As with a function, parameters are specified in parentheses:

```
[](int a, int b){ return a + b };
```

If there are no parameters, specifiers, or trailing return type, the parentheses are optional. A specifier or trailing return type makes the parentheses required:

```
[]() -> int { return 47 + 73 };
```

The mutable modifier (optional)

A lambda expression defaults to `const`-qualified unless you specify the `mutable` modifier. This allows it to be used in `const` context, but it also means that it cannot modify any of its captured-by-copy variables. For example:

```
[a]{ return ++a; };
```

This will fail to compile with an error message like this:

```
In lambda function:
error: increment of read-only variable 'a'
```

With the `mutable` modifier, the lambda is no longer `const`-qualified and the captured variable may be changed:

```
[a]() mutable { return ++a; };
```

The constexpr specifier (optional)

You may use `constexpr` to explicitly specify that you want your lambda to be considered a *constant expression*. This means that it may be evaluated at compile time. If the lambda meets the requirements, it may be considered `constexpr` even without the specifier.

The exception attribute (optional)

You can use the `noexcept` specifier to declare that your lambda does not throw any exceptions.

The trailing return type (optional)

By default, the lambda return type is deduced from the `return` statement, as if it were an `auto` return type. You may optionally specify a *trailing return type* with the `->` operator:

```
[](int a, int b) -> long { return a + b; };
```

The parameter parentheses are required if you use any of the optional specifiers or the trailing return type.

> **Note**
>
> Some compilers, including GCC, allow empty parameter parentheses to be omitted even when there's a specifier or trailing return type. This is not correct. According to the specification, the parameters, specifiers, and trailing return type are all part of the *lambda-declarator* and the parentheses are required when any part of it is included. This may change in a future version of C++.

Use lambdas as predicates with the algorithm library

Some functions in the `algorithm` library require the use of a *predicate* function. A predicate is a function (or functor or lambda) that tests a condition and returns a Boolean `true`/`false` response.

How to do it...

For this recipe, we will experiment with the `count_if()` algorithm using different types of predicates:

- First, let's create a function for use as a predicate. A predicate takes a certain number of arguments and returns a `bool`. A predicate for `count_if()` takes one argument:

```
bool is_div4(int i) {
    return i % 4 == 0;
}
```

This predicate checks whether an `int` value is divisible by 4.

- In `main()`, we'll define a vector of `int` values, and use it to test our predicate function with `count_if()`:

```
int main() {
    const vector<int> v{ 1, 7, 4, 9, 4, 8, 12, 10, 20 };
    int count = count_if(v.begin(), v.end(), is_div4);
    cout << format("numbers divisible by 4: {}\n",
        count);
}
```

The output is as follows:

`numbers divisible by 4: 5`

(The 5 divisible numbers are: 4, 4, 8, 12, and 20.)

The `count_if()` algorithm uses the predicate function to determine which elements of the sequence to count. It calls the predicate with each element as a parameter, and only counts the element if the predicate returns `true`.

In this case, we used a function as a predicate.

- We could also use a *functor* as a predicate:

```
struct is_div4 {
    bool operator()(int i) {
        return i % 4 == 0;
    }
};
```

The only change here is that we need to use an *instance* of the class as the predicate:

```
int count = count_if(v.begin(), v.end(), is_div4());
```

The advantage of a functor is that it can carry context and access class and instance variables. This was the common way to use predicates before C++11 introduced lambda expressions.

- With a lambda expression, we have the best of both worlds: the simplicity of a function and the power of a functor. We can use a lambda as a variable:

```
auto is_div4 = [](int i){ return i % 4 == 0; };
int count = count_if(v.begin(), v.end(), is_div4);
```

Or we can use an anonymous lambda:

```
int count = count_if(v.begin(), v.end(),
    [](int i){ return i % 4 == 0; });
```

- We can take advantage of the lambda capture by wrapping the lambda in a function, and using that function context to produce the same lambda with different parameters:

```
auto is_div_by(int divisor) {
    return [divisor](int i){ return i % divisor == 0; };
}
```

This function returns a predicate lambda with the divisor from the capture context.

We can then use that predicate with count_if():

```
for( int i : { 3, 4, 5 } ) {
    auto pred = is_div_by(i);
    int count = count_if(v.begin(), v.end(), pred);
    cout << format("numbers divisible by {}: {}\n", i,
        count);
}
```

Each call to is_div_by() returns a predicate with a different divisor from i. Now we get this output:

```
numbers divisible by 3: 2
numbers divisible by 4: 5
numbers divisible by 5: 2
```

How it works...

The type of a function pointer is represented as a pointer followed by the function call () operator:

```
void (*)()
```

You can declare a function pointer and initialize it with the name of an existing function:

```
void (*fp)() = func;
```

Once declared, a function pointer may be dereferenced and used as if it were the function itself:

```
func();  // do the func thing
```

A lambda expression has the same type as a function pointer:

```
void (*fp)() = []{ cout << "foo\n"; };
```

This means that wherever you use a function pointer with a certain signature, you may also use a lambda with the same signature. This allows function pointers, functors, and lambdas to work interchangeably:

```
bool (*fp)(int) = is_div4;
bool (*fp)(int) = [](int i){ return i % 4 == 0; };
```

Because of this interchangeability, an algorithm such as count_if() accepts a function, functor, or lambda where it expects a predicate with a particular function signature.

This applies to any algorithm that uses a predicate.

Use std::function as a polymorphic wrapper

The class template std::function is a thin polymorphic wrapper for functions. It can store, copy, and invoke any function, lambda expression, or other function objects. It can be useful in places where you would like to store a reference to a function or lambda. Using std::function allows you to store functions and lambdas with different signatures in the same container, and it maintains the context of lambda captures.

How to do it...

This recipe uses the std::function class to store different specializations of a lambda in a vector:

- This recipe is contained in the main() function, where we start by declaring three containers of different types:

```
int main() {
    deque<int> d;
    list<int> l;
    vector<int> v;
```

These containers, deque, list, and vector, will be referenced by a *template* lambda.

- We'll declare a simple print_c lambda function for printing out the containers:

```
auto print_c = [] (auto& c) {
    for(auto i : c) cout << format ("{} ", i);
    cout << '\n';
};
```

- Now we declare a lambda that returns an *anonymous* lambda:

```
auto push_c = [] (auto& container) {
    return [&container] (auto value) {
        container.push_back(value);
    };
};
```

The push_c lambda takes a reference to a container, which is *captured* by the anonymous lambda. The anonymous lambda calls the push_back() member on the captured container. The return value from push_c is the anonymous lambda.

- Now we declare a vector of std::function elements, and populate it with three instances of push_c():

```
const vector<std::function<void(int)>>
    consumers { push_c(d), push_c(l), push_c(v) };
```

Each of the elements in the initializer list is a function call to the push_c lambda. push_c returns an instance of the anonymous lambda, which gets stored in the vector via the function wrapper. The push_c lambda is called with the three containers, d, l, and v. The containers are passed as *captures* with the anonymous lambda.

- Now we loop through the consumers vector, and call each of the lambda elements 10 times, populating the three containers with integers 0–9 in each container:

```
for(auto &consume : consumers) {
    for (int i{0}; i < 10; ++i) {
        consume(i);
    }
}
```

- Now our three containers, the deque, list, and vector, should all be populated with integers. Let's print them out:

```
print_c(d);
print_c(l);
print_c(v);
```

Our output should be:

```
0 1 2 3 4 5 6 7 8 9
0 1 2 3 4 5 6 7 8 9
0 1 2 3 4 5 6 7 8 9
```

How it works...

Lambdas are often used with indirection and this recipe is a good example of such. For example, the push_c lambda returns an anonymous lambda:

```
auto push_c = [](auto& container) {
    return [&container](auto value) {
        container.push_back(value);
    };
};
```

This anonymous lambda is the one that's stored in the vector:

```
const vector<std::function<void(int)>>
    consumers { push_c(d), push_c(l), push_c(v) };
```

This is the definition of the consumers container. It is initialized with three elements, where each element is initialized with a call to push_c, which returns an anonymous lambda. It's the anonymous lambda that gets stored in the vector, not the push_c lambda.

The vector definition uses the std::function class as the type of the elements. The function constructor takes any callable object and stores its reference as the function target:

```
template< class F >
function( F&& f );
```

When its function call () operator is invoked, the `function` object calls the target function with the intended parameters:

```
for(auto &c : consumers) {
    for (int i{0}; i < 10; ++i) {
        c(i);
    }
}
```

This calls each *anonymous lambda*, as stored in the `consumers` container, 10 times, thus populating the d, l, and v containers.

There's more...

The nature of the `std::function` class makes it useful for many purposes. You can think of it as a polymorphic function container. It can store a standalone function:

```
void hello() {
    cout << "hello\n";
}
int main() {
    function<void(void)> h = hello;
    h();
}
```

It can store a member function, using `std::bind` to bind function parameters:

```
struct hello {
    void greeting() const { cout << "Hello Bob\n"; }
};
int main() {
    hello bob{};
    const function<void(void)> h =
        std::bind(&hello::greeting, &bob);
    h();
}
```

Or it can store any executable object:

```
struct hello {
    void operator()() const { cout << "Hello Bob\n"; }
};
int main() {
    const function<void(void)> h = hello();
    h();
}
```

The output is as follows:

```
Hello Bob
```

Concatenate lambdas with recursion

You can stack lambdas so that the output of one is the input of the next, using a simple recursive function. This creates a simple way to build one function upon another.

How to do it...

This is a short and simple recipe that uses one recursive function to do most of the work:

- We'll start by defining the concatenation function concat():

```
template <typename T, typename ...Ts>
auto concat(T t, Ts ...ts) {
    if constexpr (sizeof...(ts) > 0) {
        return [&](auto ...parameters) {
            return t(concat(ts...)(parameters...));
        };
    } else {
        return t;
    }
}
```

This function returns an anonymous lambda, which in turn calls the function again, until the parameter pack is exhausted.

- In the `main()` function, we create a couple of lambdas and call the `concat()` function with them:

```cpp
int main() {
    auto twice = [](auto i) { return i * 2; };
    auto thrice = [](auto i) { return i * 3; };
    auto combined = concat(thrice, twice,
        std::plus<int>{});
    std::cout << format("{}\n", combined(2, 3));
}
```

The `concat()` function is called with three parameters: two lambdas, and the `std::plus()` function.

As the recursion unravels, the functions are called right-to-left, starting with `plus()`. The `plus()` function takes two arguments and returns the sum. The return value from `plus()` is passed to `twice()`, and its return value is passed to `thrice()`. The result is then printed to the console with `format()`:

```
30
```

How it works...

The `concat()` function is simple, but may be confusing due to the *recursion* and the *indirection* of the returned lambda:

```cpp
template <typename T, typename ...Ts>
auto concat(T t, Ts ...ts) {
    if constexpr (sizeof...(ts) > 0) {
        return [&](auto ...parameters) {
            return t(concat(ts...)(parameters...));
        };
    } else {
        return t;
    }
}
```

The `concat()` function is called with a parameter pack. With ellipses, the `sizeof...` operator returns the number of elements in the parameter pack. This is used to test for the end of the recursion.

The `concat()` function returns a lambda. The lambda recursively calls the `concat()` function. Because the first argument of `concat()` is not part of the parameter pack, each recursive call peels off the first element of the pack.

The outer `return` statement returns the lambda. The inner `return` is from the lambda. The lambda calls the function that was passed to `concat()` and returns its value.

Feel free to take this apart and study it. There's value in this technique.

Combine predicates with logical conjunction

This example wraps a lambda in a function to create a custom conjunction for use with an algorithm predicate.

How to do it...

The `copy_if()` algorithm requires a predicate that takes one parameter. In this recipe, we will create a predicate lambda from three other lambdas:

- First, we'll write the `combine()` function. This function returns a lambda for use with the `copy_if()` algorithm:

```
template <typename F, typename A, typename B>
auto combine(F binary_func, A a, B b) {
    return [=] (auto param) {
        return binary_func(a(param), b(param));
    };
}
```

The `combine()` function takes three function parameters – a binary conjunction and two predicates – and returns a lambda that calls the conjunction with the two predicates.

- In the `main()` function, we create the lambdas for use with `combine()`:

```
int main() {
    auto begins_with = [] (const string &s) {
        return s.find("a") == 0;
    };
    auto ends_with = [] (const string &s) {
```

```
              return s.rfind("b") == s.length() - 1;
      };
      auto bool_and = [](const auto& l, const auto& r){
              return l && r;
      };
```

The begins_with and ends_with lambdas are simple filter predicates to find strings that begin with 'a' and end with 'b', respectively. The bool_and lambda is the conjunction.

- Now we can call the copy_if algorithm with combine():

```
      std::copy_if(istream_iterator<string>{cin}, {},
                   ostream_iterator<string>{cout, " "},
                   combine(bool_and, begins_with,
                      ends_with));
      cout << '\n';
```

The combine() function returns a lambda that combines the two predicates with the conjunction.

The output looks like the following:

```
      $ echo aabb bbaa foo bar abazb | ./conjunction
      aabb abazb
```

How it works...

The std::copy_if() algorithm requires a predicate function that takes one parameter, but our conjunction requires two parameters, each of which require one parameter. We resolve this with a function that returns a lambda specifically for this context:

```
template <typename F, typename A, typename B>
auto combine(F binary_func, A a, B b) {
    return [=](auto param) {
        return binary_func(a(param), b(param));
    };
}
```

The combine() function creates a lambda from three parameters, each of which is a function. The returned lambda takes the one parameter that's required of the predicate function. Now we can call copy_if() with the combine() function:

```
std::copy_if(istream_iterator<string>{cin}, {},
              ostream_iterator<string>{cout, " "},
              combine(bool_and, begins_with, ends_with));
```

This passes the combined lambda to the algorithm so it can operate within that context.

Call multiple lambdas with the same input

You can easily create multiple instances of a lambda with different capture values by wrapping the lambda in a function. This allows you to call different versions of a lambda with the same input.

How to do it...

This is a simple example of a lambda that wraps a value in different types of braces:

- We'll start by creating the wrapper function braces():

```
auto braces (const char a, const char b) {
    return [a, b](const char v) {
        cout << format("{}{}{} ", a, v, b);
    };
}
```

The braces() function wraps a lambda that returns a three-value string, where the first and last values are characters passed to the lambda as captures, and the middle value is passed as a parameter.

- In the main() function, we use braces() to create four lambdas, using four different sets of braces:

```
auto a = braces('(', ')');
auto b = braces('[', ']');
auto c = braces('{', '}');
auto d = braces('|', '|');
```

- Now we can call our lambdas from a simple for() loop:

```
for( int i : { 1, 2, 3, 4, 5 } ) {
    for( auto x : { a, b, c, d } ) x(i);
    cout << '\n';
}
```

This is two nested for() loops. The outer loop simply counts from 1 to 5, passing an integer to the inner loop. The inner loop calls the lambdas with the braces.

Both loops use an *initializer list* as the container in a range-based for() loop. This is a convenient technique for looping through a small set of values.

- The output from our program looks like this:

```
(1)  [1]  {1}  |1|
(2)  [2]  {2}  |2|
(3)  [3]  {3}  |3|
(4)  [4]  {4}  |4|
(5)  [5]  {5}  |5|
```

The output shows each of the integers, in each combination of braces.

How it works...

This is a simple example of how to use a wrapper for a lambda. The braces() function constructs a lambda using the braces passed to it:

```
auto braces (const char a, const char b) {
    return [a, b] (const auto v) {
        cout << format("{}{}{} ", a, v, b);
    };
}
```

By passing the braces() function parameters to the lambda, it can return a lambda with that context. So, each of the assignments in the main function carries those parameters with it:

```
auto a = braces('(', ')');
auto b = braces('[', ']');
auto c = braces('{', '}');
auto d = braces('|', '|');
```

When these lambdas are called with a digit, they will return a string with that digit in the corresponding braces.

Use mapped lambdas for a jump table

A jump table is a useful pattern when you want to select an action from a user or other input. Jump tables are often implemented in if/else or switch structures. In this recipe, we'll build a concise jump table using only an STL map and anonymous lambdas.

How to do it...

It's easy to build a simple jump table from a map and lambdas. The map provides simple indexed navigation and the lambda can be stored as payload. Here's how to do it:

- First, we'll create a simple prompt() function to get input from the console:

```cpp
const char prompt(const char * p) {
    std::string r;
    cout << format("{} > ", p);
    std::getline(cin, r, '\n');

    if(r.size() < 1) return '\0';
    if(r.size() > 1) {
        cout << "Response too long\n";
        return '\0';
    }
    return toupper(r[0]);
}
```

The C-string parameter is used as a prompt. std::getline() is called to get input from the user. The response is stored in r, checked for length, then if it's one character in length, it's converted to uppercase and returned.

- In the main() function, we declare and initialize a map of lambdas:

```cpp
using jumpfunc = void(*)();
map<const char, jumpfunc> jumpmap {
    { 'A', []{ cout << "func A\n"; } },
    { 'B', []{ cout << "func B\n"; } },
    { 'C', []{ cout << "func C\n"; } },
```

```
            { 'D', []{ cout << "func D\n"; } },
            { 'X', []{ cout << "Bye!\n"; } }
    };
```

The map container is loaded with anonymous lambdas for the jump table. These lambdas could easily call other functions or perform simple tasks.

The `using` alias is for convenience. We're using the function pointer type `void(*)()` for the lambda payload. If you prefer, you could use `std::function()` if you need more flexibility or if you just find it more readable. It has very little overhead:

```
using jumpfunc = std::function<void()>;
```

- Now we can prompt for user input and select an action from the `map`:

```
char select{};
while(select != 'X') {
    if((select = prompt("select A/B/C/D/X"))) {
        auto it = jumpmap.find(select);
        if(it != jumpmap.end()) it->second();
        else cout << "Invalid response\n";
    }
}
```

This is how we use the map-based jump table. We loop until `'X'` is selected for exit. We call `prompt()` with a prompt string, call `find()` on the `map` object, then call the lambda with `it->second()`.

How it works...

The `map` container makes an excellent jump table. It's concise and easy to navigate:

```
using jumpfunc = void(*)();
map<const char, jumpfunc> jumpmap {
    { 'A', []{ cout << "func A\n"; } },
    { 'B', []{ cout << "func B\n"; } },
    { 'C', []{ cout << "func C\n"; } },
    { 'D', []{ cout << "func D\n"; } },
    { 'X', []{ cout << "Bye!\n"; } }
};
```

Anonymous lambdas are stored as payload in the map container. The keys are the character responses from the menu of actions.

You can test the validity of a key and select a lambda in one action:

```
auto it = jumpmap.find(select);
if(it != jumpmap.end()) it->second();
else cout << "Invalid response\n";
```

This is a simple, elegant solution, where we would have otherwise used awkward branching code.

6

STL Algorithms

Much of the power of the STL is in the standardization of container interfaces. If a container has a particular capability, there's a good chance that the interface for that capability is standardized across container types. This standardization makes possible a library of *algorithms* that operate seamlessly across containers and sequences sharing a common interface.

For example, if we want to sum all the elements in a vector of int, we could use a loop:

```
vector<int> x { 1, 2, 3, 4, 5 };
long sum{};
for( int i : x ) sum += i;                        // sum is 15
```

Or we could use an algorithm:

```
vector<int> x { 1, 2, 3, 4, 5 };
auto sum = accumulate(x.begin(), x.end(), 0);   // sum is 15
```

This same syntax works with other containers:

```
deque<int> x { 1, 2, 3, 4, 5 };
auto sum = accumulate(x.begin(), x.end(), 0);   // sum is 15
```

The algorithm version is not necessarily shorter, but it is easier to read and easier to maintain. And an algorithm is often more efficient than the equivalent loop.

Beginning with C++20, the `ranges` library provides a set of alternative algorithms that operate with *ranges* and *views*. This book will demonstrate those alternatives where appropriate. For more information on ranges and views, refer to the recipe *Create views into containers with ranges* in *Chapter 1, New C++20 Features*, of this book.

Most of the algorithms are in the `algorithm` header. Some numeric algorithms, notably `accumulate()`, are in the `numeric` header, and some memory-related algorithms are in the `memory` header.

We will cover STL algorithms in the following recipes:

- Copy from one iterator to another
- Join container elements into a string
- Sort containers with `std::sort`
- Modify containers with `std::transform`
- Find items in a container
- Limit the values of a container to a range with `std::clamp`
- Sample data sets with `std::sample`
- Generate permutations of data sequences
- Merge sorted containers

Technical requirements

You can find the code files for this chapter on GitHub at `https://github.com/PacktPublishing/CPP-20-STL-Cookbook/tree/main/chap06`.

Copy from one iterator to another

The *copy algorithms* are generally used to copy from and to containers, but in fact, they work with iterators, which is far more flexible.

How to do it...

In this recipe, we will experiment with `std::copy` and `std::copy_n` to get a good understanding of how they work:

- Let's start with a function to print a container:

```
void printc(auto& c, string_view s = "") {
    if(s.size()) cout << format("{}: ", s);
    for(auto e : c) cout << format("[{}] ", e);
    cout << '\n';
}
```

- In `main()`, we define a `vector` and print it with `printc()`:

```
int main() {
    vector<string> v1
        { "alpha", "beta", "gamma", "delta",
          "epsilon" };
    printc(v1);
}
```

We get this output:

v1: [alpha] [beta] [gamma] [delta] [epsilon]

- Now, let's create a second `vector` with enough space to copy the first `vector`:

```
vector<string> v2(v1.size());
```

- We can copy `v1` to `v2` using the `std::copy()` algorithm:

```
std::copy(v1.begin(), v1.end(), v2.begin());
printc(v2);
```

The `std::copy()` algorithm takes two iterators for the range of the copy source, and one iterator for the destination. In this case, we give it the `begin()` and `end()` iterators of `v1` to copy the entire `vector`. The `begin()` iterator of `v2` serves as the destination for the copy.

Our output is now:

v1: [alpha] [beta] [gamma] [delta] [epsilon]
v2: [alpha] [beta] [gamma] [delta] [epsilon]

- The `copy()` algorithm does not allocate space for the destination. So, v2 must already have the space for the copy. Alternately, you can use the `back_inserter()` iterator adapter to insert the elements at the back of the `vector`:

```
vector<string> v2{};
std::copy(v1.begin(), v1.end(), back_inserter(v2))
```

- We can also use the `ranges::copy()` algorithm to copy an entire *range*. A container object serves as a range so we can use `v1` as the source. We still use an iterator for the destination:

```
vector<string> v2(v1.size());
ranges::copy(v1, v2.begin());
```

This also works with `back_inserter()`:

```
vector<string> v2{};
ranges::copy(v1, back_inserter(v2));
```

Output:

```
v2: [alpha] [beta] [gamma] [delta] [epsilon]
```

- You can copy a certain number of elements using `copy_n()`:

```
vector<string> v3{};
std::copy_n(v1.begin(), 3, back_inserter(v3));
printc(v3, "v3");
```

In the second argument, the `copy_n()` algorithm is a *count* for the number of elements to copy. The output is:

```
v3: [alpha] [beta] [gamma]
```

- There's also a `copy_if()` algorithm that uses a Boolean *predicate function* to determine which elements to copy:

```
vector<string> v4{};
std::copy_if(v1.begin(), v1.end(), back_inserter(v4),
    [](string& s){ return s.size() > 4; });
printc(v4, "v4");
```

There's also a ranges version of `copy_if()`:

```
vector<string> v4{};
ranges::copy_if(v1, back_inserter(v4),
```

```
    [](string& s){ return s.size() > 4; });
printc(v4, "v4");
```

The output includes only strings longer than 4 characters:

v4: [alpha] [gamma] [delta] [epsilon]

Notice that the value beta is excluded.

- You can use any of these algorithms to copy to or from any sequence, including a stream iterator:

```
ostream_iterator<string> out_it(cout, " ");
ranges::copy(v1, out_it)
cout << '\n';
```

Output:

alpha beta gamma delta epsilon

How it works...

The std::copy() algorithm is very simple. An equivalent function would look like this:

```
template<typename Input_it, typename Output_it>
Output_it bw_copy(Input_it begin_it, Input_it end_it,
                  Output_it dest_it) {
    while (begin_it != end_it) {
        *dest_it++ = *begin_it++;
    }
    return dest_it;
}
```

The copy() function uses the destination iterator's assignment operator to copy from the input iterator to the output iterator until it reaches the end of the input range.

There is also a version of this algorithm called std::move(), which moves elements instead of copying them:

```
std::move(v1.begin(), v1.end(), v2.begin());
printc(v1, "after move: v1");
printc(v2, "after move: v2");
```

This performs a move instead of copy assignment. After the move operation, the elements in v1 will be empty, and the elements that were in v1 are now in v2. The output looks like this:

```
after move1: v1: [] [] [] [] []
after move1: v2: [alpha] [beta] [gamma] [delta] [epsilon]
```

There is also a `ranges` version of the `move()` algorithm that performs the same operation:

```
ranges::move(v1, v2.begin());
```

The power of these algorithms lies in their simplicity. By letting the iterators manage the data, these simple, elegant functions allow you to seamlessly copy or move between any of the STL containers that support the required iterators.

Join container elements into a string

Sometimes, there is no algorithm in the library to accomplish a task at hand. We can use iterators, with the same techniques as the `algorithms` library, to easily write one.

For example, we often need to join elements from a container, with separators, into a string. One common solution is to use a simple `for()` loop:

```
for(auto v : c) cout << v << ', ';
```

The problem with this otherwise simple solution is that it leaves a trailing separator:

```
vector<string> greek{ "alpha", "beta", "gamma",
                      "delta", "epsilon" };
for(auto v : greek) cout << v << ", ";
cout << '\n';
```

Output:

```
alpha, beta, gamma, delta, epsilon,
```

This may be fine in a testing environment, but in any production system, that trailing comma is unacceptable.

The `ranges::views` library has a `join()` function, but it doesn't provide a separator:

```
auto greek_view = views::join(greek);
```

The `views::join()` function returns a `ranges::view` object. This requires a separate step to display or turn into a string. We can cycle through the view with a `for()` loop:

```
for(const char c : greek_view) cout << c;
cout << '\n';
```

The output looks like this:

alphabetagammadeltaepsilon

It's all there, but we need a proper separator between the elements to make it useful for our purposes.

Since the `algorithms` library does not have a function that suits our needs, we'll write one.

How to do it...

For this recipe, we will take the elements of a container and join them into a string with separators:

- In our `main()` function, we declare a vector of strings:

```
int main() {
    vector<string> greek{ "alpha", "beta", "gamma",
        "delta", "epsilon" };
    ...
}
```

- Now, let's write a simple `join()` function that uses an `ostream` object to join elements with a separator:

```
namespace bw {
    template<typename I>
    ostream& join(I it, I end_it, ostream& o,
                string_view sep = "") {
        if(it != end_it) o << *it++;
        while(it != end_it) o << sep << *it++;
        return o;
    }
}
```

I've put this in my own bw namespace to avoid name collisions.

We can call it with `cout` like this:

```
bw::join(greek.begin(), greek.end(), cout, ", ") << '\n';
```

Because it returns the ostream object, we can follow it with << to add a *newline* to the stream.

Output:

```
alpha, beta, gamma, delta, epsilon
```

- We'll often want a `string`, instead of directly writing to `cout`. We can overload this function for a version that returns a `string` object:

```
template<typename I>
string join(I it, I end_it, string_view sep = "") {
    ostringstream ostr;
    join(it, end_it, ostr, sep);
    return ostr.str();
}
```

This also goes in the bw namespace. This function creates an `ostringstream` object to pass to the ostream version of `bw::join()`. It returns a `string` object from the `str()` method of the `ostringstream` object.

We can use it like this:

```
string s = bw::join(greek.begin(), greek.end(), ", ");
cout << s << '\n';
```

Output:

```
alpha, beta, gamma, delta, epsilon
```

- Let's add one final overload to make this easier to use:

```
string join(const auto& c, string_view sep = "") {
    return join(begin(c), end(c), sep);
}
```

This version just takes a container and a separator, which should satisfy most use cases nicely:

```
string s = bw::join(greek, ", ");
cout << s << '\n';
```

Output:

```
alpha, beta, gamma, delta, epsilon
```

How it works...

Most of the work in this recipe is done by the iterators and the ostream object:

```
namespace bw {
    template<typename I>
    ostream& join(I it, I end_it, ostream& o,
                  string_view sep = "") {
        if(it != end_it) o << *it++;
        while(it != end_it) o << sep << *it++;
        return o;
    }
}
```

The separators go after the first element, between each of the successive elements, and stop before the final element. This means we can either add a separator *before* each element, skipping the first, or *after* each element, skipping the last. The logic is simpler if we test for, and skip, the first element. We do that in the line just before the while() loop:

```
if(it != end_it) o << *it++;
```

Once we have the first element out of the way, we can simply add a separator before each remaining element:

```
while(it != end_it) o << sep << *it++;
```

We return the ostream object as a convenience. This allows the user to easily add a newline, or other objects, to the stream:

```
bw::join(greek.begin(), greek.end(), cout, ", ") << '\n';
```

Output:

```
alpha, beta, gamma, delta, epsilon
```

There's more...

As with any of the library algorithms, the `join()` function will work with any container that supports *forward iterators*. For example, here's a `list` of `double` constants from the `numbers` library:

```
namespace num = std::numbers;
list<double> constants { num::pi, num::e, num::sqrt2 };
cout << bw::join(constants, ", ") << '\n';
```

Output:

```
3.14159, 2.71828, 1.41421
```

It will even work with a `ranges::view` object, like the `greek_view` defined earlier in this recipe:

```
cout << bw::join(greek_view, ":") << '\n';
```

Output:

```
a:l:p:h:a:b:e:t:a:g:a:m:m:a:d:e:l:t:a:e:p:s:i:l:o:n
```

Sort containers with std::sort

The problem of how to efficiently sort comparable elements is essentially solved. For most applications, there's no reason to re-invent this wheel. The STL provides an excellent sorting solution via the `std::sort()` algorithm. While the standard does not specify a sorting algorithm, it does specify a worst-case complexity of $O(n \log n)$, when applied to a range of n elements.

Just a few decades ago, the *quicksort* algorithm was considered a good compromise for most uses and was generally faster than other comparable algorithms. Today we have *hybrid* algorithms that choose between different approaches according to the circumstances, often switching algorithms on the fly. Most current C++ libraries use a hybrid approach with some combination of *introsort* and an *insertion sort*. `std::sort()` provides exceptional performance under most common circumstances.

How to do it...

In this recipe, we'll examine the `std::sort()` algorithm. The `sort()` algorithm works with any container with random-access iterators. Here, we will use a `vector` of `int`:

- We'll start with a function to test if a container is sorted:

```
void check_sorted(auto &c) {
    if(!is_sorted(c.begin(), c.end())) cout << "un";
    cout << "sorted: ";
}
```

This uses the `std::is_sorted()` algorithm and prints either `"sorted:"` or `"unsorted:"` according to the result.

- We'll need a function to print our `vector`:

```
void printc(const auto &c) {
    check_sorted(c);
    for(auto& e : c) cout << e << ' ';
    cout << '\n';
}
```

This function calls `check_sorted()` to display the status of the container before the value.

- Now we can define and print a `vector` of `int` in the `main()` function:

```
int main() {
    vector<int> v{ 1, 2, 3, 4, 5, 6, 7, 8, 9, 10 };
    printc(v);
    ...
}
```

The output looks like this:

```
sorted: 1 2 3 4 5 6 7 8 9 10
```

- In order to test the `std::sort()` algorithm, we need an unsorted vector. Here's a simple function to randomize our container:

```
void randomize(auto& c) {
    static std::random_device rd;
    static std::default_random_engine rng(rd());
    std::shuffle(c.begin(), c.end(), rng);
}
```

The `std::random_device` class uses your system's hardware *entropy* source. Most modern systems have one, otherwise the library will simulate it. The `std::default_random_engine()` function generates random numbers from the entropy source. This is used by `std::shuffle()` to randomize the container.

We can now call `randomize()` with our container and print the result:

```
randomize(v);
printc(v);
```

Output:

unsorted: 6 3 4 8 10 1 2 5 9 7

Of course, your output will be different because it's randomized. In fact, I get a different result every time I run it:

```
for(int i{3}; i; --i) {
    randomize(v);
    printc(v);
}
```

Output:

unsorted: 3 1 8 5 10 2 7 9 6 4
unsorted: 7 6 5 1 3 9 10 2 4 8
unsorted: 4 2 3 10 1 9 5 6 8 7

• To sort the vector, we simply call `std::sort()`:

```
std::sort(v.begin(), v.end());
printc(v);
```

Output:

sorted: 1 2 3 4 5 6 7 8 9 10

By default, the `sort()` algorithm uses the < operator to sort the elements in the range specified by the supplied iterators.

• The `partial_sort()` algorithm will sort part of the container:

```
cout << "partial_sort:\n";
randomize(v);
auto middle{ v.begin() + (v.size() / 2) };
std::partial_sort(v.begin(), middle, v.end());
printc(v);
```

`partial_sort()` takes three iterators: beginning, middle, and end. It sorts the container such that the elements before the middle are sorted. The elements after the middle are not guaranteed to be in the original order. Here's the output:

```
unsorted: 1 2 3 4 5 10 7 6 8 9
```

Notice that the first five elements are sorted, and the rest are not.

- The `partition()` algorithm *does not* sort anything. It rearranges the container so that certain elements appear at the front of the container:

```
coutrandomize(v);
printc(v);
partition(v.begin(), v.end(), [](int i)
    { return i > 5; });
printc(v);
```

The third argument is a *predicate* lambda that determines which elements will be moved to the front.

Output:

```
unsorted: 4 6 8 1 9 5 2 7 3 10
unsorted: 10 6 8 7 9 5 2 1 3 4
```

Notice that the values >5 are moved to the front of the container.

- The `sort()` algorithms support an optional comparison function that may be used for non-standard comparisons. For example, given a class called `things`:

```
struct things {
    string s_;
    int i_;
    string str() const {
        return format("({}, {})", s_, i_);
    }
};
```

We can create a `vector` of `things`:

```
vector<things> vthings{ {"button", 40},
    {"hamburger", 20}, {"blog", 1000},
    {"page", 100}, {"science", 60} };
```

We'll need a function to print them out:

```
void print_things(const auto& c) {
    for (auto& v : c) cout << v.str() << ' ';
    cout << '\n';
}
```

- Now we can sort and print the vector of things:

```
std::sort(vthings.begin(), vthings.end(),
        [](const things &lhs, const things &rhs) {
    return lhs.i_ < rhs.i_;
});
print_things(vthings);
```

Output:

```
(hamburger, 20) (button, 40) (science, 60) (page, 100)
(blog, 1000)
```

Notice the comparison function sorts on the i_ member, so the result is sorted by i_. We could instead sort on the s_ member:

```
std::sort(vthings.begin(), vthings.end(),
        [](const things &lhs, const things &rhs) {
    return lhs.s_ < rhs.s_;
});
print_things(vthings);
```

Now we get this output:

```
(blog, 1000) (button, 40) (hamburger, 20) (page, 100)
(science, 60)
```

How it works...

The sort() functions work by applying a sorting algorithm to a range of elements indicated by two iterators, for the beginning and end of the range.

By default, these algorithms use the < operator to compare elements. Optionally, they may use a *comparison function*, often provided as a lambda:

```
std::sort(vthings.begin(), vthings.end(),
        [](const things& lhs, const things& rhs) {
    return lhs.i_ < rhs.i_;
});
```

The comparison function takes two arguments and returns a `bool`. It has a signature equivalent to this:

```
bool cmp(const Type1& a, const Type2& b);
```

The `sort()` functions use `std::swap()` to move elements. This is efficient in both compute cycles and memory usage, as it relieves the need to allocate space for reading and writing the objects being sorted. This is also why the `partial_sort()` and `partition()` functions cannot guarantee the order of unsorted elements.

Modify containers with std::transform

The `std::transform()` function is remarkably powerful and flexible. One of the more commonly deployed algorithms in the library, it applies a *function* or *lambda* to each element in a container, storing the results in another container while leaving the original in place.

Given its power, it's deceptively simple to use.

How to do it...

In this recipe, we will explore a few applications for the `std::transform()` function:

- We'll start with a simple function that prints the contents of a container:

```
void printc(auto& c, string_view s = "") {
    if(s.size()) cout << format("{}: ", s);
    for(auto e : c) cout << format("{} ", e);
    cout << '\n';
}
```

    We'll use this to view the results of our transformations.

- In the `main()` function, let's declare a couple of vectors:

```
int main() {
    vector<int> v1{ 1, 2, 3, 4, 5, 6, 7, 8, 9, 10 };
    vector<int> v2;
    printc(v1, "v1");
    ...
}
```

This prints out the contents of v1:

```
v1: 1 2 3 4 5 6 7 8 9 10
```

- Now we can use the transform() function to insert the square of each value into v2:

```
cout << "squares:\n";
transform(v1.begin(), v1.end(), back_inserter(v2),
    [](int x){ return x * x; });
printc(v2, "v2");
```

The transform() function takes four arguments. The first two are the begin() and end() iterators for the source range. The third argument is the begin() iterator for the destination range. In this case, we're using the back_inserter() algorithm to insert the results in v2. The fourth argument is the transformation function. In this case, we're using a simple lambda to square the value.

Output:

```
squares:
v2: 1 4 9 16 25 36 49 64 81 100
```

- Of course, we can use transform() with any type. Here's an example that converts a vector of string objects to lowercase. First, we need a function to return the lowercase value of a string:

```
string str_lower(const string& s) {
    string outstr{};
    for(const char& c : s) {
        outstr += tolower(c);
    }
    return outstr;
}
```

Now we can use the str_lower() function with transform:

```
vector<string> vstr1{ "Mercury", "Venus", "Earth",
    "Mars", "Jupiter", "Saturn", "Uranus", "Neptune",
    "Pluto" };
vector<string> vstr2;
printc(vstr1, "vstr1");
cout << "str_lower:\n";
```

```
transform(vstr1.begin(), vstr1.end(),
    back_inserter(vstr2),
    [](string& x){ return str_lower(x); });
printc(vstr2, "vstr2");
```

This calls `str_lower()` for every element in `vstr1` and inserts the results into `vstr2`. The result is:

vstr: Mercury Venus Earth Mars Jupiter Saturn Uranus Neptune Pluto

str_lower:

vstr: mercury venus earth mars jupiter saturn uranus neptune pluto

(Yes, Pluto will always be a planet to me.)

- There's also a `ranges` version of transform:

```
cout << "ranges squares:\n";
auto view1 = views::transform(v1, [](int x){
    return x * x; });
printc(view1, "view1");
```

The `ranges` version has a more succinct syntax and returns a `view` object, rather than populating another container.

How it works...

The `std::transform()` function works very much like `std::copy()`, with the addition of the user-provided function. Each element in the input range is passed to the function, and the return value from the function is copy-assigned to the destination iterator. This makes `transform()` a singularly useful and powerful algorithm.

It's worth noting that `transform()` does not guarantee the elements will be processed in order. If you need to ensure the order of the transformation, you will want to use a `for` loop instead:

```
v2.clear();     // reset vector v2 to empty state
for(auto e : v1) v2.push_back(e * e);
printc(v2, "v2");
```

Output:

v2: 1 4 9 16 25 36 49 64 81 100

Find items in a container

The `algorithm` library contains a set of functions for finding elements in a container. The `std::find()` function, and its derivatives, search sequentially through a container and return an iterator pointing to the first matching element, or the `end()` element if there's no match.

How to do it...

The `find()` algorithm works with any container that satisfies the *Forward* or *Input* iterator qualifications. For this recipe, we'll use `vector` containers. The `find()` algorithm searches sequentially for the first matching element in a container. In this recipe, we'll walk through a few examples:

- We'll start by declaring a `vector` of `int` in the `main()` function:

```
int main() {
    const vector<int> v{ 1, 2, 3, 4, 5, 6, 7, 8, 9, 10 };
    ...
}
```

- Now, let's search for the element with the value 7:

```
auto it1 = find(v.begin(), v.end(), 7);
if(it1 != v.end()) cout << format("found: {}\n", *it1);
else cout << "not found\n";
```

  The `find()` algorithm takes three arguments: the `begin()` and `end()` iterators, and the value to search. It returns an iterator to the first element it finds, or the `end()` iterator if the search failed to find a match.

  Output:

  found: 7

- We can also search for something more complex than a scalar. The object needs to support the equality comparison operator, `==`. Here's a simple struct with an `operator==()` overload:

```
struct City {
    string name{};
    unsigned pop{};
    bool operator==(const City& o) const {
        return name == o.name;
```

```
    }
    string str() const {
        return format("[{}, {}]", name, pop);
    }
};
```

Notice that the `operator=()` overload only compares the `name` members.

I've also included an `str()` function that returns a `string` representation of a `City` element.

- Now we can declare a `vector` of `City` elements:

```
const vector<City> c{
    { "London", 9425622 },
    { "Berlin", 3566791 },
    { "Tokyo",  37435191 },
    { "Cairo",  20485965 }
};
```

- We can search the `vector` of `City` just as we did with the `vector` of `int`:

```
auto it2 = find(c.begin(), c.end(), City{"Berlin"});
if(it2 != c.end()) cout << format("found: {}\n",
    it2->str());
else cout << "not found\n";
```

Output:

found: [Berlin, 3566791]

- If we want to search on the `pop` member instead of `name`, we can use the `find_if()` function with a predicate:

```
auto it3 = find_if(begin(c), end(c),
    [](const City& item)
        { return item.pop > 20000000; });
if(it3 != c.end()) cout << format("found: {}\n",
    it3->str());
else cout << "not found\n";
```

The predicate tests the pop member, so we get this output:

```
found: [Tokyo, 37435191]
```

- Notice that the result from find_if() returns only the first element that satisfies the predicate, even though there are two elements in the vector with pop values greater than 20,000,000.

The find() and find_if() functions return only one iterator. The ranges library provides ranges::views::filter(), a *view adapter* that will give us all the matching iterators without disturbing our vector:

```
auto vw1 = ranges::views::filter(c,
        [](const City& c){ return c.pop > 20000000; });
for(const City& e : vw1) cout << format("{}\n", e.str());
```

This gives us both matching elements in our output:

```
[Tokyo, 37435191]
[Cairo, 20485965]
```

How it works...

The find() and find_if() functions search sequentially through a container, checking each element until it finds a match. If it finds a match, it returns an iterator pointing to that match. If it reaches the end() iterator without finding a match, it returns the end() iterator to indicate no match was found.

The find() function takes three arguments, the begin() and end() iterators, and a search value. The signature looks like this:

```
template<class InputIt, class T>
constexpr InputIt find(InputIt, InputIt, const T&)
```

The find_if() function uses a predicate instead of a value:

```
template<class InputIt, class UnaryPredicate>
constexpr InputIt find_if(InputIt, InputIt, UnaryPredicate)
```

There's more...

Both `find()` functions search sequentially and return when they find the first match. If you want to find more matching elements, you can use the `filter()` function from the `ranges` library:

```
template<ranges::viewable_range R, class Pred>
constexpr ranges::view auto ranges::views::filter(R&&, Pred&&);
```

The `filter()` function returns a *view*, a non-destructive window into the container with only the filtered elements. We can then use the view as we would any other container:

```
auto vw1 = std::ranges::views::filter(c,
    [](const City& c){ return c.pop > 20000000; });
for(const City& e : vw1) cout << format("{}\n", e.str());
```

Output:

```
[Tokyo, 37435191]
[Cairo, 20485965]
```

Limit the values of a container to a range with std::clamp

Introduced with C++17, the `std::clamp()` function can be used to limit the range of a numeric scalar to within minimum and maximum values. The function is optimized to use *move semantics*, where possible, for maximum speed and efficiency.

How to do it...

We can use `clamp()` to constrain the values of a container by using it in a loop, or with the `transform()` algorithm. Let's look at some examples.

- We'll start with a simple function for printing out the values of a container:

```
void printc(auto& c, string_view s = "") {
    if(s.size()) cout << format("{}: ", s);
    for(auto e : c) cout << format("{:>5} ", e);
    cout << '\n';
}
```

Notice the *format string* "`{:>5}`". This right-aligns each value to 5 spaces, for a tabular view.

- In the `main()` function, we'll define an *initializer list* for use with our container. This allows us to use the same values more than once:

```
int main() {
    auto il = { 0, -12, 2001, 4, 5, -14, 100, 200,
      30000 };

    ...

}
```

That's a nice range of values to work with `clamp()`.

- Let's also define some constants for use as our limits:

```
constexpr int ilow{0};
constexpr int ihigh{500};
```

We'll use these values in our calls to `clamp()`.

- Now we can define a container in our `main()` function. We'll use a `vector` of `int`:

```
vector<int> voi{ il };
cout << "vector voi before:\n";
printc(voi);
```

Using the values from our initializer list, the output is:

```
vector voi before:
    0   -12   2001      4      5    -14    100    200 30000
```

- Now we can use a `for` loop with `clamp()` to limit the values to between 0 and 500:

```
cout << "vector voi after:\n";
for(auto& e : voi) e = clamp(e, ilow, ihigh);
printc(voi);
```

This applies the `clamp()` function to each value in the container, using 0 and 500 for the low and high limits, respectively. Now, the output is:

```
vector voi before:
    0   -12   2001      4      5    -14    100    200 30000
vector voi after:
    0     0    500      4      5      0    100    200    500
```

After the `clamp()` operation, the negative values are 0 and the values greater than
. 500 are 500.

- We can do the same thing with the `transform()` algorithm, using `clamp()` in a
  lambda. This time we'll use a `list` container:

```
cout << "list loi before:\n";
list<int> loi{ il };
printc(loi);
transform(loi.begin(), loi.end(), loi.begin(),
    [=](auto e){ return clamp(e, ilow, ihigh); });
cout << "list loi after:\n";
printc(loi);
```

The output is the same as in the version with a `for` loop:

```
list loi before:
    0   -12   2001      4      5   -14    100    200 30000
list loi after:
    0     0    500      4      5     0    100    200    500
```

How it works...

The `clamp()` algorithm is a simple function that looks something like this:

```
template<class T>
constexpr const T& clamp( const T& v, const T& lo,
    const T& hi ) {
    return less(v, lo) ? lo : less(hi, v) ? hi : v;
}
```

If the value of v is less than `lo`, it returns `lo`. If `hi` is less than v, it returns `hi`.
The function is fast and efficient.

In our examples, we used a `for` loop to apply `clamp()` to a container:

```
for(auto& v : voi) v = clamp(v, ilow, ihigh);
```

We also used the `transform()` algorithm with `clamp()` in a lambda:

```
transform(loi.begin(), loi.end(), loi.begin(),
    [=](auto v){ return clamp(v, ilow, ihigh); });
```

In my experiments, both versions gave the same results, and both produced similar code from the GCC compiler. There was a slight difference in compiled size (the version with the for loop was smaller, as expected) and a negligible difference in performance.

In general, I prefer the for loop, but the transform() version may be more flexible in other applications.

Sample data sets with std::sample

The std::sample() algorithm takes a random *sample* of a sequence of values and populates a destination container with the sample. It is useful for analyzing a larger set of data, where the random sample is taken to be representative of the whole.

A sample set allows us to approximate the characteristics of a large set of data, without analyzing the full set. This provides efficiency in exchange for accuracy, a fair trade-off in many circumstances.

How to do it...

In this recipe, we'll use an array of 200,000 random integers, with *standard normal distribution*. We'll sample a few hundred values to create a histogram of the frequency of each value.

- We'll start with a simple function to return a rounded int from a double. The standard library lacks such a function and we'll need it later:

```
int iround(const double& d) {
    return static_cast<int>(std::round(d));
}
```

  The standard library provides several versions of std::round(), including one that returns a long int. But we need an int, and this is a simple solution that avoids compiler warnings about narrowing conversion while hiding away the unsightly static_cast.

- In the main() function, we'll start with some useful constants:

```
int main() {
    constexpr size_t n_data{ 200000 };
    constexpr size_t n_samples{ 500 };
    constexpr int mean{ 0 };
    constexpr size_t dev{ 3 };
    ...
}
```

We have values for n_data and n_samples, used for the size of the data and sample containers, respectively. We also have values for mean and dev, the *mean* and *standard deviation* parameters for the *normal distribution* of random values.

* We now set up our *random number generator* and *distribution* objects. These are used to initialize the source data set:

```
std::random_device rd;
std::mt19937 rng(rd());
std::normal_distribution<> dist{ mean, dev };
```

The random_device object provides access to the hardware random number generator. The mt19937 class is an implementation of the *Mersenne Twister* random number algorithm, a high-quality algorithm that will perform well on most systems with a data set of the size we're using. The normal_distribution class provides a distribution of random numbers around the *mean* with the *standard deviation* provided.

* Now we populate an array with an n_data number of random int values:

```
array<int, n_data> v{};
for(auto& e : v) e = iround(dist(rng));
```

The array container is fixed in size, so the template parameters include a size_t value for the number of elements to allocate. We use a for() loop to populate the array.

The rng object is the hardware random number generator. This is passed to dist(), our normal_distribution object, and then to iround(), our integer rounding function.

* At this point, we have an array with 200,000 data points. That's a lot to analyze, so we'll use the sample() algorithm to take a sample of 500 values:

```
array<int, n_samples> samples{};
sample(data.begin(), data.end(), samples.begin(),
    n_samples, rng);
```

We define another array object to hold the samples. This one is n_samples in size. Then we use the sample() algorithm to populate the array with n_samples random data points.

- We create a histogram to analyze the samples. A map structure is perfect for this as we can easily map the frequency of each value:

```
std::map<int, size_t> hist{};
for (const int i : samples) ++hist[i];
```

The for() loop takes each value from the samples container and uses it as a key in the map. The increment expression ++hist[i] counts the number of occurrences of each value in the sample set.

- We print out the histogram using the C++20 format() function:

```
constexpr size_t scale{ 3 };
cout << format("{:>3} {:>5} {:<}/{}\n",
    "n", "count", "graph", scale);
for (const auto& [value, count] : hist) {
    cout << format("{:>3} ({:>3}) {}\n",
        value, count, string(count / scale, '*'));
}
```

The format() specifiers that look like { :>3} make space for a certain number of characters. The angle bracket specifies alignment, right or left.

The string(count, char) constructor creates a string with a character repeated the number of times specified, in this case, *n* asterisk characters *, where *n* is count/scale, the frequency of a value in the histogram, divided by the scale constant.

The output looks like this:

```
$ ./sample
 n count graph/3
-9 (  2)
-7 (  5) *
-6 (  9) ***
-5 ( 22) *******
-4 ( 24) ********
-3 ( 46) ***************
-2 ( 54) *****************
-1 ( 59) ******************
 0 ( 73) ************************
 1 ( 66) *********************
```

```
2 ( 44) **************
3 ( 34) **********
4 ( 26) ********
5 ( 18) ******
6 (  9) ***
7 (  5) *
8 (  3) *
9 (  1)
```

This is a nice graphical representation of the histogram. The first number is the value, the second number is the frequency of the value, and the asterisks are a visual representation of the frequency, where each asterisk represents scale (3) occurrences in the sample set.

Your output will differ each time you run the code.

How it works...

The `std::sample()` function selects a specific number of elements from random locations in the source container and copies them to the destination container.

The signature of `sample()` looks like this:

```
OutIter sample(SourceIter, SourceIter, OutIter,
    SampleSize, RandNumGen&&);
```

The first two arguments are `begin()` and `end()` iterators on a container with the full data set. The third argument is an iterator for the destination of the samples. The fourth argument is the sample size, and the final argument is a random number generator function.

The `sample()` algorithm uses *uniform distribution*, so each data point has the same chance of being sampled.

Generate permutations of data sequences

There are many use cases for permutations, including testing, statistics, research, and more. The `next_permutation()` algorithm generates permutations by re-ordering a container to the next *lexicographical* permutation.

How to do it...

For this recipe, we will print out the permutations of a set of three strings:

- We'll start by creating a short function for printing the contents of a container:

```
void printc(const auto& c, string_view s = "") {
    if(s.size()) cout << format("{}: ", s);
    for(auto e : c) cout << format("{} ", e);
    cout << '\n';
}
```

We'll use this simple function to print our data set and permutations.

- In the main() function, we declare a vector of string objects and sort it with the sort() algorithm.

```
int main() {
    vector<string> vs{ "dog", "cat", "velociraptor" };
    sort(vs.begin(), vs.end());

    ...
}
```

The next_permutation() function requires a sorted container.

- Now we can list the permutations with next_permutation() in a do loop:

```
do {
    printc(vs);
} while (next_permutation(vs.begin(), vs.end()));
```

The next_permutation() function modifies the container and returns true if there is another permutation, or false if not.

The output lists six permutations of our three pets:

```
cat dog velociraptor
cat velociraptor dog
dog cat velociraptor
dog velociraptor cat
velociraptor cat dog
velociraptor dog cat
```

How it works...

The `std::next_permutation()` algorithm generates *lexicographical* permutations of a set of values, that is, permutations based on dictionary ordering. The input must be sorted because the algorithm steps through permutations in lexicographical order. So, if you start with a set like 3, 2, 1, it will terminate immediately as this is the last lexicographical order of those three elements.

For example:

```
vector<string> vs{ "velociraptor", "dog", "cat" };
do {
    printc(vs);
} while (next_permutation(vs.begin(), vs.end()));
```

This gives us the following output:

```
velociraptor dog cat
```

While the term *lexicographical* implies alphabetical ordering, the implementation uses standard comparison operators, so it works on any sortable values.

Likewise, if values in the set repeat, they are only counted according to *lexicographical* order. Here we have a `vector` of `int` with two repeating sequences of five values:

```
vector<int> vi{ 1, 2, 3, 4, 5, 1, 2, 3, 4, 5 };
sort(vi.begin(), vi.end());
printc(vi, "vi sorted");
long count{};
do {
    ++count;
} while (next_permutation(vi.begin(), vi.end()));
cout << format("number of permutations: {}\n", count);
```

Output:

```
Vi sorted: 1 1 2 2 3 3 4 4 5 5
number of permutations: 113400
```

There are 113,400 permutations of these values. Notice that it's not *10!* (3,628,800) because some values repeat. Since *3,3* and *3,3* sort the same, they are not different *lexicographical* permutations.

In other words, if I list the permutations of this short set:

```
vector<int> vi2{ 1, 3, 1 };
sort(vi2.begin(), vi2.end());
do {
    printc(vi2);
} while (next_permutation(vi2.begin(), vi2.end()));
```

We get only three permutations, not *3!* (9), because of the repeating values:

```
1 1 3
1 3 1
3 1 1
```

Merge sorted containers

The std::merge() algorithm takes two sorted sequences and creates a third merged and sorted sequence. This technique is often used as part of a *merge sort*, allowing very large amounts of data to be broken down into chunks, sorted separately, and merged into one sorted target.

How to do it...

For this recipe, we'll take two sorted vector containers and merge them into a third vector using std::merge().

- We'll start with a simple function to print the contents of a container:

```
void printc(const auto& c, string_view s = "") {
    if(s.size()) cout << format("{}: ", s);
    for(auto e : c) cout << format("{} ", e);
    cout << '\n';
}
```

We'll use this to print the source and destination sequences.

- In the `main()` function, we'll declare our source vectors, along with the destination vector, and print them out:

```
int main() {
    vector<string> vs1{ "dog", "cat",
        "velociraptor" };
    vector<string> vs2{ "kirk", "sulu", "spock" };
    vector<string> dest{};
    printc(vs1, "vs1");
    printc(vs2, "vs2");

    ...

}
```

The output is:

vs1: dog cat velociraptor
vs2: kirk sulu spock

- Now we can sort our vectors and print them again:

```
sort(vs1.begin(), vs1.end());
sort(vs2.begin(), vs2.end());
printc(vs1, "vs1 sorted");
printc(vs2, "vs2 sorted");
```

Output:

vs1 sorted: cat dog velociraptor
vs2 sorted: kirk spock sulu

- Now that our source containers are sorted, we can merge them for our final merged result:

```
merge(vs1.begin(), vs1.end(), vs2.begin(), vs2.end(),
    back_inserter(dest));
printc(dest, "dest");
```

Output:

dest: cat dog kirk spock sulu velociraptor

This output represents the merge of the two sources into one sorted vector.

How it works...

The merge() algorithm takes begin() and end() iterators from both the sources and an output iterator for the destination:

```
OutputIt merge(InputIt1, InputIt1, InputIt2, InputIt2,
OutputIt)
```

It takes the two input ranges, performs its merge/sort operation, and sends the resulting sequence to the output iterator.

7
Strings, Streams, and Formatting

The STL `string` class is a powerful, full-featured tool for storing, manipulating, and displaying character-based data. It has much of the convenience you would find in a high-level scripting language, yet remains as quick and agile as you would expect from C++.

The `string` class is based on `basic_string`, a contiguous container class that may be instantiated with any character type. Its class signature looks like this:

```
template<
    typename CharT,
    typename Traits = std::char_traits<CharT>,
    typename Allocator = std::allocator<CharT>
> class basic_string;
```

The `Traits` and `Allocator` template parameters are usually left to their default values.

The underlying storage of `basic_string` is a contiguous sequence of `CharT`, and can be accessed with the `data()` member function:

```
const std::basic_string<char> s{"hello"};
const char * sdata = s.data();
for(size_t i{0}; i < s.size(); ++i) {
    cout << sdata[i] << ' ';
}
cout << '\n';
```

Output:

```
h e l l o
```

The `data()` member function returns a `CharT*` that points to the underlying array of characters. Since C++11, the array returned by `data()` is null-terminated, making `data()` equivalent to `c_str()`.

The `basic_string` class includes many of the methods you would find in other contiguous-storage classes, including `insert()`, `erase()`, `push_back()`, `pop_back()`, and others. These methods operate on the underlying array of `CharT`.

`std::string` is a type alias for `std::basic_string<char>`:

```
using std::string = std::basic_string<char>;
```

For most purposes, you'll use `std::string`.

String formatting

String formatting has traditionally been a weak point with the STL. Until recently, we've been left with an imperfect choice between the cumbersome STL `iostreams` or the archaic legacy `printf()`. Beginning with C++20 and the `format` library, STL string formatting has finally grown up. Closely based on Python's `str.format()` method, the new `format` library is fast and flexible, providing many of the advantages of both `iostreams` and `printf()`, along with good memory management and type safety.

For more about the `format` library, see the *Format text with the new format library* recipe in *Chapter 1, New C++20 Features*.

While we no longer need to use `iostreams` for string formatting, it is still quite useful for other purposes, including file and stream I/O, and some type conversions.

In this chapter, we will cover these subjects and more in the following recipes:

- Use `string_view` as a lightweight string object
- Concatenate strings
- Transform strings
- Format text with C++20's `format` library
- Trim whitespace from strings
- Read strings from user input
- Count words in a file
- Initialize complex structures from file input
- Customize a string class with `char_traits`
- Parse strings with Regular Expressions

Technical requirements

You can find code files for this chapter on GitHub at `https://github.com/PacktPublishing/CPP-20-STL-Cookbook/tree/main/chap07`.

Use string_view as a lightweight string object

The `string_view` class provides a lightweight alternative to the `string` class. Instead of maintaining its own data store, `string_view` operates on a *view* of a C-string. This makes `string_view` smaller and more efficient than `std::string`. It's useful in cases where you need a string object but don't need the more memory- and computation-intensive features of `std::string`.

How to do it...

The `string_view` class looks deceptively similar to the STL `string` class, but it works a bit differently. Let's consider some examples:

- Here's an STL `string` initialized from a C-string (array of `char`):

```
char text[]{ "hello" };
string greeting{ text };
text[0] = 'J';
cout << text << ' ' << greeting << '\n';
```

Output:

```
Jello hello
```

Notice that the `string` does not change when we modify the array. This is because the `string` constructor creates its own copy of the underlying data.

- When we do the same with a `string_view`, we get a different result:

```
char text[]{ "hello" };
string_view greeting{ text };
text[0] = 'J';
cout << text << ' ' << greeting << '\n';
```

Output:

```
Jello Jello
```

The `string_view` constructor creates a *view* of the underlying data. It does not make its own copy. This results in significant efficiencies but also allows for side effects.

- Because `string_view` doesn't copy the underlying data, the source data must remain in scope for the duration of the `string_view` object. So, this does not work:

```
string_view sv() {
    const char text[]{ "hello" };   // temporary storage
    string_view greeting{ text };
    return greeting;
}
int main() {
    string_view greeting = sv();   // data out of scope
    cout << greeting << '\n';   // output undefined
}
```

Because the underlying data goes out of scope after the `sv()` function returns, the `greeting` object in `main()` is no longer valid by the time we use it.

- The string_view class has constructors that make sense for the underlying data. This includes character arrays (const char*), contiguous *ranges* (including std::string), and other string_view objects. This example uses the *ranges* constructor:

```
string str{ "hello" };
string_view greeting{ str };
cout << greeting << '\n';
```

Output:

```
hello
```

- There is also a string_view literal operator sv, defined in the std::literals namespace:

```
using namespace std::literals;
cout << "hello"sv.substr(1, 4) << '\n';
```

This constructs a constexpr string_view object and calls its method substr() to get the 4 values starting at index 1.

Output:

```
ello
```

How it works...

The string_view class is effectively an *iterator adapter* on a contiguous sequence of characters. The implementation typically has two members: a const CharT * and a size_t. It works by wrapping a contiguous_iterator around the source data.

This means that you can use it like std::string for many purposes, with a few important distinctions:

- The copy constructor does not copy the data. This means that when you make a copy of a string_view, each copy operates on the same underlying data:

```
char text[]{ "hello" };
string_view sv1{ text };
string_view sv2{ sv1 };
string_view sv3{ sv2 };
string_view sv4{ sv3 };
cout << format("{} {} {} {}\n", sv1, sv2, sv3, sv4);
```

```
text[0] = 'J';
cout << format("{} {} {} {}\n", sv1, sv2, sv3, sv4);
```

Output:

```
hello hello hello hello
Jello Jello Jello Jello
```

• Keep in mind that when you pass a string_view to a function, it uses the copy constructor:

```
void f(string_view sv) {
    if(sv.size()) {
        char* x = (char*)sv.data();   // dangerous
        x[0] = 'J';  // modifies the source
    }
    cout << format("f(sv): {} {}\n", (void*)sv.data(),
        sv);
}
int main() {
    char text[]{ "hello" };
    string_view sv1{ text };
    cout << format("sv1: {} {}\n", (void*)sv1.data(),
        sv1);
    f(sv1);
    cout << format("sv1: {} {}\n", (void*)sv1.data(),
        sv1);
}
```

Output:

```
sv1: 0x7ffd80fa7b2a hello
f(sv): 0x7ffd80fa7b2a Jello
sv1: 0x7ffd80fa7b2a Jello
```

Notice that the address of the underlying data (returned by the data() member function) is the same for all instances of the string_view. That's because the copy constructor does not make a copy of the underlying data. Even though the string_view member pointer is const-qualified, it's still possible to cast away the const qualifier, though it's *not recommended* because it could cause unintended side effects. But it is worth noting that the data is never copied.

- The `string_view` class lacks methods that directly operate on the underlying string. Methods such as `append()`, `operator+()`, `push_back()`, `pop_back()`, `replace()`, and `resize()`, which are supported in `string`, are not supported in `string_view`.

If you need to concatenate strings with the + operator, you'll need a `std::string`. For example, this does not work with `string_view`:

```
sv1 = sv2 + sv3 + sv4; // does not work
```

You'll need to use `string` instead:

```
string str1{ text };
string str2{ str1 };
string str3{ str2 };
string str4{ str3 };

str1 = str2 + str3 + str4; // works
cout << str1 << '\n';
```

Output:

```
JelloJelloJello
```

Concatenate strings

There are several ways to concatenate strings in C++. In this recipe, we will look at the three most common: the `string` class `operator+()`, the `string` class `append()` function, and the `ostringstream` class `operator<<()`. New in C++20, we also have the `format()` function. Each of these has its advantages, disadvantages, and use cases.

How to do it...

In this recipe, we will examine ways to concatenate strings. We will then perform some benchmarks and consider the different use cases.

- We'll start with a couple of `std::string` objects:

```
string a{ "a" };
string b{ "b" };
```

The `string` objects are constructed from literal C-strings.

The C-string constructor makes a copy of the literal string and uses the local copy as the underlying data for the `string` object.

- Now, let's construct a new empty string object and concatenate a and b with a separator and a newline:

```
string x{};
x += a + ", " + b + "\n";
cout << x;
```

Here, we used the `string` object's += and + operators to concatenate the a and b strings, along with literal strings ", " and "\n". The resulting string has the elements concatenated together:

a, b

- We could instead use the `string` object's `append()` member function:

```
string x{};
x.append(a);
x.append(", ");
x.append(b);
x.append("\n");
cout << x;
```

This gives us the same result:

a, b

- Or, we could construct an `ostringstream` object, which uses the stream interface:

```
ostringstream x{};
x << a << ", " << b << "\n";
cout << x.str();
```

We get the same result:

a, b

- We could also use the C++20 `format()` function:

```
string x{};
x = format("{}, {}\n", a, b);
cout << x;
```

Again, we have the same result:

a, b

How it works...

The `string` object has two distinct methods for concatenating a string, the + operator and the `append()` member function.

The `append()` member function adds data to the end of the `string` object's data. It must allocate and manage memory to accomplish this.

The + operator uses the `operator+()` overload to construct a new `string` object with the old and new data, and returns the new object.

The `ostringstream` object works like an `ostream` but stores its output for use as a string.

The C++20 `format()` function uses a format string with variadic arguments and returns a newly constructed `string` object.

There's more...

How do you decide which concatenation strategy is right for your code? We can start with some benchmarks.

Benchmarks

I performed these tests using GCC 11 on Debian Linux:

- First, we'll create a `timer` function using the `<chrono>` library:

```
using std::chrono::high_resolution_clock;
using std::chrono::duration;

void timer(string(*f)()) {
    auto t1 = high_resolution_clock::now();
    string s{ f() };
    auto t2 = high_resolution_clock::now();
    duration<double, std::milli> ms = t2 - t1;
    cout << s;
    cout << format("duration: {} ms\n", ms.count());
}
```

The `timer` function calls the function passed to it, marking the time before and after the function call. It then displays the duration using `cout`.

- Now, we create a function that concatenates strings, using the `append()` member function:

```
string append_string() {
    cout << "append_string\n";
    string a{ "a" };
    string b{ "b" };
    long n{0};
    while(++n) {
        string x{};
        x.append(a);
        x.append(", ");
        x.append(b);
        x.append("\n");
        if(n >= 10000000) return x;
    }
    return "error\n";
}
```

For benchmarking purposes, this function repeats the concatenation 10 million times. We call this function from `main()` with `timer()`:

```
int main() {
    timer(append_string);
}
```

We get this output:

append_string

a, b

duration: 425.361643 ms

So, on this system, our concatenation ran 10 million iterations in about 425 milliseconds.

- Now, let's create the same function with the + operator overload:

```
string concat_string() {
    cout << "concat_string\n";
    string a{ "a" };
    string b{ "b" };
    long n{0};
```

```
    while(++n) {
        string x{};
        x += a + ", " + b + "\n";
        if(n >= 10000000) return x;
    }
    return "error\n";
}
```

Our benchmark output:

concat_string

a, b

duration: 659.957702 ms

This version performed 10 million iterations in about 660 milliseconds.

- Now, let's try it with ostringstream:

```
string concat_ostringstream() {
    cout << "ostringstream\n";
    string a { "a" };
    string b { "b" };
    long n{0};
    while(++n) {
        ostringstream x{};
        x << a << ", " << b << "\n";
        if(n >= 10000000) return x.str();
    }
    return "error\n";
}
```

Our benchmark output:

ostringstream

a, b

duration: 3462.020587 ms

This version ran 10 million iterations in about 3.5 seconds.

- Here's the format() version:

```
string concat_format() {
    cout << "append_format\n";
    string a{ "a" };
    string b{ "b" };
    long n{0};
    while(++n) {
        string x{};
        x = format("{}, {}\n", a, b);
        if(n >= 10000000) return x;
    }
    return "error\n";
}
```

Our benchmark output:

append_format

a, b

duration: 782.800547 ms

The format() version ran 10 million iterations in about 783 milliseconds.

- Summary of the results:

Concatenation method	Benchmark in milliseconds
append()	425 ms
operator+()	660 ms
format()	783 ms
ostringstream	3,462 ms

A comparison of concatenation performance

Why the performance discrepancies?

We can see from these benchmarks that the ostringstream version takes many times longer than the string-based versions.

The append() method is slightly faster than the + operator. It needs to allocate memory but does not construct new objects. Some optimizations may be possible due to repetition.

The + operator overload probably calls the append() method. The extra function call could make it incrementally slower than the append() method.

The format() version creates one new string object but without the overhead of the iostream system.

The ostringstream operator << overload creates a new ostream object for each operation. Given the complexity of the stream object, along with managing the stream state, this makes it much slower than either of the string-based versions.

Why would I choose one over another?

Some measure of personal preference will be involved. The operator overloads (+ or <<) can be convenient. Performance may or may not be an issue for you.

The ostringstream class has one distinct advantage over the string methods: it specializes the << operator for each different type, so it's able to operate in circumstances where you may have different types calling the same code.

The format() function offers the same type-safety and customization options and is significantly faster than the ostringstream class.

The string object's + operator overload is fast, easy to use, and easy to read but is incrementally slower than append().

The append() version is fastest but requires a separate function call for each item.

For my purposes, I like the format() function or the string object's + operator for most circumstances. I'll use append() if every bit of speed matters. I'll use ostringstream where I need its unique features and performance is not an issue.

Transform strings

The std::string class is a *contiguous container*, much like a vector or an array. It supports the contiguous_iterator concept and all corresponding algorithms.

The string class is a specialization of basic_string with a char type. This means that the elements of the container are of type char. Other specializations are available, but string is most common.

Because it is fundamentally a contiguous container of char elements, string may be used with the transform() algorithm, or any other technique that uses the contiguous_iterator concept.

How to do it...

There are several ways to do transformations, depending on the application. This recipe will explore a few of them.

- We'll start with a few predicate functions. A predicate function takes a transformation element and returns a related element. For example, here is a simple predicate that returns an upper-case character:

```
char char_upper(const char& c) {
    return static_cast<char>(std::toupper(c));
}
```

This function is a wrapper around `std::toupper()`. Because the `toupper()` function returns an `int` and `string` elements are type `char`, we cannot use the `toupper()` function directly in a transformation.

Here is a corresponding `char_lower()` function:

```
char char_lower(const char& c) {
    return static_cast<char>(std::tolower(c));
}
```

- The `rot13()` function is a fun transformation predicate for demonstration purposes. It's a simple substitution cypher, *not suitable for encryption* but commonly used for *obfuscation*:

```
char rot13(const char& x) {
    auto rot13a = [] (char x, char a)->char {
        return a + (x - a + 13) % 26;
    };
    if (x >= 'A' && x <= 'Z') return rot13a(x, 'A');
    if (x >= 'a' && x <= 'z') return rot13a(x, 'a');
    return x;
}
```

- We can use these predicates with the `transform()` algorithm:

```
main() {
    string s{ "hello jimi\n" };
    cout << s;
    std::transform(s.begin(), s.end(), s.begin(),
        char_upper);
```

```
cout << s;
...
```

The `transform()` function calls `char_upper()` with each element of `s`, puts the result back in `s` and transforms all the characters to uppercase:

Output:

hello jimi
HELLO JIMI

- Instead of `transform()`, we can also use a simple `for` loop with a *predicate function*:

```
for(auto& c : s) c = rot13(c);
cout << s;
```

Starting with our uppercase string object, the result is:

URYYB WVZV

- The fun thing about the `rot13` cypher is that it unscrambles itself. Because there are 26 letters in the *ASCII* alphabet, rotating 13 and then rotating 13 again results in the original string. Let's transform to lowercase and `rot13` again to restore our string:

```
for(auto& c : s) c = rot13(char_lower(c));
cout << s;
```

Output:

hello jimi

Because of their uniform interface, the predicate functions may be *chained* as parameters of each other. We could also use `char_lower(rot13(c))` with the same result.

- If your requirement is too complex for a simple character-by-character transformation, you may use `string` iterators as you would with any contiguous container. Here's a simple function that transforms a lowercase string to *Title Case* by capitalizing the first character and every character that follows a space:

```
string& title_case(string& s) {
    auto begin = s.begin();
    auto end = s.end();
    *begin++ = char_upper(*begin);   // first element
    bool space_flag{ false };
```

```
    for(auto it{ begin }; it != end; ++it) {
        if(*it == ' ') {
            space_flag = true;
        } else {
            if(space_flag) *it = char_upper(*it);
            space_flag = false;
        }
    }
    return s;
}
```

Because it returns a reference to the transformed string, we can call it with `cout`, like this:

```
cout << title_case(s);
```

Output:

Hello Jimi

How it works...

The `std::basic_string` class, and its specializations (including `string`), are supported by iterators fully compliant with `contiguous_iterator`. This means that any technique that works with any contiguous container also works with `string`.

Note

These transformations will not work with `string_view` objects because the underlying data is `const`-qualified.

Format text with C++20's format library

C++20 introduces the new `format()` function, which returns a formatted representation of its arguments in a string. `format()` uses a Python-style formatting string, with concise syntax, type safety, and excellent performance.

The `format()` function takes a format string and a template, *parameter pack*, for its arguments:

```
template< class... Args >
string format(const string_view fmt, Args&&... args );
```

The format string uses curly braces { } as a placeholder for the formatted arguments:

```
const int a{47};
format("a is {}\n", a);
```

Output:

```
a is 47
```

It also uses the braces for format specifiers, for example:

```
format("Hex: {:x} Octal: {:o} Decimal {:d} \n", a, a, a);
```

Output:

```
Hex: 2f Octal: 57 Decimal 47
```

This recipe will show you how to use the `format()` function for some common string formatting solutions.

> **Note**
>
> This chapter was developed using a preview release of the Microsoft Visual C++ compiler on Windows 10. At the time of writing, this is the only compiler that fully supports the C++20 < format > library. Final implementations may differ in some details.

How to do it...

Let's consider some common formatting solutions using the `format()` function:

- We'll start with some variables to format:

```
const int inta{ 47 };
const char * human{ "earthlings" };
const string_view alien{ "vulcans" };
const double df_pi{ pi };
```

The pi constant is in the `<numbers>` header and the `std::numbers` namespace.

- We can display the variables using `cout`:

```
cout << "inta is " << inta << '\n'
    << "hello, " << human << '\n'
    << "All " << alien << " are welcome here\n"
    << "π is " << df_pi << '\n';
```

We get this output:

```
a is 47
hello, earthlings
All vulcans are welcome here
π is 3.14159
```

- Now, let's look at each of these with `format()`, starting with the C-string, human:

```
cout << format("Hello {}\n", human);
```

This is the simplest form of the `format()` function. The format string has one placeholder `{}` and one corresponding variable, human. The output is:

```
Hello earthlings
```

- The `format()` function returns a string, and we use `cout <<` to display the string.

The original proposal for the `format()` library included a `print()` function, using the same parameters as `format()`. That would allow us to print our formatted strings in one step:

```
print("Hello {}\n", cstr);
```

Unfortunately, `print()` didn't make it into the C++20 standard, although it is expected to be included in C++23.

We can provide the same functionality with a simple function, using `vformat()`:

```
template<typename... Args>
constexpr void print(const string_view str_fmt,
                     Args&&... args) {
    fputs(std::vformat(str_fmt,
          std::make_format_args(args...)).c_str(),
          stdout);
}
```

This simple one-line function gives us a serviceable `print()` function. We can use it in place of the `cout << format()` combination:

```
print("Hello {}\n", human);
```

Output:

Hello earthlings

A more complete version of this function may be found in the `include` directory of the example files.

- The format string also provides positional options:

```
print("Hello {} we are {}\n", human, alien);
```

Output:

Hello earthlings we are vulcans

We can change the order of the arguments by using positional options in the format string:

```
print("Hello {1} we are {0}\n", human, alien);
```

Now, we get this output:

Hello vulcans we are earthlings

Notice that the arguments remain the same. Only the positional values in the braces have changed. The positional indices are zero-based, just like the `[]` operator.

This feature can be useful for internationalization, as different languages use different orders for parts of speech in a sentence.

- There are many formatting options for numbers:

```
print("π is {}\n", df_pi);
```

Output:

π is 3.141592653589793

We can specify the number of digits of precision:

```
print("π is {:.5}\n", df_pi);
```

Output:

π is 3.1416

The colon character : is used to separate positional indices from formatting arguments:

```
print("inta is {1:}, π is {0:.5}\n", df_pi, inta);
```

Output:

```
inta is 47, π is 3.1416
```

- If we want a value to take up a certain amount of space, we can specify the number of characters like this:

```
print("inta is [{:10}]\n", inta);
```

Output:

```
inta is [        47]
```

We can align it left or right:

```
print("inta is [{:<10}]\n", inta);
print("inta is [{:>10}]\n", inta);
```

Output:

```
inta is [47        ]
inta is [        47]
```

By default, it fills with space characters, but we can change that:

```
print("inta is [{:*<10}]\n", inta);
print("inta is [{:0>10}]\n", inta);
```

Output:

```
inta is [47********]
inta is [0000000047]
```

We can also center a value:

```
print("inta is [{:^10}]\n", inta);
print("inta is [{:_^10}]\n", inta);
```

Output:

```
inta is [    47    ]
inta is [____47____]
```

- We can format integer numbers as hexadecimal, octal, or the default decimal representation:

```
print("{:>8}: [{:04x}]\n", "Hex", inta);
print("{:>8}: [{:4o}]\n", "Octal", inta);
print("{:>8}: [{:4d}]\n", "Decimal", inta);
```

Output:

```
    Hex: [002f]
  Octal: [  57]
Decimal: [  47]
```

Notice that I used right alignment to line up the labels.

Use a capital X for uppercase hexadecimal:

```
print("{:>8}: [{:04X}]\n", "Hex", inta);
```

Output:

```
    Hex: [002F]
```

> **Tip**
>
> By default, Windows uses uncommon character encodings. Recent versions may default to UTF-16 or UTF-8 BOM. Older versions may default to "code page" 1252, a superset of the ISO 8859-1 ASCII standard. No Windows system defaults to the more common UTF-8 (no BOM).
>
> By default, Windows will not display the standard UTF-8 π character. To make Windows compatible with UTF-8 encoding (and the rest of the world), use the compiler switch /utf-8 and issue the command chcp 65001 on the command line when testing. Now, you can have your π and eat it too.

How it works...

The <format> library uses a template *parameter pack* to pass arguments to the formatter. This allows the arguments to be individually inspected for class and type. The library function, make_format_args() takes a parameter pack and returns a format_args object, which provides a *type erased* list of arguments to be formatted.

We can see this in action in our print() function:

```
template<typename... Args>
constexpr void print(const string_view str_fmt, Args&&... args)
{
    fputs(vformat(str_fmt,
```

```
    make_format_args(args...)).c_str(),
        stdout);
}
```

The make_format_args() function takes a parameter pack and returns a format_args object. The vformat() function takes a format string and the format_args object, and returns a std::string. We use the c_str() method to get a C-string for use with fputs().

There's more...

It's common practice to overload the ostream << operator for custom classes. For example, given a class Frac that holds the values of a fraction:

```
template<typename T>
struct Frac {
    T n;
    T d;
};
...
Frac<long> n{ 3, 5 };
cout << "Frac: " << n << '\n';
```

We want to print the object as a fraction like 3 / 5. So, we would write a simple operator<< specialization like this:

```
template <typename T>
std::ostream& operator<<(std::ostream& os, const Frac<T>& f) {
    os << f.n << '/' << f.d;
    return os;
}
```

Now our output is:

Frac: 3/5

To provide `format()` support for our custom class, we need to create a `formatter` object specialization, like this:

```
template <typename T>
struct std::formatter<Frac<T>> : std::formatter<unsigned> {
    template <typename Context>
    auto format(const Frac<T>& f, Context& ctx) const {
        return format_to(ctx.out(), "{}/{}", f.n, f.d);
    }
};
```

The specialization of the `std::formatter` class overloads its `format()` method. We inherit from the `formatter<unsigned>` specialization for simplicity. The `format()` method is called with a `Context` object, which provides the output context for the formatted string. For the return value, we use the `format_to()` function with `ctx.out`, a normal format string, and parameters.

Now, we can now use our `print()` function with the `Frac` class:

```
print("Frac: {}\n", n);
```

The formatter now recognizes our class and provides our desired output:

```
Frac: 3/5
```

Trim whitespace from strings

It is common for input from users to include extraneous whitespace at one or both ends of a string. This can be problematic, so we often need to remove it. In this recipe, we'll use the `string` class methods, `find_first_not_of()` and `find_last_not_of()`, to trim whitespace from the ends of a string.

How to do it...

The `string` class includes methods for finding elements that are, or are not, included in a list of characters. We'll use these methods to trim `string`:

* We start by defining `string` with input from a hypothetical ten-thumbed user:

```
int main() {
    string s{" \t  ten-thumbed input   \t   \n \t "};
    cout << format("[{}]\n", s);
    ...
```

Our input has a few extra tab \t and newline \n characters before and after the content. We print it with surrounding brackets to show the whitespace:

```
[        ten-thumbed input
        ]
```

- Here's a `trimstr()` function to remove all the whitespace characters from both ends of `string`:

```cpp
string trimstr(const string& s) {
    constexpr const char * whitespace{ " \t\r\n\v\f" };
    if(s.empty()) return s;
    const auto first{ s.find_first_not_of(whitespace) };
    if(first == string::npos) return {};
    const auto last{ s.find_last_not_of(whitespace) };
    return s.substr(first, (last - first + 1));
}
```

We defined our set of whitespace characters as *space*, *tab*, *return*, *newline*, *vertical tab*, and *form feed*. Some of these are more common than others, but that's the canonical set.

This function uses the `find_first_not_of()` and `find_last_not_of()` methods of the `string` class to find the first/last elements that are *not* a member of the set.

- Now, we can call the function to get rid of all that unsolicited whitespace:

```cpp
cout << format("[{}]\n", trimstr(s));
```

Output:

[ten-thumbed input]

How it works...

The `string` class's various `find...()` member functions return a position as a `size_t` value:

```cpp
size_t find_first_not_of( const CharT* s, size_type pos = 0 );
size_t find_last_not_of( const CharT* s, size_type pos = 0 );
```

The return value is the zero-based position of the first matching character (*not* in the s list of characters) or the special value, `string::npos`, if not found. `npos` is a static member constant that represents an invalid position.

We test for (`first == string::npos`) and return an empty string { } if there is no match. Otherwise, we use the `first` and `last` positions with the `s.substr()` method to return the string without whitespace.

Read strings from user input

The STL provides character-based input from the standard input stream using the `std::cin` object. The `cin` object is a global *singleton* that reads input from the console as an `istream` input stream.

By default, `cin` reads *one word at a time* until it reaches the end of the stream:

```
string word{};
cout << "Enter words: ";
while(cin >> word) {
    cout << format("[{}] ", word);
}
cout << '\n';
```

Output:

```
$ ./working
Enter words: big light in sky↵
[big] [light] [in] [sky]
```

This is of limited usefulness, and it may lead some to dismiss `cin` as minimally functional.

While `cin` certainly has its quirks, it can be easily wrangled into providing line-oriented input.

How to do it...

To get basic line-oriented functionality from `cin`, there are two significant behaviors that need to be understood. One is the ability to get a line at a time, instead of a word at a time. The other is the ability to reset the stream after an error condition. Let's look at these in some detail:

- First, we need to prompt the user for input. Here's a simple `prompt` function:

```
bool prompt(const string_view s, const string_view s2 =
"") {
    if(s2.size()) cout << format("{} ({}): ", s, s2);
    else cout << format("{}: ", s);
    cout.flush();
    return true;
}
```

The `cout.flush()` function call ensures that the output is displayed immediately. Sometimes, when the output doesn't include a newline, the output stream may not flush automatically.

- The `cin` class has a `getline()` method that gets a line of text from the input stream and puts it in a C-string array:

```
constexpr size_t MAXLINE{1024 * 10};
char s[MAXLINE]{};
const char * p1{ "Words here" };
prompt(p1);
cin.getline(s, MAXLINE, '\n');
cout << s << '\n';
```

Output:

Words here: big light in sky↵
big light in sky

The `cin.getline()` method takes three arguments:

```
getline(char* s, size_t count, char delim );
```

The first argument is a C-string array for the destination. The second is the size of the array. The third is the delimiter for the end of the line.

The function will not put more than `count-1` characters in the array, leaving room for a *null* terminator.

The delimiter defaults to the newline `'\n'` character.

- The STL also provides a stand-alone `getline()` function that works with an STL `string` object:

```
string line{};
const char * p1a{ "More words here" };
prompt(p1a, "p1a");
getline(cin, line, '\n');
cout << line << '\n';
```

Output:

```
$ ./working
More words here (p1a): slated to appear in east↵
slated to appear in east
```

The stand-alone `std::getline()` function takes three arguments:

```
getline(basic_istream&& in, string& str, char delim );
```

The first argument is the output stream, second is a reference to a `string` object, and the third is the end-of-line delimiter.

If not specified, the delimiter defaults to the newline `'\n'` character.

I find the standalone `getline()` more convenient than the `cin.getline()` method.

- We can use `cin` to get a specific type from the input stream. To do this, we must be able to handle an error condition.

When `cin` encounters an error, it sets the stream to an error condition and stops accepting input. To retry input after an error, we must reset the state of the stream. Here's a function that resets the input stream after an error:

```
void clearistream() {
    string s{};
    cin.clear();
    getline(cin, s);
}
```

The `cin.clear()` function resets the error flags on the input stream but leaves text in the buffer. We then clear the buffer by reading a line and discarding it.

- We can accept numeric input by using `cin` with numeric type variables:

```
double a{};
double b{};
const char * p2{ "Please enter two numbers" };
for(prompt(p2); !(cin >> a >> b); prompt(p2)) {
    cout << "not numeric\n";
    clearistream();
}
cout << format("You entered {} and {}\n", a, b);
```

Output:

```
$ ./working
Please enter two numbers: a b⏎
not numeric
Please enter two numbers: 47 73⏎
You entered 47 and 73
```

The `cin >> a >> b` expression accepts input from the console and attempts to convert the first two words to types compatible with a and b (`double`). If it fails, we call `clearistream()` and try again.

- We can use the `getline()` separator parameter to get comma-separated input:

```
line.clear();
prompt(p3);
while(line.empty()) getline(cin, line);
stringstream ss(line);
while(getline(ss, word, ',')) {
    if(word.empty()) continue;
    cout << format("word: [{}]\n", trimstr(word));
}
```

Output:

```
$ ./working
Comma-separated words: this, that, other
word: [this]
word: [that]
word: [other]
```

Because this code runs after the numbers code, and because `cin` is messy, there may still be a line ending in the buffer. The `while(line.empty())` loop will optionally eat any empty lines.

We use a `stringstream` object to process the words, so we don't have to do it with `cin`. This allows us to use `getline()` to get one line without waiting for the end-of-file state.

Then, we call `getline()` on the `stringstream` object to parse out words separated by commas. This gives us words but with leading whitespace. We use the `trimstr()` function from the *Trim whitespace from strings* recipe in this chapter to trim the whitespace.

How it works...

The `std::cin` object is more useful than it may appear, but it can be a challenge to use. It tends to leave line endings on the stream, and in the case of errors, it can end up ignoring input.

The solution is to use `getline()` and, when necessary, put the line into a `stringstream` for convenient parsing.

Count words in a file

By default, the `basic_istream` class reads one word at a time. We can take advantage of this property to use an `istream_iterator` to count words.

How to do it...

This is a simple recipe to count words using an `istream_iterator`:

- We'll start with a simple function to count words using an `istream_iterator` object:

```
size_t wordcount(auto& is) {
    using it_t = istream_iterator<string>;
    return distance(it_t{is}, it_t{});
}
```

The distance() function takes two iterators and returns the number of steps between them. The using statement creates an alias it_t for the istream_iterator class with a string specialization. We then call distance() with an iterator, initialized with the input stream it_t{is}, and another with the default constructor, which gives us an end-of-stream sentinel.

* We call wordcount() from main():

```
int main() {
    const char * fn{ "the-raven.txt" };
    std::ifstream infile{fn, std::ios_base::in};
    size_t wc{ wordcount(infile) };
    cout << format("There are {} words in the
        file.\n", wc);
}
```

This calls wordcount() with our fstream object and prints the number of words in the file. When I call it with the text of Edgar Allan Poe's *The Raven*, we get this output:

```
There are 1068 words in the file.
```

How it works...

Because basic_istream defaults to word-by-word input, the number of steps in a file will be the number of words. The distance() function will measure the number of steps between two iterators, so calling it with the beginning and the sentinel of a compatible object will count the number of words in the file.

Initialize complex structures from file input

One strength of the *input stream* is its ability to parse different types of data from a text file and convert them to their corresponding fundamental types. Here's a simple technique for importing data into a container of structures using an input stream.

How to do it...

In this recipe, we'll take a data file and import its disparate fields into a `vector` of `struct` objects. The data file represents cities with their populations and map coordinates:

- This is `cities.txt`, the data file we'll read:

```
Las Vegas
661903 36.1699 -115.1398
New York City
8850000 40.7128 -74.0060
Berlin
3571000 52.5200 13.4050
Mexico City
21900000 19.4326 -99.1332
Sydney
5312000 -33.8688 151.2093
```

The city name is on a line by itself. The second line is population, followed by longitude and latitude. This pattern repeats for each of the five cities.

- We'll define our filename in a constant so that we can open it later:

```
constexpr const char * fn{ "cities.txt" };
```

- Here's a `City` struct to hold the data:

```
struct City {
    string name;
    unsigned long population;
    double latitude;
    double longitude;
};
```

- We would like to read the file and populate a `vector` of `City` objects:

```
vector<City> cities;
```

- Here's where the input stream makes this easy. We can simply specialize
  `operator>>` for our `City` class like this:

```
std::istream& operator>>(std::istream& in, City& c) {
    in >> std::ws;
    std::getline(in, c.name);
    in >> c.population >> c.latitude >> c.longitude;
    return in;
}
```

The `std::ws` input manipulator discards leading whitespace from the input
stream.

We use `getline()` to read the city name, as it could be one or more words.

This leverages the `>>` operator for the `population` (`unsigned long`), and
`latitude` and `longitude` (both `double`) elements to populate the correct type.

- Now, we can open the file and use the `>>` operator to read the file directly into the
  vector of `City` objects:

```
ifstream infile(fn, std::ios_base::in);
if(!infile.is_open()) {
    cout << format("failed to open file {}\n", fn);
    return 1;
}
for(City c{}; infile >> c;) cities.emplace_back(c);
```

- We can display the vector using `format()`:

```
for (const auto& [name, pop, lat, lon] : cities) {
    cout << format("{:.<15} pop {:<10} coords {}, {}\n",
        name, make_commas(pop), lat, lon);
}
```

Output:

```
$ ./initialize_container < cities.txt
Las Vegas...... pop 661,903    coords 36.1699, -115.1398
New York City.. pop 8,850,000  coords 40.7128, -74.006
Berlin......... pop 3,571,000  coords 52.52, 13.405
Mexico City.... pop 21,900,000 coords 19.4326, -99.1332
Sydney......... pop 5,312,000  coords -33.8688, 151.2093
```

- The make_commas() function was also used in the *Use structured binding to return multiple values* recipe in *Chapter 2, General STL Features*. It takes a numeric value and returns a string object, with commas added for readability:

```
string make_commas(const unsigned long num) {
    string s{ std::to_string(num) };
    for(int l = s.length() - 3; l > 0; l -= 3) {
        s.insert(l, ",");
    }
    return s;
}
```

How it works...

The heart of this recipe is the istream class operator>> overload:

```
std::istream& operator>>(std::istream& in, City& c) {
    in >> std::ws;
    std::getline(in, c.name);
    in >> c.population >> c.latitude >> c.longitude;
    return in;
}
```

By specifying our City class in the function header, this function will be called every time a City object appears on the right-hand side of an input stream >> operator:

```
City c{};
infile >> c;
```

This allows us to specify exactly how the input stream reads data into a City object.

There's more...

When you run this code on a Windows system, you'll notice that the first word of the first line gets corrupted. That's because Windows always includes a **Byte Order Mark (BOM)** at the head of any UTF-8 file. So, when you read a file on Windows, the BOM will be included in the first object you read. The BOM is anachronistic, but at the time of writing, there is no way to stop Windows from employing it.

The solution is to call a function that checks the first three bytes of a file for the BOM. The BOM for UTF-8 is EF BB BF. Here's a function that searches for, and skips, a UTF-8 BOM:

```
// skip BOM for UTF-8 on Windows
void skip_bom(auto& fs) {
    const unsigned char boms[]{ 0xef, 0xbb, 0xbf };
    bool have_bom{ true };
    for(const auto& c : boms) {
        if((unsigned char)fs.get() != c) have_bom = false;
    }
    if(!have_bom) fs.seekg(0);
    return;
}
```

This reads the first three bytes of the file and checks them for the UTF-8 BOM signature. If any of the three bytes do not match, it resets the input stream to the beginning of the file. If the file has no BOM, there's no harm done.

You simply call this function before you begin reading from a file:

```
int main() {
    ...
    ifstream infile(fn, std::ios_base::in);
    if(!infile.is_open()) {
        cout << format("failed to open file {}\n", fn);
        return 1;
    }
    skip_bom(infile);
    for(City c{}; infile >> c;) cities.emplace_back(c);
    ...
}
```

This will ensure that the BOM is not included in the first string of the file.

> **Note**
>
> Because the cin input stream is not seekable, the skip_bom() function will not work on the cin stream. It will only work with a seekable text file.

Customize a string class with char_traits

The `string` class is an alias of the `basic_string` class, with the signature:

```
class basic_string<char, std::char_traits<char>>;
```

The first template parameter provides the type of character. The second template parameter provides a character traits class, which provides basic character and string operations for the specified character type. We normally use the default `char_traits<char>` class.

We can modify the behavior of a string by providing our own custom character traits class.

How to do it...

In this recipe, we will create a *character traits class* for use with `basic_string` that will ignore casing for comparison purposes:

- First, we'll need a function to convert characters to a common case. We'll use lowercase here, but it's an arbitrary choice. Uppercase would work just as well:

```
constexpr char char_lower(const char& c) {
    if(c >= 'A' && c <= 'Z') return c + ('a' - 'A');
    else return c;
}
```

This function must be `constexpr` (for C++20 and later), so the existing `std::tolower()` function won't work here. Fortunately, it's a simple solution to a simple problem.

- Our traits class is called `ci_traits` (*ci* stands for case-independent). It inherits from `std::char_traits<char>`:

```
class ci_traits : public std::char_traits<char> {
public:
    ...
};
```

The inheritance allows us to override only the functions that we need.

- The comparison functions are called `lt()` for less than and `eq()` for equal to:

```
static constexpr bool lt(char_type a, char_type b)
noexcept {
    return char_lower(a) < char_lower(b);
}
static constexpr bool eq(char_type a, char_type b)
noexcept {
    return char_lower(a) == char_lower(b);
}
```

  Notice that we compare the *lowercase* versions of characters.

- There's also a `compare()` function, which compares two C-strings. It returns +1 for greater than, -1 for less than, and 0 for equal to. We can use the spaceship `<=>` operator for this:

```
static constexpr int compare(const char_type* s1,
        const char_type* s2, size_t count) {
    for(size_t i{0}; i < count; ++i) {
        auto diff{ char_lower(s1[i]) <=>
          char_lower(s2[i]) };
        if(diff > 0) return 1;
        if(diff < 0) return -1;
    }
    return 0;
}
```

- Finally, we need to implement a `find()` function. This returns a pointer to the first instance of a found character, or `nullptr` if not found:

```
static constexpr const char_type* find(const char_type*
p,
        size_t count, const char_type& ch) {
    const char_type find_c{ char_lower(ch) };
    for(size_t i{0}; i < count; ++i) {
        if(find_c == char_lower(p[i])) return p + i;
    }
    return nullptr;
}
```

- Now that we have a `ci_traits` class, we can define an alias for our `string` class:

  ```
  using ci_string = std::basic_string<char, ci_traits>;
  ```

- In our `main()` function, we define a `string` and a `ci_string`:

  ```
  int main() {
      string s{"Foo Bar Baz"};
      ci_string ci_s{"Foo Bar Baz"};
      ...
  ```

- We want to print them using `cout`, but this won't work:

  ```
  cout << "string: " << s << '\n';
  cout << "ci_string: " << ci_s << '\n';
  ```

  First, we need an operator overload for the `operator<<`:

  ```
  std::ostream& operator<<(std::ostream& os,
          const ci_string& str) {
      return os << str.c_str();
  }
  ```

  Now, we get this output:

  ```
  string: Foo Bar Baz
  ci_string: Foo Bar Baz
  ```

- Let's compare two `ci_string` objects with different cases:

  ```
  ci_string compare1{"CoMpArE StRiNg"};
  ci_string compare2{"compare string"};
  if (compare1 == compare2) {
      cout << format("Match! {} == {}\n", compare1,
          compare2);
  } else {
      cout << format("no match {} != {}\n", compare1,
          compare2);
  }
  ```

  Output:

  ```
  Match! CoMpArE StRiNg == compare string
  ```

  The comparison works as expected.

- Using the `find()` function on the `ci_s` object, we search for a lowercase b and find an uppercase B:

```
size_t found = ci_s.find('b');
cout << format("found: pos {} char {}\n", found,
ci_s[found]);
```

Output:

found: pos 4 char B

> **Note**
>
> Notice that the `format()` function doesn't require a specialization. This was tested with the `fmt.dev` reference implementation. It did not work with the preview release of MSVC's `format()`, even with a specialization. Hopefully, this will be fixed in a future release.

How it works...

This recipe works by replacing the `std::char_traits` class in the template specialization of the `string` class with a `ci_traits` class of our own. The `basic_string` class uses the traits class for its fundamental character-specific functions, such as comparisons and searching. When we replace it with our own class, we can change these fundamental behaviors.

There's more...

We can also override the `assign()` and `copy()` member functions to create a class that stores lowercase characters:

```
class lc_traits : public std::char_traits<char> {
public:
    static constexpr void assign( char_type& r, const
      char_type& a )
            noexcept {
        r = char_lower(a);
    }
    static constexpr char_type* assign( char_type* p,
            std::size_t count, char_type a ) {
        for(size_t i{}; i < count; ++i) p[i] =
          char_lower(a);
```

```
        return p;
    }
    static constexpr char_type* copy(char_type* dest,
            const char_type* src, size_t count) {
        for(size_t i{0}; i < count; ++i) {
            dest[i] = char_lower(src[i]);
        }
        return dest;
    }
};
```

Now, we can create an `lc_string` alias, and the object stores lowercase characters:

```
using lc_string = std::basic_string<char, lc_traits>;
...
lc_string lc_s{"Foo Bar Baz"};
cout << "lc_string: " << lc_s << '\n';
```

Output:

```
lc_string: foo bar baz
```

> **Note**
>
> These techniques work as expected on GCC and Clang but not on the preview release of MSVC. I expect that this will be fixed in a future release.

Parse strings with Regular Expressions

Regular Expressions (commonly abbreviated as *regex*) are commonly used for lexical analysis and pattern-matching on streams of text. They are common in Unix text-processing utilities, such as `grep`, `awk`, and `sed`, and are an integral part of the *Perl* language. There are a few common variations in the syntax. A POSIX standard was approved in 1992, while other common variations include *Perl* and *ECMAScript* (JavaScript) dialects. The C++ `regex` library defaults to the ECMAScript dialect.

The `regex` library was first introduced to the STL with C++11. It can be very useful for finding patterns in text files.

To learn more about Regular Expression syntax and usage, I recommend the book, *Mastering Regular Expressions* by Jeffrey Friedl.

How to do it...

For this recipe, we will extract hyperlinks from an HTML file. A hyperlink is coded in HTML like this:

```
<a href="http://example.com/file.html">Text goes here</a>
```

We will use a `regex` object to extract both the link and the text, as two separate strings.

- Our example file is called `the-end.html`. It's taken from my website (`https://bw.org/end/`), and is included in the GitHub repository:

  ```
  const char * fn{ "the-end.html" };
  ```

- Now, we define our `regex` object with a regular expression string:

  ```
  const std::regex
      link_re{ "<a href=\"([^\"]*)\"[^<]*>([^<]*)</a>" };
  ```

  Regular expressions can look intimidating at first, but they're actually rather simple.

  This is parsed as follows:

  I.   Match the whole string.

  II. Find the substring `<a href="`.

  III. Store everything up to the next `"` as sub-match 1.

  IV. Skip past the `>` character.

  V.   Store everything up to the string `</a>` as sub-match 2.

- Now, we read our file entirely into a string:

  ```
  string in{};
  std::ifstream infile(fn, std::ios_base::in);
  for(string line{}; getline(infile, line);) in += line;
  ```

This opens the HTML file, reads it line by line, and appends each line to the `string` object, `in`.

- To extract the link strings, we set up an `sregex_token_iterator` object to step through the file and extract each of the matched elements:

```
std::sregex_token_iterator it{ in.begin(), in.end(),
    link_re, {1, 2} };
```

The 1 and 2 correspond to the sub-matches in the regular expression.

- We have a corresponding function to step through the results with the iterator:

```
template<typename It>
void get_links(It it) {
    for(It end_it{}; it != end_it; ) {
        const string link{ *it++ };
        if(it == end_it) break;
        const string desc{ *it++ };
        cout << format("{:.<24} {}\n", desc, link);
    }
}
```

We call the function with the `regex` iterator:

```
get_links(it);
```

And we get this result with our descriptions and links:

```
Bill Weinman............ https://bw.org/
courses................. https://bw.org/courses/
music................... https://bw.org/music/
books................... https://packt.com/
back to the internet.... https://duckduckgo.com/
```

How it works...

The STL `regex` engine operates as a *generator* that evaluates and yields one result at a time. We set up the iterator using `sregex_iterator` or `sregex_token_iterator`. While `sregex_token_iterator` supports sub-matches, `sregex_iterator` does not.

The parentheses in our regex serve as *sub-matches*, numbered 1 and 2 respectively:

```
const regex link_re{ "<a href=\"([^\"]*)\"[^<]*>([^<]*)</a>" };
```

Each part of the `regex` matches is illustrated here:

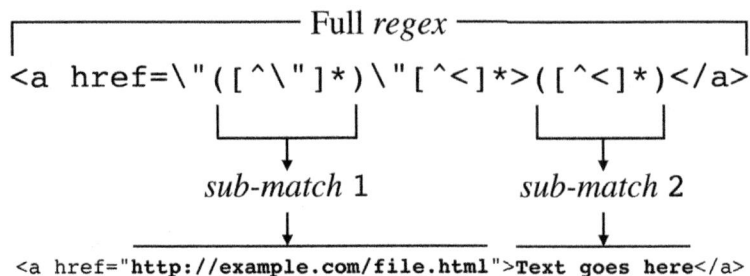

```
┌──────────────── Full regex ────────────────┐
<a href=\"([^\"]*)\"[^<]*>([^<]*)</a>
         └───┬───┘         └──┬──┘
         sub-match 1      sub-match 2
              │                │
              ↓                ↓
<a href="http://example.com/file.html">Text goes here</a>
```

Figure 7.1 – A Regular Expression with sub-matches

This allows us to match a string and use parts of that string as our results:

```cpp
sregex_token_iterator it{ in.begin(), in.end(), link_re, {1, 2}
};
```

The sub-matches are numbered, beginning with 1. Sub-match 0 is a special value that represents the entire match.

Once we have our iterator, we use it as we would any other iterator:

```cpp
for(It end_it{}; it != end_it; ) {
    const string link{ *it++ };
    if(it == end_it) break;
    const string desc{ *it++ };

    cout << format("{:.<24} {}\n", desc, link);
}
```

This simply steps through our results via the `regex` iterator, giving us the formatted output:

```
Bill Weinman............ https://bw.org/
courses................. https://bw.org/courses/
music................... https://bw.org/music/
books................... https://packt.com/
back to the internet.... https://duckduckgo.com/
```

8
Utility Classes

The C++ Standard Library includes an assortment of utility classes designed for specific tasks. Some are common, and you've probably seen many of these classes in other recipes in this book.

This chapter covers a broad range of utilities, including time measurement, generic types, smart pointers, and more, in the following recipes:

- Manage optional values with `std::optional`
- Use `std::any` for type safety
- Store different types with `std::variant`
- Time events with `std::chrono`
- Use fold expressions for variadic tuples
- Manage allocated memory with `std::unique_ptr`
- Share objects with `std::shared_ptr`
- Use weak pointers with shared objects
- Share members of a managed object
- Compare random number engines
- Compare random number distribution generators

Technical requirements

The code files for this chapter can be found on GitHub at `https://github.com/ PacktPublishing/CPP-20-STL-Cookbook/tree/main/chap08`.

Manage optional values with std::optional

Introduced with C++17, the `std::optional` class holds an *optional value*.

Consider the case where you have a function that may or may not return a value – for example, a function that checks if a number is *prime* but returns the first factor if there is one. This function should return either a value or a `bool` status. We could create a `struct` that carries both value and status:

```
struct factor_t {
    bool is_prime;
    long factor;
};
factor_t factor(long n) {
    factor_t r{};
    for(long i = 2; i <= n / 2; ++i) {
        if (n % i == 0) {
            r.is_prime = false;
            r.factor = i;
            return r;
        }
    }
    r.is_prime = true;
    return r;
}
```

It's a clumsy solution but it works, and it's not uncommon.

It could be made a lot simpler with the `optional` class:

```
optional<long> factor(long n) {
    for (long i = 2; i <= n / 2; ++i) {
        if (n % i == 0) return {i};
    }
    return {};
}
```

With `optional`, we can return a value or a non-value.

We can call it, like this:

```
long a{ 42 };
long b{ 73 };
auto x = factor(a);
auto y = factor(b);
if(x) cout << format("lowest factor of {} is {}\n", a, *x);
else cout << format("{} is prime\n", a);
if(y) cout << format("lowest factor of {} is {}\n", b, *y);
else cout << format("{} is prime\n", b);
```

Our output is:

```
lowest factor of 42 is 2
73 is prime
```

The optional class allows us to easily return the optional value and easily test for a value.

How to do it...

In this recipe, we'll look at some examples of how to use the `optional` class:

- The `optional` class is quite simple. We construct an optional value using standard template notation:

  ```
  optional<int> a{ 42 };
  cout << *a << '\n';
  ```

  We access the value of the `optional` with the * pointer dereference operator.

  Output:

  ```
  42
  ```

- We test if the `optional` has a value using its `bool` operator:

  ```
  if(a) cout << *a << '\n';
  else cout << "no value\n";
  ```

  If a were constructed without a value:

  ```
  optional<int> a{};
  ```

The output would reflect the `else` condition:

```
no value
```

- We can further simplify this by declaring a *type alias*:

```
using oint = std::optional<int>;
oint a{ 42 };
oint b{ 73 };
```

- If we want to operate on `oint` objects, with `oint` objects as the result, we can provide operator overloads:

```
oint operator+(const oint& a, const oint& b) {
    if(a && b) return *a + *b;
    else return {};
}
oint operator+(const oint& a, const int b) {
    if(a) return *a + b;
    else return {};
}
```

Now, we can operate on the `oint` objects directly:

```
auto sum{ a + b };
if(sum) {
    cout << format("{} + {} = {}\n", *a, *b, *sum);
} else {
    cout << "NAN\n";
}
```

Output:

```
42 + 73 = 115
```

- Suppose we declare b with the default constructor:

```
oint b{};
```

Now, we get the `else` branch output:

```
NAN
```

How it works...

The `std::optional` class is made for simplicity. It provides operator overloads for many common functions. It also includes member functions for further flexibility.

The `optional` class provides an `operator bool` overload for determining if the object has a value:

```
optional<int> n{ 42 };
if(n) ... // has a value
```

Or, you may use the `has_value()` member function:

```
if(n.has_value()) ... // has a value
```

To access the value, you may use the `operator*` overload:

```
x = *n;   // * retruns the value
```

Or, you may use the `value()` member function:

```
x = n.value();   // * retruns the value
```

The `reset()` member function destroys the value and resets the state of the `optional` object:

```
n.reset();        // no longer has a value
```

There's more...

The `optional` class provides exception support with the `value()` method:

```
b.reset();
try {
    cout << b.value() << '\n';
} catch(const std::bad_optional_access& e) {
    cout << format("b.value(): {}\n", e.what());
}
```

Output:

b.value(): bad optional access

> **Important Note**
>
> Only the value() method throws an exception. The behavior of the *
> operator is *undefined* for an invalid value.

Use std::any for type safety

Introduced with C++17, the std::any class provides a type-safe container for a single object of any type.

For example, this is a default-constructed any object:

```
any x{};
```

This object has no value. We can test that with the has_value() method:

```
if (x.has_value()) cout << "have value\n";
else cout << "no value\n";
```

Output:

no value

We assign a value to the any object with the assignment operator:

```
x = 42;
```

Now, the any object has a value, and a type:

```
if (x.has_value()) {
    cout << format("x has type: {}\n", x.type().name());
    cout << format("x has value: {}\n", any_cast<int>(x));
} else {
    cout << "no value\n";
}
```

Output:

```
x has type: i
x has value: 42
```

The `type()` method returns a `type_info` object. The `type_info::name()` method returns an implementation-defined name for the type in a C-string. In this case, for GCC, the `i` means `int`.

We use the `any_cast<`*type*`>()` non-member function to cast the value for use.

We can re-assign the any object with different values of different types:

```
x = "abc"s;
cout << format("x is type {} with value {}\n",
    x.type().name(), any_cast<string>(x))
```

Output:

```
x is type NSt7__cxx1112basic_string... with value abc
```

I've abbreviated the long type name from GCC but you get the idea. The same any object that once held an `int` now contains an STL `string` object.

The main usefulness of the any class is in creating a polymorphic function. Let's examine how to do that in this recipe:

How to do it...

In this recipe, we'll build a polymorphic function using the any class. A polymorphic function is one that can take objects of different types in its parameters:

- Our polymorphic function takes an any object and prints its type and value:

```
void p_any(const any& a) {
    if (!a.has_value()) {
        cout << "None.\n";
    } else if (a.type() == typeid(int)) {
        cout << format("int: {}\n", any_cast<int>(a));
    } else if (a.type() == typeid(string)) {
        cout << format("string: \"{}\"\n",
            any_cast<const string&>(a));
    } else if (a.type() == typeid(list<int>)) {
```

```
            cout << "list<int>: ";
            for(auto& i : any_cast<const list<int>&>(a))
                cout << format("{} ", i);
            cout << '\n';
        } else {
            cout << format("something else: {}\n",
                a.type().name());
        }
    }
```

The p_any() function first tests to see if the object has a value. It then tests the type() method against various types and takes appropriate action for each type.

Before the any class, we would have had to write four different specializations for this function, and we still wouldn't be able to easily handle the default case.

- We call this function from main(), like this:

```
p_any({});
p_any(47);
p_any("abc"s);
p_any(any(list{ 1, 2, 3 }));
p_any(any(vector{ 1, 2, 3 }));
```

Output:

```
None.
int: 47
string: "abc"
list<int>: 1 2 3
something else: St6vectorIiSaIiEE
```

Our polymorphic function handles the various types with a minimum of code.

How it works...

The std::any copy constructor and assignment operator use *direct initialization* to make a non-const copy of the target object as the *contained* object. The type of the contained object is stored separately as a typeid object.

Once initialized, the any object has the following methods:

- emplace() replaces the contained object, constructing the new object in place.

- reset() destroys the contained object.

- `has_value()` returns `true` if there is a contained object.
- `type()` returns a `typeid` object, representing the type of the contained object.
- `operator=()` replaces the contained object by a *copy* or *move* operation.

The any class also supports the following non-member functions:

- `any_cast<T>()`, a template function, provides type-safe access to the contained object.

  Keep in mind that the `any_cast<T>()` function returns a copy of the contained object. You may use `any_cast<T&>()` to return a reference.
- `std::swap()` specializes the `std::swap` algorithm.

If you try to cast an any object with the wrong type, it throws a `bad_any_cast` exception:

```
try {
    cout << any_cast<int>(x) << '\n';
} catch(std::bad_any_cast& e) {
    cout << format("any: {}\n", e.what());
}
```

Output:

any: bad any_cast

Store different types with std::variant

Introduced with C++17, the `std::variant` class may hold different values, one at a time, where each value must fit in the same allocated memory space. It's useful for holding alternative types for use in a single context.

Differences from the primitive union structure

The `variant` class is a *tagged union*. It differs from the primitive `union` structure in that only one type may be in effect at a time.

The primitive `union` type, inherited from C, is a structure where the same datum may be accessed as different types. For example:

```
union ipv4 {
    struct {
        uint8_t a; uint8_t b; uint8_t c; uint8_t d;
```

```
    } quad;
    uint32_t int32;
} addr;
addr.int32 = 0x2A05A8C0;
cout << format("ip addr dotted quad: {}.{}.{}.{}\n",
    addr.quad.a, addr.quad.b, addr.quad.c, addr.quad.d);
cout << format("ip addr int32 (LE): {:08X}\n", addr.int32);
```

Output:

```
ip addr dotted quad: 192.168.5.42
ip addr int32 (LE): 2A05A8C0
```

In this example, the union has two members, types struct and uint32_t, where struct has four uint8_t members. This gives us two *different perspectives of the same 32-bit memory space*. We can view the same ipv4 address as either a 32-bit unsigned integer (**Little Endian** or **LE**) or four 8-bit unsigned integers in the common *dotted quad* notation. This provides a bitwise polymorphy that can be useful at the systems level.

variant doesn't work like that. The variant class is a *tagged union*, where each datum is tagged with its type. If we store a value as uint32_t, we may only access it as uint32_t. This makes variant type safe but not a replacement for union.

How to do it...

In this recipe, we demonstrate the use of std::variant with a small catalogue of household pets of various species.

- We'll start with a simple class to hold an Animal:

```
class Animal {
    string_view _name{};
    string_view _sound{};
    Animal();
public:
    Animal(string_view n, string_view s)
        : _name{ n }, _sound{ s } {}
    void speak() const {
        cout << format("{} says {}\n", _name, _sound);
    }
    void sound(string_view s) {
```

```
        _sound = s;
    }
};
```

The name of the animal and the sound that the animal makes are passed in the constructor.

- Individual species classes inherit from `Animal`:

```
class Cat : public Animal {
public:
    Cat(string_view n) : Animal(n, "meow") {}
};
class Dog : public Animal {
public:
    Dog(string_view n) : Animal(n, "arf!") {}
};
class Wookie : public Animal {
public:
    Wookie(string_view n) : Animal(n, "grrraarrgghh!") {}
};
```

Each of these classes set the sound for their specific species by calling the parent constructor.

- Now, we can define our `variant` type in an alias:

```
using v_animal = std::variant<Cat, Dog, Wookie>;
```

This `variant` can hold any of the types, `Cat`, `Dog`, or `Wookie`.

- In `main()`, we create a `list` using our `v_animal` alias as the type:

```
int main() {
    list<v_animal> pets{
        Cat{"Hobbes"}, Dog{"Fido"}, Cat{"Max"},
        Wookie{"Chewie"}
    };
    ...
```

Each element in the list is of a type included in the `variant` definition.

- The `variant` class provides several different ways to access elements. First, we'll look at the `visit()` function.

  `visit()` calls a *functor* with the object currently contained in the `variant`. First, let's define a functor that accepts any of our pets:

  ```
  struct animal_speaks {
      void operator()(const Dog& d) const { d.speak(); }
      void operator()(const Cat& c) const { c.speak(); }
      void operator()(const Wookie& w) const {
        w.speak(); }
  };
  ```

  This is a simple functor class with overloads for each of the `Animal` sub-classes. We call it with `visit()`, with each of our `list` elements:

  ```
  for (const v_animal& a : pets) {
      visit(animal_speaks{}, a);
  }
  ```

  We get this output:

  ```
  Hobbes says meow
  Fido says arf!
  Max says meow
  Chewie says grrraarrgghh!
  ```

- The `variant` class also provides an `index()` method:

  ```
  for(const v_animal &a : pets) {
      auto idx{ a.index() };
      if(idx == 0) get<Cat>(a).speak();
      if(idx == 1) get<Dog>(a).speak();
      if(idx == 2) get<Wookie>(a).speak();
  }
  ```

  Output:

  ```
  Hobbes says meow
  Fido says arf!
  Max says meow
  Chewie says grrraarrgghh!
  ```

Each `variant` object is indexed, based on the order in which the types were declared in the template arguments. Our `v_animal` type was defined with `std::variant<Cat, Dog, Wookie>`, and these types are indexed as 0 – 2, in that order.

- The `get_if<T>()` function tests a given element against a type:

```
for (const v_animal& a : pets) {
    if(const auto c{ get_if<Cat>(&a) }; c) {
        c->speak();
    } else if(const auto d{ get_if<Dog>(&a) }; d) {
        d->speak();
    } else if(const auto w{ get_if<Wookie>(&a) }; w) {
        w->speak();
    }
}
```

Output:

```
Hobbes says meow
Fido says arf!
Max says meow
Chewie says grrraarrgghh!
```

The `get_if<T>()` function returns a pointer if the type of the element matches `T`; otherwise, it returns `nullptr`.

- Finally, the `holds_alternative<T>()` function returns `true` or `false`. We can use this to test a type against an element, without returning the element:

```
size_t n_cats{}, n_dogs{}, n_wookies{};
for(const v_animal& a : pets) {
    if(holds_alternative<Cat>(a)) ++n_cats;
    if(holds_alternative<Dog>(a)) ++n_dogs;
    if(holds_alternative<Wookie>(a)) ++n_wookies;
}
cout << format("there are {} cat(s), "
               "{} dog(s), "
               "and {} wookie(s)\n",
               n_cats, n_dogs, n_wookies);
```

Output:

```
there are 2 cat(s), 1 dog(s), and 1 wookie(s)
```

How it works...

The `std::variant` class is a single-object container. An instance of `variant<X, Y, Z>` must hold exactly one object of type X, Y, or Z. It holds both the value and the type of its current object.

The `index()` method tells us the type of the current object:

```
if(v.index() == 0) // if variant is type X
```

The `holds_alternative<T>()` non-member function returns `true` if T is the type of the current object:

```
if(holds_alternative<X>(v))  // if current variant obj is type
X
```

We can retrieve the current object with the `get()` non-member function:

```
auto o{ get<X>(v) };  // current variant obj must be type X
```

We can combine the test for type and retrieval with the `get_if()` non-member function:

```
auto* p{ get_if<X>(v) };  // nullptr if current obj not type X
```

The `visit()` non-member function invokes a callable object with the current variant object as its single parameter:

```
visit(f, v);  // calls f(v) with current variant obj
```

The `visit()` function is the only way to retrieve an object without testing its type. In combination with a functor that can handle each type, this can be very flexible:

```
struct animal_speaks {
    void operator()(const Dog& d) const { d.speak(); }
    void operator()(const Cat& c) const { c.speak(); }
    void operator()(const Wookie& v) const { v.speak(); }
};
main() {
    for (const v_animal& a : pets) {
```

```
        visit(animal_speaks{}, a);
    }
}
```

Output:

```
Hobbes says meow
Fido says arf!
Max says meow
Chewie says grrraarrgghh!
```

Time events with std::chrono

The `std::chrono` library provides tools for measuring and reporting time and intervals.

Many of these classes and functions were introduced with C++11. There have been significant changes and updates for C++20, but at the time of writing, many of those updates are not yet implemented on the systems I've tested.

Using the `chrono` library, this recipe explores techniques for timing events.

How to do it...

The `system_clock` class is used for reporting the current date and time. The `steady_clock` and `high_resolution_clock` classes are used for timing events. Let's look at the differences between these clocks:

- Because these names can be long and unwieldy, we'll use some type aliases throughout this recipe:

```
using std::chrono::system_clock;
using std::chrono::steady_clock;
using std::chrono::high_resolution_clock;
using std::chrono::duration;
using seconds = duration<double>;
using milliseconds = duration<double, std::milli>;
using microseconds = duration<double, std::micro>;
using fps24 = duration<unsigned long, std::ratio<1, 24>>;
```

The `duration` class represents an interval between two points in time. These aliases are convenient for using different intervals.

- We can get the current time and date by using the `system_clock` class:

```
auto t = system_clock::now();
cout << format("system_clock::now is {:%F %T}\n", t);
```

The `system_clock::now()` function returns a `time_point` object. The `<chrono>` library includes a `format()` specialization for `time_point` that uses `strftime()` format specifiers.

The output is:

```
system_clock::now is 2022-02-05 13:52:15
```

The `<iomanip>` header includes `put_time()`, which works like `strftime()` for `ostream`:

```
std::time_t now_t = system_clock::to_time_t(t);
cout << "system_clock::now is "
    << std::put_time(std::localtime(&now_t), "%F %T")
    << '\n';
```

`put_time()` takes a pointer to a C-style `time_t*` value. `system_clock::to_time_t` converts a `time_point` object to `time_t`.

This gives the same output as our `format()` example:

```
system_clock::now is 2022-02-05 13:52:15
```

- We can also use `system_clock` to time an event. First, we need something to time. Here's a function that counts prime numbers:

```
constexpr uint64_t MAX_PRIME{ 0x1FFFF }
uint64_t count_primes() {
    constexpr auto is_prime = [](const uint64_t n) {
        for(uint64_t i{ 2 }; i < n / 2; ++i) {
            if(n % i == 0) return false;
        }
        return true;
    };
    uint64_t count{ 0 };
    uint64_t start{ 2 };
    uint64_t end{ MAX_PRIME };
    for(uint64_t i{ start }; i <= end ; ++i) {
        if(is_prime(i)) ++count;
```

```
    }
    return count;
}
```

This function counts the prime numbers between 2 and 0x1FFFF (131,071), which should take a few seconds on most modern systems.

- Now, we write a timer function to time our count_primes():

```
seconds timer(uint64_t(*f)()) {
    auto t1{ system_clock::now() };
    uint64_t count{ f() };
    auto t2{ system_clock::now() };
    seconds secs{ t2 - t1 };
    cout << format("there are {} primes in range\n",
        count);
    return secs;
}
```

This function takes an function f and returns duration<double>. We use system_clock::now() to mark the time before and after the call to f(). We take the difference between the two times and return it in a duration object.

- We can call our timer() from main(), like this:

```
int main() {
    auto secs{ timer(count_primes) };
    cout << format("time elapsed: {:.3f} seconds\n",
        secs.count());

    ...
```

This passes the count_primes() function to timer() and stores the duration object in secs.

Output:

```
there are 12252 primes in range
time elapsed: 3.573 seconds
```

The count() method on the duration object returns the duration in the specified units – in this case, double, representing *seconds* of duration.

This was run on a VM running *Debian* with GCC. The exact time will vary on different systems.

- The `system_clock` class is designed to provide the current *wall clock* time. While its resolution may support timing purposes, it is not guaranteed to be *monotonic*. In other words, it may not always provide consistent *ticks* (timing intervals).

  The `chrono` library provides a more suitable clock in `steady_clock`. It has the same interface as `system_clock` but provides more reliable ticks for timing purposes:

  ```
  seconds timer(uint64_t(*f)()) {
      auto t1{ steady_clock::now() };
      uint64_t count{ f() };
      auto t2{ steady_clock::now() };
      seconds secs{ t2 - t1 };
      cout << format("there are {} primes in range\n",
          count);
      return secs;
  }
  ```

  `steady_clock` is designed to provide reliably consistent monotonic ticks, suitable for timing events. It uses a relative time reference, so it's not useful for wall clock time. While `system_clock` measures by beginning from a fixed point in time (1 January 1970, 00:00 UTC), `steady_clock` uses a relative time.

  Another option is `high_resolution_clock`, which provides the shortest tick period available on a given system but is not implemented consistently across different implementations. It may be an alias for `system_clock` or `steady_clock`, and it may or may not be monotonic. `high_resolution_clock` is not recommended for general-purpose use.

- Our `timer()` function returns `seconds`, which is an alias for `duration<double>`:

  ```
  using seconds = duration<double>;
  ```

  The duration class takes an optional second template parameter, a `std::ratio` class:

  ```
  template<class Rep, class Period = std::ratio<1>>
  class duration;
  ```

  The `<chrono>` header provides convenience types for many decimal ratios, including `milli` and `micro`:

  ```
  using milliseconds = duration<double, std::milli>;
  using microseconds = duration<double, std::micro>;
  ```

If we require something else, we may provide our own:

```
using fps24 = duration<unsigned long, std::ratio<1, 24>>;
```

fps24 represents the number of frames of film shot at the standard 24 frames per second. The ratio is 1/24 of a second.

This allows us to easily convert between different ranges of duration:

```
cout << format("time elapsed: {:.3f} sec\n", secs.
count());
cout << format("time elapsed: {:.3f} ms\n",
    milliseconds(secs).count());
cout << format("time elapsed: {:.3e} μs\n",
    microseconds(secs).count());
cout << format("time elapsed: {} frames at 24 fps\n",
    floor<fps24>(secs).count());
```

Output:

```
time elapsed: 3.573 sec
time elapsed: 3573.077 ms
time elapsed: 3.573e+06 μs
time elapsed: 85 frames at 24 fps
```

Because the fps24 alias uses unsigned long instead of double, a type conversion is required. The floor function provides this by discarding the fractional part. round() and ceil() are also available in this context.

- For convenience, the chrono library provides format() specializations for the standard duration ratios:

```
cout << format("time elapsed: {:.3}\n", secs);
cout << format("time elapsed: {:.3}\n",
milliseconds(secs));
cout << format("time elapsed: {:.3}\n",
microseconds(secs));
```

Output:

```
time elapsed: 3.573s
time elapsed: 3573.077ms
time elapsed: 3573076.564μs
```

These results will vary on different implementations.

How it works...

There are two major pieces to the chrono library, the *clock* classes and the duration class.

The clock classes

The clock classes include:

- system_clock – provides wall clock time.

- steady_clock – provides guaranteed monotonic ticks for duration measurements.

- high_resolution_clock – provides the shortest available tick period. It may be an alias of system_clock or steady_clock on some systems.

We use system_clock to display the current time and date. We use steady_clock to measure intervals.

Each of the clock classes has a now() method that returns time_point, representing the current value of the clock. now() is a static member function, so it's called on the class without instantiating an object:

```
auto t1{ steady_clock::now() };
```

The std::duration class

The duration class is used to hold a time interval – that is, the difference between two time_point objects. It is generally constructed with a time_point object's subtraction (-) operator.

```
duration<double> secs{ t2 - t1 };
```

The time_point subtraction operator doubles as a constructor for duration:

```
template<class C, class D1, class D2>
constexpr duration<D1,D2>
operator-( const time_point<C,D1>& pt_lhs,
    const time_point<C,D2>& pt_rhs );
```

The duration class has template parameters for type representation and a ratio object:

```
template<class Rep, class Period = std::ratio<1>>
class duration;
```

The `Period` template parameter defaults to a `ratio` of 1:1, which is seconds.

The library provides `ratio` aliases (such as `micro` and `milli`) for powers-of-10 from `atto` (1/1,000,000,000,000,000,000) through `exa` (1,000,000,000,000,000,000/1). This allows us to create standard durations, as we did in our example:

```
using milliseconds = duration<double, std::milli>;
using microseconds = duration<double, std::micro>;
```

The `count()` method gives us the duration in the `Rep` type:

```
constexpr Rep count() const;
```

This allows us to easily access the duration for display or other purposes:

```
cout << format("duration: {}\n", secs.count());
```

Use fold expressions for variadic tuples

The `std::tuple` class is essentially a more complex, and less convenient, `struct`. The interface for `tuple` is cumbersome, although *class template argument deduction* and *structured binding* have made it somewhat easier.

I tend to use `struct` before `tuple` for most applications, with one significant exception: the one real advantage of `tuple` is that it can be used with *fold expressions* in a variadic context.

Fold expressions

Designed to make it easier to expand a variadic parameter pack, *fold expressions* are a new feature with C++17. Prior to fold expressions, expanding a parameter pack required a recursive function:

```
template<typename T>
void f(T final) {
    cout << final << '\n';
}
template<typename T, typename... Args>
void f(T first, Args... args) {
    cout << first;
    f(args...);
}
```

```
int main() {
    f("hello", ' ', 47, ' ', "world");
}
```

Output:

hello 47 world

Using a fold expression, this is much simpler:

```
template<typename... Args>
void f(Args... args) {
    (cout << ... << args);
    cout << '\n';
}
```

Output:

hello 47 world

There are four types of fold expressions:

- Unary right fold: `(args op ...)`
- Unary left fold: `(... op args)`
- Binary right fold: `(args op ... op init)`
- Binary left fold: `(init op ... op args)`

The expression in the example above is a *binary left fold*:

```
(cout << ... << args);
```

This expands to:

```
cout << "hello" << ' ' << 47 << ' ' << "world";
```

Fold expressions are a great convenience for many purposes. Let's look at how we can use them with tuples.

How to do it...

In this recipe, we'll create a template function that operates on a tuple with varying numbers and types of elements:

- The heart of this recipe is a function that takes a tuple of unknown size and type and prints each element with `format()`:

```cpp
template<typename... T>
constexpr void print_t(const tuple<T...>& tup) {
    auto lpt =
        [&tup] <size_t... I>
            (std::index_sequence<I...>)
              constexpr {
              (..., ( cout <<
                  format((I? ", {}" : "{}"),
                      get<I>(tup))
              ));
              cout << '\n';
        };
    lpt(std::make_index_sequence<sizeof...(T)>());
}
```

The heart of this function is in the lambda expression. It uses the `index_sequence` object to generate a parameter pack of index values. We then use a fold expression to call `get<I>` with each index value. The templated lambda requires C++20.

You could use a separate function in place of the lambda, but I like keeping it in a single scope.

- We can now call this from `main()` with a variety of tuples:

```cpp
int main() {
    tuple lables{ "ID", "Name", "Scale" };
    tuple employee{ 123456, "John Doe", 3.7 };
    tuple nums{ 1, 7, "forty-two", 47, 73L, -111.11 };

    print_t(lables);
    print_t(employee);
    print_t(nums);
}
```

Output:

```
ID, Name, Scale
123456, John Doe, 3.7
1, 7, forty-two, 47, 73, -111.11
```

How it works...

The challenge with `tuple` is its restrictive interface. You can retrieve elements with `std::tie()`, with *structured bindings*, or the `std::get<>` function. None of these techniques are useful if you don't know the number and type of elements in the `tuple`.

We get around this limitation by using the `index_sequence` class. `index_sequence` is a specialization of `integer_sequence` that provides a parameter pack of the `size_t` elements, which we can use to index our `tuple`. We call our lambda function with `make_index_sequence` to set up a parameter pack in the lambda:

```
lpt(std::make_index_sequence<sizeof...(T)>());
```

The templated lambda is constructed with a parameter pack of `size_t` indexes for the `get()` function:

```
[&tup] <size_t... I> (std::index_sequence<I...>) constexpr {
    ...
};
```

The `get()` function takes the index value as a template parameter. We use a *unary left fold expression* to call `get<I>()`:

```
(..., ( cout << format("{} ", std::get<I>(tup))));
```

The fold expression takes each element of the function's parameter pack and applies the comma operator. The right-hand side of the comma has a `format()` function that prints each element of the tuple.

This makes it possible to deduce the number of elements in the tuple, which makes it useable in a variadic context. Keep in mind that, as with template functions in general, the compiler will generate a separate specialization of this function for each combination of `tuple` parameters.

There's more...

We can use this technique for other tasks. For example, here's a function that returns the sum of all the int values in a tuple of unknown size:

```
template<typename... T>
constexpr int sum_t(const tuple<T...>& tup) {
    int accum{};
    auto lpt =
        [&tup, &accum] <size_t... I>
            (std::index_sequence<I...>)
        constexpr {
            (..., (
                accum += get<I>(tup)
            ));
        };
    lpt(std::make_index_sequence<sizeof...(T)>());
    return accum;
}
```

We can call this with several tuple objects of varying numbers of int values:

```
tuple ti1{ 1, 2, 3, 4, 5 };
tuple ti2{ 9, 10, 11, 12, 13, 14, 15 };
tuple ti3{ 47, 73, 42 };
auto sum1{ sum_t(ti1) };
auto sum2{ sum_t(ti2) };
auto sum3{ sum_t(ti3) };
cout << format("sum of ti1: {}\n", sum1);
cout << format("sum of ti2: {}\n", sum2);
cout << format("sum of ti3: {}\n", sum3);
```

Output:

```
sum of ti1: 15
sum of ti2: 84
sum of ti3: 162
```

Manage allocated memory with std::unique_ptr

Smart pointers are an excellent tool for managing allocated *heap memory*.

Heap memory is managed at the lowest level by the C functions, `malloc()` and `free()`. `malloc()` allocates a block of memory from the heap, and `free()` returns it to the heap. These functions do not perform initialization and do not call constructors or destructors. If you fail to return allocated memory to the heap with a call to `free()`, the behavior is undefined and often leads to memory leaks and security vulnerabilities.

C++ provides the `new` and `delete` operators to allocate and free heap memory, in place of `malloc()` and `free()`. The `new` and `delete` operators call object constructors and destructors but still do not manage memory. If you allocate memory with `new` and fail to free it with `delete`, you will leak memory.

Introduced with C++14, smart pointers comply with the **Resource Acquisition Is Initialization (RAII)** idiom. This means that when memory is allocated for an object, that object's constructor is called. And when the object's destructor is called, the memory is automatically returned to the heap.

For example, when we create a new smart pointer with `make_unique()`:

```
{   // beginning of scope
    auto p = make_unique<Thing>(); // memory alloc'd,
                                   // ctor called
    process_thing(p);    // p is unique_ptr<Thing>
}   // end of scope, dtor called, memory freed
```

`make_unique()` allocates memory for a `Thing` object, calls the `Thing` default constructor, constructs a `unique_ptr<Thing>` object, and returns the `unique_ptr`. When p goes out of scope, the `Thing` destructor is called, and the memory is automatically returned to the heap.

Aside from the memory management, a smart pointer works very much like a primitive pointer:

```
auto x = *p;   // *p derefs the pointer, returns Thing object
auto y = p->thname; // p-> derefs the pointer, returns member
```

`unique_ptr` is a smart pointer that allows only one instance of the pointer. It may be moved, but it may not be copied. Let's take a closer look at how to use `unique_ptr`.

How to do it...

In this recipe, we examine `std::unique_ptr` with a demonstration class that prints when its constructors and destructor are called:

- First, we'll create a simple demonstration class:

```cpp
struct Thing {
    string_view thname{ "unk" };
    Thing() {
        cout << format("default ctor: {}\n", thname);
    }
    Thing(const string_view& n) : thname(n) {
        cout << format("param ctor: {}\n", thname);
    }
    ~Thing() {
        cout << format("dtor: {}\n", thname);
    }
};
```

This class has a default constructor, a parameterized constructor, and a destructor. Each of these has a simple print statement to tell us what was called.

- When we just construct a `unique_ptr`, it does not allocate memory or construct a managed object:

```cpp
int main() {
    unique_ptr<Thing> p1;
    cout << "end of main()\n";
}
```

Output:

```
end of main()
```

- When we use the new operator, it allocates memory and constructs a `Thing` object:

```
int main() {
    unique_ptr<Thing> p1{ new Thing };
    cout << "end of main()\n";
}
```

Output:

```
default ctor: unk
end of main()
dtor: unk
```

The new operator constructs a `Thing` object by calling the default constructor. The `unique_ptr<Thing>` destructor calls the `Thing` destructor when the smart pointer reaches the end of its scope.

The `Thing` default constructor does not initialize the `thname` string, leaving its default value, `"unk"`.

- We can use `make_unique()` to get the same result:

```
int main() {
    auto p1 = make_unique<Thing>();
    cout << "end of main()\n";
}
```

Output:

```
default ctor: unk
end of main()
dtor: unk
```

The `make_unique()` helper function takes care of the memory allocation and returns a `unique_ptr` object. This is the recommended way to construct a `unique_ptr`.

- Any arguments you pass to `make_unique()` are used in constructing the target object:

```
int main() {
    auto p1 = make_unique<Thing>("Thing 1") };
    cout << "end of main()\n";
}
```

Output:

```
param ctor: Thing 1
end of main()
dtor: Thing 1
```

The parameterized constructor assigns a value to thname, so our Thing object is now "Thing 1".

- Let's write a function that takes a unique_ptr<Thing> argument:

```
void process_thing(unique_ptr<Thing> p) {
    if(p) cout << format("processing: {}\n",
      p->thname);
    else cout << "invalid pointer\n";
}
```

If we try to pass a unique_ptr to this function, we get a compiler error:

```
process_thing(p1);
```

Compiler error:

```
error: use of deleted function...
```

This is because the function call tries to make a copy of the unique_ptr object, but the unique_ptr copy constructor is *deleted* to prevent copying. The solution is to have the function take a const& reference:

```
void process_thing(const unique_ptr<Thing>& p) {
    if(p) cout << format("processing: {}\n",
      p->thname);
    else cout << "invalid pointer\n";
}
```

Output:

```
param ctor: Thing 1
processing: Thing 1
end of main()
dtor: Thing 1
```

- We can call process_thing() with a temporary object, which is immediately destroyed at the end of the function scope:

```
int main() {
    auto p1{ make_unique<Thing>("Thing 1") };
    process_thing(p1);
    process_thing(make_unique<Thing>("Thing 2"));
    cout << "end of main()\n";
}
```

Output:

```
param ctor: Thing 1
processing: Thing 1
param ctor: Thing 2
processing: Thing 2
dtor: Thing 2
end of main()
dtor: Thing 1
```

How it works...

A *smart pointer* is simply an object that presents a pointer interface while owning and managing the resources of another object.

The unique_ptr class is distinguished by its deleted copy constructor and copy assignment operator, which prevents the smart pointer from being copied.

You may not copy a unique_ptr:

```
auto p2 = p1;
```

Compiler error:

```
error: use of deleted function...
```

But you can move a unique_ptr:

```
auto p2 = std::move(p1);
process_thing(p1);
process_thing(p2);
```

After the `move`, p1 is invalid and p2 is "Thing 1".

Output:

```
invalid pointer
processing: Thing 1
end of main()
dtor: Thing 1
```

The `unique_ptr` interface has a method to reset a pointer:

```
p1.reset();  // pointer is now invalid
process_thing(p1);
```

Output:

```
dtor: Thing 1
invalid pointer
```

The `reset()` method may also be used to replace the managed object with another of the same type:

```
p1.reset(new Thing("Thing 3"));
process_thing(p1);
```

Output:

```
param ctor: Thing 3
dtor: Thing 1
processing: Thing 3
```

Share objects with std::shared_ptr

The `std::shared_ptr` class is a smart pointer that owns its managed object and maintains a *use counter* to keep track of copies. This recipe explores the use of `shared_ptr` to manage memory while sharing copies of the pointer.

> **Note**
>
> For more detail about smart pointers, see the introduction to the *Manage allocated memory with std::unique_ptr* recipe earlier in this chapter.

How to do it...

In this recipe, we examine `std::shared_ptr` with a demonstration class that prints when its constructors and destructor are called:

- First, we create a simple demonstration class:

```
struct Thing {
    string_view thname{ "unk" };
    Thing() {
        cout << format("default ctor: {}\n", thname);
    }
    Thing(const string_view& n) : thname(n) {
        cout << format("param ctor: {}\n", thname);
    }
    ~Thing() {
        cout << format("dtor: {}\n", thname);
    }
};
```

This class has a default constructor, a parameterized constructor, and a destructor. Each of these has a simple print statement to tell us what was called.

- The `shared_ptr` class works very much like other smart pointers, in that it may be constructed with the `new` operator or with its helper, the `make_shared()` function:

```
int main() {
    shared_ptr<Thing> p1{ new Thing("Thing 1") };
    auto p2 = make_shared<Thing>("Thing 2");
    cout << "end of main()\n";
}
```

Output:

```
param ctor: Thing 1
param ctor: Thing 2
end of main()
dtor: Thing 2
dtor: Thing 1
```

The make_shared() function is recommended, as it manages the construction process and is less prone to error.

As with the other smart pointers, the managed object is destroyed, and its memory is returned to the heap when the pointer goes out of scope.

- Here's a function to check the use count of a shared_ptr object:

```
void check_thing_ptr(const shared_ptr<Thing>& p) {
    if(p) cout << format("{} use count: {}\n",
        p->thname, p.use_count());
    else cout << "invalid pointer\n";
}
```

thname is a member of the Thing class, so we access it through the pointer with the p-> member dereference operator. The use_count() function is a member of the shared_ptr class, so we access it with the p. object member operator.

Let's call this with our pointers:

```
check_thing_ptr(p1);
check_thing_ptr(p2);
```

Output:

```
Thing 1 use count: 1
Thing 2 use count: 1
```

- When we make copies of our pointers, the use count increases, but no new objects are constructed:

```
cout << "make 4 copies of p1:\n";
auto pa = p1;
auto pb = p1;
auto pc = p1;
auto pd = p1;
check_thing_ptr(p1);
```

Output:

```
make 4 copies of p1:
Thing 1 use count: 5
```

- When we check any of the other copies, we get the same result:

```
check_thing_ptr(pa);
check_thing_ptr(pb);
check_thing_ptr(pc);
check_thing_ptr(pd);
```

Output:

```
Thing 1 use count: 5
Thing 1 use count: 5
Thing 1 use count: 5
Thing 1 use count: 5
```

Each pointer reports the same use count.

- When the copies go out of scope, they are destroyed, and the use count is decremented:

```
{    // new scope
    cout << "make 4 copies of p1:\n";
    auto pa = p1;
    auto pb = p1;
    auto pc = p1;
    auto pd = p1;
    check_thing_ptr(p1);
}    // end of scope
check_thing_ptr(p1);
```

Output:

```
make 4 copies of p1:
Thing 1 use count: 5
Thing 1 use count: 1
```

- Destroying a copy reduces the use count but does not destroy the managed object. The object is destroyed when the final copy goes out of scope and the use count reaches zero:

```
{
    cout << "make 4 copies of p1:\n";
    auto pa = p1;
    auto pb = p1;
```

```
            auto pc = p1;
            auto pd = p1;
            check_thing_ptr(p1);
            pb.reset();
            p1.reset();
            check_thing_ptr(pd);
    }    // end of scope
```

Output:

```
make 4 copies of p1:
Thing 1 use count: 5
Thing 1 use count: 3
dtor: Thing 1
```

Destroying pb (a copy) and p1 (the original) leaves three copies of the pointer (pa, bc, and pd), so the managed object remains.

The remaining three pointer copies are destroyed at the end of the scope in which they were created. Then the object is destroyed and its memory returned to the heap.

How it works...

The shared_ptr class is distinguished by its management of multiple pointers to the same managed object.

The shared_ptr object's copy constructor and copy assignment operator increment a *use counter*. The destructor decrements the use counter until it reaches zero, then destroys the managed object, and returns its memory to the heap.

The shared_ptr class manages both the managed object and a heap-allocated *control block*. The control block contains the use counter, along with other housekeeping objects. The control block is managed and shared between copies along with the managed object. This allows the original shared_ptr object to cede control to its copies, so that the last remaining shared_ptr may manage the object and its memory.

Use weak pointers with shared objects

Strictly speaking, std::weak_ptr is not a smart pointer. Rather, it's an *observer* that operates in cooperation with shared_ptr. A weak_ptr object does not hold a pointer on its own.

There are circumstances where shared_ptr objects may create dangling pointers or race conditions, which could lead to memory leaks or other problems. The solution is to use weak_ptr objects with shared_ptr.

How to do it...

In this recipe, we examine the use of std::weak_ptr with std::shared_ptr, using a demonstration class that prints when its constructors and destructor are called.

- We start with the same class we've used to demonstrate shared_ptr and unique_ptr:

```cpp
struct Thing {
    string_view thname{ "unk" };
    Thing() {
        cout << format("default ctor: {}\n", thname);
    }
    Thing(const string_view& n) : thname(n) {
        cout << format("param ctor: {}\n", thname);
    }
    ~Thing() {
        cout << format("dtor: {}\n", thname);
    }
};
```

This class has a default constructor, a parameterized constructor, and a destructor. Each of these has a simple print statement to tell us what was called.

- We also need a function to examine a weak_ptr object:

```cpp
void get_weak_thing(const weak_ptr<Thing>& p) {
    if(auto sp = p.lock()) cout <<
        format("{}: count {}\n", sp->thname,
            p.use_count());
    else cout << "no shared object\n";
}
```

A weak_ptr does not operate as a pointer on its own; it requires the use of a shared_ptr. The lock() function returns a shared_ptr object, which can then be used to access the managed object.

- Because weak_ptr requires an associated shared_ptr, we'll start main() by creating a shared_ptr<Thing> object. When we create a weak_ptr object without assigning the shared_ptr, the expired flag is initially set:

```
int main() {
    auto thing1 = make_shared<Thing>("Thing 1");
    weak_ptr<Thing> wp1;
    cout << format("expired: {}\n", wp1.expired());
    get_weak_thing(wp1);
}
```

Output:

```
param ctor: Thing 1
expired: true
no shared object
```

The make_shared() function allocates memory and constructs a Thing object.

The weak_ptr<Thing> declaration constructs a weak_ptr object without assigning a shared_ptr. So, when we check the expired flag, it's true, indicating that there is no associated shared_ptr.

The get_weak_thing() function is not able to obtain a lock because there is no shared_ptr available.

- When we assign the shared_ptr to the weak_ptr, we can use the weak_ptr to access the managed object:

```
wp1 = thing1;
get_weak_thing(wp1);
```

Output:

```
Thing 1: count 2
```

The get_weak_thing() function is now able to obtain a lock and access the managed object. The lock() method returns a shared_ptr, and the use_count() reflects the fact that there is now a second shared_ptr managing the Thing object.

The new `shared_ptr` is destroyed at the end of the `get_weak_thing()` scope.

- The `weak_ptr` class has a constructor that takes a `shared_ptr` for one-step construction:

```
weak_ptr<Thing> wp2(thing1);
get_weak_thing(wp2);
```

Output:

Thing 1: count 2

The `use_count()` is 2 again. Remember that the previous `shared_ptr` was destroyed when its enclosing `get_weak_thing()` scope ended.

- When we reset `shared_ptr`, its associated `weak_ptr` objects are expired:

```
thing1.reset();
get_weak_thing(wp1);
get_weak_thing(wp2);
```

Output:

```
dtor: Thing 1
no shared object
no shared object
```

After the `reset()`, the use count reaches zero, and the managed object is destroyed and the memory released.

How it works...

A `weak_ptr` object is an *observer* that holds a non-owning reference to a `shared_ptr` object. The `weak_ptr` observes the `shared_ptr` so that it knows when the managed object is, and is not, available. This allows use of a `shared_ptr` in circumstances where you may not always know if the managed object is active.

The `weak_ptr` class has a `use_count()` function that returns the use count of `shared_ptr`, or 0 if the managed object has been deleted:

```
long use_count() const noexcept;
```

`weak_ptr` also has an `expired()` function that reports if the managed object has been deleted:

```
bool expired() const noexcept;
```

The `lock()` function is the preferred way to access the shared pointer. It checks `expired()` to see if the managed object is available. If so, it returns a new `shared_ptr` that shares ownership with the managed object. Otherwise, it returns an empty `shared_ ptr`. It does all that as one atomic operation:

```
std::shared_ptr<T> lock() const noexcept;
```

There's more...

One important use case for `weak_ptr` is when there's a possibility of circular references to `shared_ptr` objects. For example, consider the case of two classes that link to each other (perhaps in a hierarchy):

```
struct circB;
struct circA {
    shared_ptr<circB> p;
    ~circA() { cout << "dtor A\n"; }
};
struct circB {
    shared_ptr<circA> p;
    ~circB() { cout << "dtor B\n"; }
};
```

We have print statements in the destructors, so we can see when the objects are destroyed. We can now create two objects that point at each other with `shared_ptr`:

```
int main() {
    auto a{ make_shared<circA>() };
    auto b{ make_shared<circB>() };
    a->p = b;
    b->p = a;
    cout << "end of main()\n";
}
```

When we run this, notice that the destructors are never called:

end of main()

Because the objects maintain shared pointers that refer to each other, the use counts never reach zero, and the managed objects are never destroyed.

We can resolve this problem by changing one of the classes to use a `weak_ptr`:

```
struct circB {
    weak_ptr<circA> p;
    ~circB() { cout << "dtor B\n"; }
};
```

The code in `main()` remains the same, and we get this output:

```
end of main()
dtor A
dtor B
```

By changing one `shared_ptr` to a `weak_ptr`, we have resolved the circular reference, and the objects are now properly destroyed at the end of their scope.

Share members of a managed object

The `std::shared_ptr` class provides an *aliasing constructor* to share a pointer managed by another unrelated pointer:

```
shared_ptr( shared_ptr<Y>&& ref, element_type* ptr ) noexcept;
```

This returns an aliased `shared_ptr` object that uses the resources of `ref` but returns a pointer to `ptr`. The `use_count` is shared with ref. The deleter is shared with `ref`. But `get()` returns `ptr`. This allows us to share a member of a managed object without sharing the entire object, and without allowing the entire object to be deleted while we're still using the member.

How to do it...

In this recipe, we create a managed object and share members of that object:

- We start with a class for the managed object:

```
struct animal {
    string name{};
    string sound{};
    animal(const string& n, const string& a)
            : name{n}, sound{a} {
        cout << format("ctor: {}\n", name);
```

```
        }
        ~animal() {
            cout << format("dtor: {}\n", name);
        }
    };
```

This class has two members, `string` types for name and sound of the `animal` object. We also have print statements for the constructor and the destructor.

- Now, we need a function to create an animal but only share its name and sound:

```
    auto make_animal(const string& n, const string& s) {
        auto ap = make_shared<animal>(n, s);
        auto np = shared_ptr<string>(ap, &ap->name);
        auto sp = shared_ptr<string>(ap, &ap->sound);
        return tuple(np, sp);
    }
```

This function creates `shared_ptr` with an `animal` object, constructed with a name and a sound. We then create aliased `shared_ptr` objects for the name and sound. When we return the name and sound pointers, the `animal` pointer goes out of scope. It is not deleted because the aliased pointers keep the use count from reaching zero.

- In our `main()` function, we call `make_animal()` and inspect the results:

```
    int main() {
        auto [name, sound] =
            make_animal("Velociraptor", "Grrrr!");
        cout << format("The {} says {}\n", *name, *sound);
        cout << format("Use count: name {}, sound {}\n",
            name.use_count(), sound.use_count());
    }
```

Output:

```
    ctor: Velociraptor
    The Velociraptor says Grrrr!
    Use count: name 2, sound 2
    dtor: Velociraptor
```

We can see that the aliased pointers each show a `use_count` of 2. When the `make_animal()` function creates the aliased pointers, they each increase the use count of the `animal` pointer. When the function ends, the `animal` pointer goes out of scope, leaving its use count at 2, which is reflected in the aliased pointers. The aliased pointers go out of scope at the end of `main()`, which allows the `animal` pointer to be destroyed.

How it works...

The *aliased* shared pointer seems a bit abstract, but it's simpler than it appears.

A shared pointer uses a *control block* to manage its resources. One control block is associated with one managed object and is shared among the pointers that share that object. The control block generally contains:

- A pointer to the managed object
- The *deleter*
- The *allocator*
- The number of `shared_ptr` objects that own the managed object (this is the *use count*)
- The number of `weak_ptr` objects that refer to the managed object

In the case of an aliased shared pointer, the control block includes the pointer to the *aliased object*. Everything else remains the same.

Aliased shared pointers participate in the use count, just like non-aliased shared pointers, preventing the managed object from being destroyed until the use count reaches zero. The deleter is not changed, so it destroys the managed object.

> **Important Note**
> It is possible to use any pointer to construct an aliased shared pointer. Usually, the pointer refers to a member within the aliased object. If the aliased pointer does not refer to an element of the managed object, you will need to manage its construction and destruction separately.

Compare random number engines

The random library provides a selection of random number generators, each with different strategies and properties. In this recipe, we examine a function to compare the different options by creating a histogram of their output.

How to do it...

In this recipe, we compare the different random number generators provided by the C++ random library:

- We start with some constants to provide uniform parameters for the random number generators:

```
constexpr size_t n_samples{ 1000 };
constexpr size_t n_partitions{ 10 };
constexpr size_t n_max{ 50 };
```

n_samples is the number of samples to examine, n_partitions is the number of partitions in which to display the samples, and n_max is the maximum size of a bar in the histogram (this will vary some due to rounding).

These numbers provide a reasonable display of the differences between the engines. Increasing the ratio of *samples* versus *partitions* tends to smooth out the curves and obscure the differences between the engines.

- This is the function that collects random number samples and displays a histogram:

```
template <typename RNG>
void histogram(const string_view& rng_name) {
    auto p_ratio = (double)RNG::max() / n_partitions;
    RNG rng{};   // construct the engine object

    // collect the samples
    vector<size_t> v(n_partitions);
    for(size_t i{}; i < n_samples; ++i) {
        ++v[rng() / p_ratio];
    }

    // display the histogram
    auto max_el = std::max_element(v.begin(),
      v.end());
```

```
    auto v_ratio = *max_el / n_max;
    if(v_ratio < 1) v_ratio = 1;
    cout << format("engine: {}\n", rng_name);
    for(size_t i{}; i < n_partitions; ++i) {
        cout << format("{:02}:{:*<{}}\n",
            i + 1, ' ', v[i] / v_ratio);
    }
    cout << '\n';
}
```

In a nutshell, this function stores a histogram of collected samples in a vector. It then displays the histogram as a series of asterisks on the console.

- We call histogram() from main(), like this:

```
int main() {
    histogram<std::random_device>("random_device");
    histogram<std::default_random_engine>
        ("default_random_engine");
    histogram<std::minstd_rand0>("minstd_rand0");
    histogram<std::minstd_rand>("minstd_rand");
    histogram<std::mt19937>("mt19937");
    histogram<std::mt19937_64>("mt19937_64");
    histogram<std::ranlux24_base>("ranlux24_base");
    histogram<std::ranlux48_base>("ranlux48_base");
    histogram<std::ranlux24>("ranlux24");
    histogram<std::ranlux48>("ranlux48");
    histogram<std::knuth_b>("knuth_b");
}
```

Output:

```
engine: random_device
01: ****************************************************
02: ***************************************************
03: ****************************************************
04: *****************************************************
05: ***************************************************
06: ***************************************************
07: *****************************************************
08: **************************************************
09: *************************************************
10: ****************************************************
```

```
engine: default_random_engine
01: ************************************************
02: ************************************************
03: ************************************************
04: ********************************************
05: *****************************************************
06: ****************************************************
07: ****************************************************
08: ***********************************************
09: ***********************************************
10: ********************************************
```

Figure 8.1 – A screenshot of output from the first two random number engines

This screenshot shows histograms of the first two random number engines. Your output will vary.

If we raise the value of `n_samples` to 100,000, you'll see that the variance between engines becomes more difficult to discern:

```
engine: random_device
01: *******************************************************
02: *******************************************************
03: *******************************************************
04: *******************************************************
05: *******************************************************
06: *******************************************************
07: *******************************************************
08: *******************************************************
09: *******************************************************
10: *******************************************************

engine: default_random_engine
01: *******************************************************
02: *******************************************************
03: *******************************************************
04: *******************************************************
05: *******************************************************
06: *******************************************************
07: *******************************************************
08: *******************************************************
09: *******************************************************
10: *******************************************************
```

Figure 8.2 – A screenshot of output with 100,000 samples

How it works...

Each of the random number engines has a functor interface that returns the next random number in the sequence:

```
result_type operator()();
```

The functor returns a random value, evenly distributed between the min() and max() values. All the random number engines have this interface in common.

The histogram() function takes advantage of this uniformity by using the class of the random number engine in a template:

```
template <typename RNG>
```

(**RNG** is a common abbreviation for **Random Number Generator**. The library documentation refers to these classes as *engines*, which is synonymous with RNG for our purposes.)

We instantiate an object with the RNG class and create a histogram in a vector:

```
RNG rng{};
vector<size_t> v(n_partitions);
for(size_t i{}; i < n_samples; ++i) {
    ++v[rng() / p_ratio];
}
```

This allows us to easily compare the results of the various random number engines with this technique.

There's more...

Each of the random number engines in the library have different methodologies and characteristics. When you run the histogram multiple times, you'll notice that most of the engines have the same distribution each time they're run. That's because they are *deterministic* – that is, they generate the same sequence of numbers each time. std::random_device is non-deterministic on most systems. You can use it to seed one of the other engines if you need more variation. It is also common to seed an RNG with the current date and time.

The std::default_random_engine is a suitable choice for most purposes.

Compare random number distribution generators

The C++ Standard Library provides a selection of random number distribution generators, each with its own properties. In this recipe, we examine a function to compare the different options by creating a histogram of their output.

How to do it...

Like the random number engines, the distribution generators have some common interface elements. Unlike the random number engines, the distribution generators have a variety of properties to set. We can create a template function to print a histogram of the various distributions, but the initializations of the various distribution generators vary significantly:

- We start with some constants:

```
constexpr size_t n_samples{ 10 * 1000 };
constexpr size_t n_max{ 50 };
```

The n_samples constant is the number of samples to generate for each histogram – in this case, 10,000.

The n_max constant is used as a divisor while generating our histograms.

- Our histogram function takes a distribution generator as an argument and prints a histogram for that distribution algorithm:

```
void dist_histogram(auto distro,
        const string_view& dist_name) {
    std::default_random_engine rng{};
    map<long, size_t> m;

    // create the histogram map
    for(size_t i{}; i < n_samples; ++i)
        ++m[(long)distro(rng)];

    // print the histogram
    auto max_elm_it = max_element(m.begin(), m.end(),
        [](const auto& a, const auto& b)
        { return a.second < b.second; }
```

```
        );
    size_t max_elm = max_elm_it->second;
    size_t max_div = std::max(max_elm / n_max,
        size_t(1));
    cout << format("{}:\n", dist_name);
    for (const auto [randval, count] : m) {
        if (count < max_elm / n_max) continue;
        cout << format("{:3}:{:*<{}}\n",
            randval, ' ', count / max_div);
    }
}
```

The dist_histogram() function uses a map to store the histogram. It then displays the histogram as a series of asterisks on the console.

- We call dist_histogram() from main(), like this:

```
int main() {
    dist_histogram(std::uniform_int_distribution<int>
        {0, 9}, uniform_int_distribution");
    dist_histogram(std::normal_distribution<double>
        {0.0, 2.0}, "normal_distribution");
    . . .
```

Calling the dist_histogram() function is more complex than it was for the random number generators. Each random distribution class has a different set of parameters, according to its algorithm.

For the full list, refer to the distribution.cpp file in the GitHub archive.

Output:

```
uniform_int_distribution:
  0:  ********************************************
  1:  *********************************************
  2:  *******************************************
  3:  *****************************************
  4:  ********************************************
  5:  **********************************************
  6:  *********************************************
  7:  *******************************************
  8:  **********************************************
  9:  **********************************************
normal_distribution:
 -4:  *
 -3:  *****
 -2:  **********
 -1:  *****************
  0:  ********************************************
  1:  *****************
  2:  *********
  3:  ****
  4:
bernoulli_distribution:
  0:  **************
  1:  **********************************************
discrete_distribution:
  0:  *****
  1:  **********
  2:  *********************
  3:  **********************************************
```

Figure 8.3 – A screenshot of random distribution histograms

Each of the distribution algorithms produces very different output. You will want to experiment with the different options for each random distribution generator.

How it works...

Each of the distribution generators has a functor that returns the next value in the random distribution:

```
result_type operator()( Generator& g );
```

The functor takes a random number generator (RNG) object as an argument:

```
std::default_random_engine rng{};
map<long, size_t> m;
for (size_t i{}; i < n_samples; ++i) ++m[(long)distro(rng)];
```

For our purposes, we're using the `std::default_random_engine` for our RNG.

As with the RNG histogram, this is a useful tool to visualize the various random distribution algorithms available in the `random` library. You will want to experiment with the various parameters available for each algorithm.

9

Concurrency and Parallelism

Concurrency and parallelism refer to the ability to run code in separate *threads of execution*.

More specifically, *concurrency* is the ability to run threads in the background, and *parallelism* is the ability to run threads simultaneously in separate cores of a processor. The run-time library, along with the host operating system, will choose between concurrent and parallel execution models for a given thread on a given hardware environment.

In a modern multi-tasking operating system, the main() function already represents a thread of execution. When a new thread is started, it's said to be *spawned* by an existing thread. A group of threads may be called a *swarm*.

In the C++ standard library, the std::thread class provides the basic unit of threaded execution. Other classes build upon thread to provide *locks*, *mutexes*, and other concurrency patterns. Depending on system architecture, execution threads may run concurrently on one processor, or in parallel on separate cores.

In this chapter, we will cover these tools and more in the following recipes:

- Sleep for a specific amount of time
- Use `std::thread` for concurrency
- Use `std::async` for concurrency
- Run STL algorithms in parallel with execution policies
- Share data safely with mutex and locks
- Share flags and values with `std::atomic`
- Initialize threads with `std::call_once`
- Use `std::condition_variable` to resolve the producer-consumer problem
- Implement multiple producers and consumers

Technical requirements

You can find the code files for this chapter on GitHub at `https://github.com/PacktPublishing/CPP-20-STL-Cookbook/tree/main/chap09`.

Sleep for a specific amount of time

The `<thread>` header provides two functions for putting a thread to sleep, `sleep_for()` and `sleep_until()`. Both functions are in the `std::this_thread` namespace.

This recipe explores the use of these functions, as we will be using them later in this chapter.

How to do it...

Let's look at how to use the `sleep_for()` and `sleep_until()` functions:

- The sleep-related functions are in the `std::this_thread` namespace. Because it has just a few symbols, we'll go ahead and issue `using` directives for `std::this_thread` and `std::chrono_literals`:

    ```
    using namespace std::this_thread;
    using namespace std::chrono_literals;
    ```

    The `chrono_literals` namespace has symbols for representing durations, such as `1s` for one second, or `100ms` for 100 milliseconds.

- In main(), we'll mark a point in time with steady_clock::now(), so we can time our test:

```
int main() {
    auto t1 = steady_clock::now();
    cout << "sleep for 1.3 seconds\n";
    sleep_for(1s + 300ms);
    cout << "sleep for 2 seconds\n";
    sleep_until(steady_clock::now() + 2s);
    duration<double> dur1 = steady_clock::now() - t1;
    cout << format("total duration: {:.5}s\n",
        dur1.count());
}
```

The sleep_for() function takes a duration object to specify the amount of time to sleep. The argument (1s + 300ms) uses chrono_literal operators to return a duration object representing 1.3 seconds.

The sleep_until() function takes a time_point object to specify a specific time to resume from sleep. In this case, the chrono_literal operators are used to modify the time_point object returned from steady_clock::now().

This is our output:

```
sleep for 1.3 seconds
sleep for 2 seconds
total duration: 3.3005s
```

How it works...

The sleep_for(duration) and sleep_until(time_point) functions suspend execution of the current thread for the specified duration, or until the time_point is reached.

The sleep_for() function will use the steady_clock implementation, if supported. Otherwise, the duration may be subject to time adjustments. Both functions may block for longer due to scheduling or resource delays.

There's more...

Some systems support a POSIX function, `sleep()`, which suspends execution for the number of seconds specified:

```
unsigned int sleep(unsigned int seconds);
```

The `sleep()` function is part of the POSIX standard and is not part of the C++ standard.

Use std::thread for concurrency

A *thread* is a unit of concurrency. The `main()` function may be thought of as the *main thread of execution*. Within the context of the operating system, the main thread runs concurrently with other threads owned by other processes.

The `std::thread` class is the root of concurrency in the STL. All other concurrency features are built on the foundation of the `thread` class.

In this recipe, we will examine the basics of `std::thread` and how `join()` and `detach()` determine its execution context.

How to do it...

In this recipe, we create some `std::thread` objects and experiment with their execution options.

- We start with a convenience function for sleeping a thread, in milliseconds:

```
void sleepms(const unsigned ms) {
    using std::chrono::milliseconds;
    std::this_thread::sleep_for(milliseconds(ms));
}
```

The `sleep_for()` function takes a `duration` object and blocks execution of the current thread for the specified duration. This `sleepms()` function serves as a convenience wrapper that takes an `unsigned` value for the number of milliseconds to sleep.

- Now, we need a function for our thread. This function sleeps for a variable number of milliseconds, based on an integer parameter:

```
void fthread(const int n) {
    cout << format("This is t{}\n", n);

    for(size_t i{}; i < 5; ++i) {
        sleepms(100 * n);
        cout << format("t{}: {}\n", n, i + 1);
    }
    cout << format("Finishing t{}\n", n);
}
```

fthread() calls sleepms() five times, sleeping each time for 100 * n milliseconds.

- We can run this in a separate thread with std::thread from main():

```
int main() {
    thread t1(fthread, 1);
    cout << "end of main()\n";
}
```

It compiles but we get this error when we run it:

terminate called without an active exception
Aborted

(Your error message will vary. This is the error message on Debian with GCC.)

The problem is that the operating system doesn't know what to do with the thread object when it goes out of scope. We must specify if the caller waits for the thread, or if it's detached and runs independently.

- We use the join() method to indicate that the caller will wait for the thread to finish:

```
int main() {
    thread t1(fthread, 1);
    t1.join();
    cout << "end of main()\n";
}
```

Output:

```
This is t1
t1: 1
t1: 2
t1: 3
t1: 4
t1: 5
Finishing t1
end of main()
```

Now, main() waits for the thread to finish.

- If we call detach() instead of join(), then main() doesn't wait, and the program ends before the thread can run:

```
thread t1(fthread, 1);
t1.detach();
```

Output:

```
end of main()
```

- When the thread is detached, we need to give it time to run:

```
thread t1(fthread, 1);
t1.detach();
cout << "main() sleep 2 sec\n";
sleepms(2000);
```

Output:

```
main() sleep 2 sec
This is t1
t1: 1
t1: 2
t1: 3
t1: 4
t1: 5
Finishing t1
end of main()
```

- Let's start and detach a second thread and see what happens:

```
int main() {
    thread t1(fthread, 1);
    thread t2(fthread, 2);
    t1.detach();
    t2.detach();
    cout << "main() sleep 2 sec\n";
    sleepms(2000);
    cout << "end of main()\n";
}
```

Output:

```
main() sleep 2 sec
This is t1
This is t2
t1: 1
t2: 1
t1: 2
t1: 3
t2: 2
t1: 4
t1: 5
Finishing t1
t2: 3
t2: 4
t2: 5
Finishing t2
end of main()
```

Because our `fthread()` function uses its parameter as a multiplier for `sleepms()`, the second thread runs a bit slower than the first. We can see the timers interlaced in the output.

- If we do this with `join()` instead of `detatch()`, we get a similar result:

```
int main() {
    thread t1(fthread, 1);
    thread t2(fthread, 2);
    t1.join();
    t2.join();
    cout << "end of main()\n";
}
```

Output:

```
This is t1
This is t2
t1: 1
t2: 1
t1: 2
t1: 3
t2: 2
t1: 4
t1: 5
Finishing t1
t2: 3
t2: 4
t2: 5
Finishing t2
end of main()
```

Because `join()` waits for the thread to finish, we no longer need the 2-second `sleepms()` in `main()` to wait for the threads to finish.

How it works...

A `std::thread` object represents a thread of execution. There is a one-to-one relationship between object and thread. One `thread` object represents one thread, and one thread is represented by one `thread` object. A `thread` object cannot be copied or assigned, but it can be moved.

The `thread` constructor looks like this:

```
explicit thread( Function&& f, Args&&... args );
```

A thread is constructed with a function pointer and zero or more arguments. The function is called immediately with the arguments provided:

```
thread t1(fthread, 1);
```

This creates the object t1 and immediately calls the function fthread(int) with the literal value 1 as the argument.

After creating the thread, we must use either join() or detach() on the thread:

```
t1.join();
```

The join() method blocks execution of the calling thread until the t1 thread has completed:

```
t1.detach();
```

The detach() method allows the calling thread to continue independently of the t1 thread.

There's more...

C++20 provides std::jthread, which automatically joins the caller at the end of its scope:

```
int main() {
    std::jthread t1(fthread, 1);
    cout "< "end of main("\n";
}
```

Output:

```
end of main()
This is t1
t1: 1
t1: 2
t1: 3
t1: 4
t1: 5
Finishing t1
```

This allows the `t1` thread to execute independently and then automatically join the `main()` thread at the end of its scope.

Use std::async for concurrency

`std::async()` runs a target function asynchronously and returns a `std::future` object to carry the target function's return value. In this way, `async()` operates much like `std::thread` but allows return values.

Let's consider the use of `std::async()` with a few examples.

How to do it...

In its simplest forms, the `std::async()` function performs much the same task as `std::thread`, without the need to call `join()` or `detach()` and while also allowing return values via a `std::future` object.

In this recipe, we'll use a function that counts the number of primes in a range. We'll use `chrono::steady_clock` to time the execution of each thread.

- We'll start with a couple of convenience aliases:

    ```cpp
    using launch = std::launch;
    using secs = std::chrono::duration<double>;
    ```

    `std::launch` has launch policy constants, for use with the `async()` call. The `secs` alias is a `duration` class, for timing our prime number calculations.

- Our target function counts prime numbers in a range. This is essentially a way to understand the execution policies by eating some clock cycles:

    ```cpp
    struct prime_time {
        secs dur{};
        uint64_t count{};
    };
    prime_time count_primes(const uint64_t& max) {
        prime_time ret{};
        constexpr auto isprime = [](const uint64_t& n) {
            for(uint64_t i{ 2 }; i < n / 2; ++i) {
                if(n % i == 0) return false;
            }
            return true;
    ```

```
    };
    uint64_t start{ 2 };
    uint64_t end{ max };
    auto t1 = steady_clock::now();
    for(uint64_t i{ start }; i <= end ; ++i) {
        if(isprime(i)) ++ret.count;
    }
    ret.dur = steady_clock::now() - t1;
    return ret;
}
```

The prime_time structure is for the return value, with elements for duration and count. This allows us to time the loop itself. The isprime lambda returns true if a value is prime. We use steady_clock to calculate the duration of the loop that counts primes.

- In main(), we call our function and report its timing:

```
int main() {
    constexpr uint64_t MAX_PRIME{ 0x1FFFF };
    auto pt = count_primes(MAX_PRIME);
    cout << format("primes: {} {:.3}\n", pt.count,
        pt.dur);
}
```

Output:

```
primes: 12252 1.88008s
```

- Now, we can run count_primes() asynchronously with std::async():

```
int main() {
    constexpr uint64_t MAX_PRIME{ 0x1FFFF };
    auto primes1 = async(count_primes, MAX_PRIME);
    auto pt = primes1.get();
    cout << format("primes: {} {:.3}\n", pt.count,
        pt.dur);
}
```

Here, we call async() with our count_primes function and the MAX_PRIME parameter. This runs count_primes() in the background.

`async()` returns a `std::future` object, which carries the return value of an asynchronous operation. The `future` object's `get()` method blocks until the asynchronous function has completed and then returns the return object from the function.

This runs with almost the same timing as we got without `async()`:

```
primes: 12252 1.97245s
```

- The `async()` function optionally takes execution policy flags as its first parameter:

```
auto primes1 = async(launch::async, count_primes, MAX_
PRIME);
```

The choices are `async` or `deferred`. These flags are in the `std::launch` namespace.

The `async` flag enables asynchronous operation, and the `deferred` flag enables lazy evaluation. These flags are bitmapped and may be combined with the bitwise or `|` operator.

The default is for both bits to be set, as if `async | deferred` was specified.

- We can run several instances of our function simultaneously with `async()`:

```
int main() {
    constexpr uint64_t MAX_PRIME{ 0x1FFFF };
    list<std::future<prime_time>> swarm;
    cout << "start parallel primes\n";
    auto t1{ steady_clock::now() };
    for(size_t i{}; i < 15; ++i) {
        swarm.emplace_back(
            async(launch::async, count_primes,
                MAX_PRIME)
        );
    }

    for(auto& f : swarm) {
        static size_t i{};
        auto pt = f.get();
        cout << format("primes({:02}): {} {:.5}\n",
            ++i, pt.count, pt.dur);
    }
}
```

```
    secs dur_total{ steady_clock::now() - t1 };
    cout << format("total duration: {:.5}s\n",
        dur_total.count());
}
```

We know that `async` returns a `future` object. So, we can run 15 threads by storing the `future` objects in a container. Here's our output on a 6-core i7 running Windows:

```
start parallel primes
primes(01): 12252 4.1696s
primes(02): 12252 3.7754s
primes(03): 12252 3.78089s
primes(04): 12252 3.72149s
primes(05): 12252 3.72006s
primes(06): 12252 4.1306s
primes(07): 12252 4.26015s
primes(08): 12252 3.77283s
primes(09): 12252 3.77176s
primes(10): 12252 3.72038s
primes(11): 12252 3.72416s
primes(12): 12252 4.18738s
primes(13): 12252 4.07128s
primes(14): 12252 2.1967s
primes(15): 12252 2.22414s
total duration: 5.9461s
```

Even though the 6-core i7 is not able to run all the processes in separate cores, it still completes 15 instances in under 6 seconds.

It looks like it finishes the first 13 threads in about 4 seconds, and then takes another 2 seconds to finish the last 2 threads. It appears to take advantage of Intel's Hyper-Threading technology that allows 2 threads to run in one core under some circumstances.

When we run the same code on a 12-core Xeon, we get this result:

```
start parallel primes
primes(01): 12252 0.96221s
primes(02): 12252 0.97346s
primes(03): 12252 0.92189s
primes(04): 12252 0.97499s
primes(05): 12252 0.98135s
primes(06): 12252 0.93426s
primes(07): 12252 0.90294s
primes(08): 12252 0.96307s
primes(09): 12252 0.95015s
primes(10): 12252 0.94255s
primes(11): 12252 0.94971s
primes(12): 12252 0.95639s
primes(13): 12252 0.95938s
primes(14): 12252 0.92115s
primes(15): 12252 0.94122s
total duration: 0.98166s
```

The 12-core Xeon gets through all 15 processes in under a second.

How it works...

The key to understanding `std::async` is in its use of `std::promise` and `std::future`.

The `promise` class allows a `thread` to store an object that may later be retrieved asynchronously by a `future` object.

For example, let's say we have a function like this:

```
void f() {
    cout << "this is f()\n";
}
```

We can run it with `std::thread`, like this:

```
int main() {
    std::thread t1(f);
    t1.join();
    cout << "end of main()\n";
}
```

That works fine for a simple function with no return value. When we want to return a value from `f()`, we can use `promise` and `future`.

We set up the promise and future objects in the `main()` thread:

```
int main() {
    std::promise<int> value_promise;
    std::future<int> value_future =
      value_promise.get_future();
    std::thread t1(f, std::move(value_promise));
    t1.detach();
    cout << format("value is {}\n", value_future.get());
    cout << "end of main()\n";
}
```

And we pass the `promise` object to our function:

```
void f(std::promise<int> value) {
    cout << "this is f()\n";
    value.set_value(47);
}
```

Note that a `promise` object cannot be copied, so we need to use `std::move` to pass it to the function.

The `promise` object serves as a bridge to a `future` object, which allows us to retrieve the value when it becomes available.

`std::async()` is just a helper function to simplify the creation of the `promise` and `future` objects. With `async()`, we can do all of that like this:

```
int f() {
    cout << "this is f()\n";
    return 47;
}

int main() {
    auto value_future = std::async(f);
    cout << format("value is {}\n", value_future.get());
    cout << "end of main()\n";
}
```

That's the value of `async()`. For many purposes, it makes the use of `promise` and `future` much easier.

Run STL algorithms in parallel with execution policies

Beginning with C++17, many of the standard STL algorithms can run with *parallel execution*. This feature allows an algorithm to split its work into sub-tasks to run simultaneously on multiple cores. These algorithms accept an execution policy object that specifies the kind of parallelism applied to the algorithm. This feature requires hardware support.

How to do it...

Execution policies are defined in the `<execution>` header and in the `std::execution` namespace. In this recipe, we will test the available policies using the `std::transform()` algorithm:

- For timing purposes, we'll use the `duration` object with the `std::milli` ratio so that we can measure in milliseconds:

    ```
    using dur_t = duration<double, std::milli>;
    ```

- For demonstration purposes, we'll start with a `vector` of `int` with 10 million random values:

```
int main() {
    std::vector<unsigned> v(10 * 1000 * 1000);
    std::random_device rng;
    for(auto &i : v) i = rng() % 0xFFFF;
    ...
```

- Now, we apply a simple transformation:

```
auto mul2 = [](int n){ return n * 2; };
auto t1 = steady_clock::now();
std::transform(v.begin(), v.end(), v.begin(), mul2);
dur_t dur1 = steady_clock::now() - t1;
cout << format("no policy: {:.3}ms\n", dur1.count());
```

The `mul2` lambda simply multiplies a value by 2. The `transform()` algorithm applies `mul2` to every member of the vector.

This transformation does not specify an execution policy.

Output:

```
no policy: 4.71ms
```

- We can specify an execution policy in the first argument of the algorithm:

```
std::transform(execution::seq,
    v.begin(), v.end(), v.begin(), mul2);
```

The `seq` policy means that the algorithm shall not be parallelized. This is the same as no execution policy.

Output:

```
execution::seq: 4.91ms
```

Notice that the duration is roughly the same as without a policy. It will never be exact because it varies each time it's run.

- The `execution::par` policy allows the algorithm to parallelize its workload:

```
std::transform(execution::par,
    v.begin(), v.end(), v.begin(), mul2);
```

Output:

execution::par: 3.22ms

Notice that the algorithm runs somewhat faster with the parallel execution policy.

- The `execution::par_unseq` policy allows unsequenced parallel execution of the workload:

```
std::transform(execution::par_unseq,
    v.begin(), v.end(), v.begin(), mul2);
```

Output:

execution::par_unseq: 2.93ms

Here, we notice another increase in performance with this policy.

The `execution::par_unseq` policy has tighter requirements of the algorithm. The algorithm must not perform operations that require concurrent or sequential operation.

How it works...

The execution policies interface doesn't specify how the algorithm workloads are parallelized. It's designed to work with a diverse set of hardware and processors under varying loads and circumstances. It may be implemented entirely in the library or rely on compiler or hardware support.

Parallelization will show the most improvement on algorithms that do more than $O(n)$ work. For example, `sort()` shows a dramatic improvement. Here's a `sort()` with no parallelization:

```
auto t0 = steady_clock::now();
std::sort(v.begin(), v.end());
dur_t dur0 = steady_clock::now() - t0;
cout << format("sort: {:.3}ms\n", dur0.count());
```

Output:

sort: 751ms

With `execution::par`, we see significant performance gains:

```
std::sort(execution::par, v.begin(), v.end());
```

Output:

```
sort: 163ms
```

The improvement with `execution::par_unseq` is better still:

```
std::sort(execution::par_unseq, v.begin(), v.end());
```

Output:

```
sort: 152ms
```

It's a good idea to do a lot of testing when using the parallelized algorithms. If your algorithm or predicates do not lend themselves well to parallelization, you may end up with minimal performance gains or unintended side effects.

> **Note**
>
> At the time of writing, execution policies are poorly supported in GCC and not yet supported by LLVM/Clang. This recipe was tested on a 6-core i7 running Windows 10 and a preview release of Visual C++.

Share data safely with mutex and locks

The term *mutex* refers to *mutually exclusive* access to shared resources. A mutex is commonly used to avoid data corruption and race conditions, due to multiple threads of execution attempting to access the same data. A mutex will typically use *locks* to restrict access to one thread at a time.

The STL provides *mutex* and *lock* classes in the <mutex> header.

How to do it...

In this recipe, we will use a simple `Animal` class to experiment with *locking* and *unlocking* a `mutex`:

- We start by creating a `mutex` object:

    ```
    std::mutex animal_mutex;
    ```

The `mutex` is declared in the global scope, so it's accessible to all the relevant objects.

- Our `Animal` class has a name and a list of friends:

```
class Animal {
    using friend_t = list<Animal>;
    string_view s_name{ "unk" };
    friend_t l_friends{};
public:
    Animal() = delete;
    Animal(const string_view n) : s_name{n} {}
    ...
}
```

Adding and deleting friends will be a useful test case for our `mutex`.

- The equality operator is the only operator we'll need:

```
bool operator==(const Animal& o) const {
    return s_name.data() == o.s_name.data();
}
```

The `s_name` member is a `string_view` object, so we can test the address of its data store for equality.

- The `is_friend()` method tests if another `Animal` is in the `l_friends` list:

```
bool is_friend(const Animal& o) const {
    for(const auto& a : l_friends) {
        if(a == o) return true;
    }
    return false;
}
```

- The `find_friend()` method returns an `optional`, with an iterator to the `Animal` if found:

```
optional<friend_t::iterator>
find_friend(const Animal& o) noexcept {
    for(auto it{l_friends.begin()};
            it != l_friends.end(); ++it) {
```

```
            if(*it == o) return it;
        }
        return {};
    }
```

- The print() method prints s_name along with names of each of the Animal objects in the l_friends list:

```
void print() const noexcept {
    auto n_animals{ l_friends.size() };
    cout << format("Animal: {}, friends: ", s_name);
    if(!n_animals) cout << "none";
    else {
        for(auto n : l_friends) {
            cout << n.s_name;
            if(--n_animals) cout << ", ";
        }
    }
    cout << '\n';
}
```

- The add_friend() method adds an Animal object to the l_friends list:

```
bool add_friend(Animal& o) noexcept {
    cout << format("add_friend {} -> {}\n", s_name,
        o.s_name);
    if(*this == o) return false;
    std::lock_guard<std::mutex> l(animal_mutex);
    if(!is_friend(o)) l_friends.emplace_back(o);
    if(!o.is_friend(*this))
        o.l_friends.emplace_back(*this);
    return true;
}
```

- The `delete_friend()` method removes an `Animal` object from the `l_friends` list:

```cpp
bool delete_friend(Animal& o) noexcept {
    cout << format("delete_friend {} -> {}\n",
        s_name, o.s_name);
    if(*this == o) return false;
    if(auto it = find_friend(o))
        l_friends.erase(it.value());
    if(auto it = o.find_friend(*this))
        o.l_friends.erase(it.value());
    return true;
}
```

- In the `main()` function, we create some `Animal` objects:

```cpp
int main() {
    auto cat1 = std::make_unique<Animal>("Felix");
    auto tiger1 = std::make_unique<Animal>("Hobbes");
    auto dog1 = std::make_unique<Animal>("Astro");
    auto rabbit1 = std::make_unique<Animal>("Bugs");
    ...
```

- We call `add_friends()` on our objects with `async()`, to run them in separate threads:

```cpp
    auto a1 = std::async([&]{ cat1->add_friend(*tiger1); });
    auto a2 = std::async([&]{ cat1->add_friend(*rabbit1); });
    auto a3 = std::async([&]{ rabbit1->add_friend(*dog1); });
    auto a4 = std::async([&]{ rabbit1->add_friend(*cat1); });
    a1.wait();
    a2.wait();
    a3.wait();
    a4.wait();
```

  We call `wait()` to allow our threads to complete before continuing.

- We call `print()` to see our `Animals` and their relationships:

```
auto p1 = std::async([&]{ cat1->print(); });
auto p2 = std::async([&]{ tiger1->print(); });
auto p3 = std::async([&]{ dog1->print(); });
auto p4 = std::async([&]{ rabbit1->print(); });
p1.wait();
p2.wait();
p3.wait();
p4.wait();
```

- And finally, we call `delete_friend()` to remove one of our relationships:

```
auto a5 = std::async([&]{ cat1->delete_friend(*rabbit1);
});
a5.wait();
auto p5 = std::async([&]{ cat1->print(); });
auto p6 = std::async([&]{ rabbit1->print(); });
```

- At this point, our output looks like this:

```
add_friend Bugs -> Felix
add_friend Felix -> Hobbes
add_friend Felix -> Bugs
add_friend Bugs -> Astro
Animal: Felix, friends: Bugs, Hobbes
Animal: Hobbes, friends: Animal: Bugs, friends:
FelixAnimal: Astro, friends: Felix
, Astro
Bugs
delete_friend Felix -> Bugs
Animal: Felix, friends: Hobbes
Animal: Bugs, friends: Astro
```

This output is somewhat scrambled. It will be different each time you run it. It may be fine sometimes, but don't let that fool you. We need to add some mutex locks to control access to the data.

- One way to use `mutex` is with its `lock()` and `unlock()` methods. Let's add them to the `add_friend()` function:

```
bool add_friend(Animal& o) noexcept {
    cout << format("add_friend {} -> {}\n", s_name, o.s_
name);
    if(*this == o) return false;
    animal_mutex.lock();
    if(!is_friend(o)) l_friends.emplace_back(o);
    if(!o.is_friend(*this)) o.l_friends.emplace_
back(*this);
    animal_mutex.unlock();
    return true;
}
```

The `lock()` method attempts to acquire a lock on the `mutex`. If the mutex is already locked, it will wait (block execution) until the `mutex` is unlocked.

- We also need to add a lock to `delete_friend()`:

```
bool delete_friend(Animal& o) noexcept {
    cout << format("delete_friend {} -> {}\n",
        s_name, o.s_name);
    if(*this == o) return false;
    animal_mutex.lock();
    if(auto it = find_friend(o))
      l_friends.erase(it.value());
    if(auto it = o.find_friend(*this))
        o.l_friends.erase(it.value());
    animal_mutex.unlock();
    return true;
}
```

- Now, we need to add a lock to `print()` so that data is not changed while printing:

```
void print() const noexcept {
    animal_mutex.lock();
    auto n_animals{ l_friends.size() };
    cout << format("Animal: {}, friends: ", s_name);
```

```
        if(!n_animals) cout << "none";
        else {
            for(auto n : l_friends) {
                cout << n.s_name;
                if(--n_animals) cout << ", ";
            }
        }
        cout << '\n';
        animal_mutex.unlock();
    }
```

Now, our output is sensible:

```
add_friend Bugs -> Felix
add_friend Bugs -> Astro
add_friend Felix -> Hobbes
add_friend Felix -> Bugs
Animal: Felix, friends: Bugs, Hobbes
Animal: Hobbes, friends: Felix
Animal: Astro, friends: Bugs
Animal: Bugs, friends: Felix, Astro
delete_friend Felix -> Bugs
Animal: Felix, friends: Hobbes
Animal: Bugs, friends: Astro
```

Your output may have the lines in a different order due to asynchronous operation.

- The lock() and unlock() methods are rarely called directly. The std::lock_guard class manages locks with a proper **Resource Acquisition Is Initialization (RAII)** pattern that automatically releases the lock upon destruction. Here's the add_friend() method with lock_guard:

```
bool add_friend(Animal& o) noexcept {
    cout << format("add_friend {} -> {}\n", s_name, o.s_name);
    if(*this == o) return false;
    std::lock_guard<std::mutex> l(animal_mutex);
    if(!is_friend(o)) l_friends.emplace_back(o);
    if(!o.is_friend(*this))
        o.l_friends.emplace_back(*this);
```

```
        return true;
    }
```

The `lock_guard` object is created and holds a lock until it is destroyed. Like the `lock()` method, `lock_guard` also blocks until a lock is available.

- Let's apply `lock_guard` to the `delete_friend()` and `print()` methods.

Here is `delete_friend()`:

```
bool delete_friend(Animal& o) noexcept {
    cout << format("delete_friend {} -> {}\n",
        s_name, o.s_name);
    if(*this == o) return false;
    std::lock_guard<std::mutex> l(animal_mutex);
    if(auto it = find_friend(o))
      l_friends.erase(it.value());
    if(auto it = o.find_friend(*this))
        o.l_friends.erase(it.value());
    return true;
}
```

And here is `print()`:

```
void print() const noexcept {
    std::lock_guard<std::mutex> l(animal_mutex);
    auto n_animals{ l_friends.size() };
    cout << format("Animal: {}, friends: ", s_name);
    if(!n_animals) cout << "none";
    else {
        for(auto n : l_friends) {
            cout << n.s_name;
            if(--n_animals) cout << ", ";
        }
    }
    cout << '\n';
}
```

Our output remains coherent:

```
add_friend Felix -> Hobbes
add_friend Bugs -> Astro
add_friend Felix -> Bugs
add_friend Bugs -> Felix
Animal: Felix, friends: Bugs, Hobbes
Animal: Astro, friends: Bugs
Animal: Hobbes, friends: Felix
Animal: Bugs, friends: Astro, Felix
delete_friend Felix -> Bugs
Animal: Felix, friends: Hobbes
Animal: Bugs, friends: Astro
```

As before, your output may have the lines in a different order due to asynchronous operation.

How it works...

It's important to understand that a `mutex` does not lock data; it blocks execution. As shown in this recipe, when a `mutex` is applied in object methods, it can be used to enforce mutually exclusive access to data.

When one thread locks a `mutex`, with either `lock()` or `lock_guard`, that thread is said to *own* the `mutex`. Any other thread that tries to lock the same `mutex` will be blocked until it's unlocked by the owner.

The `mutex` object must not be destroyed while it's owned by any thread. Likewise, a thread must not be destroyed while it owns a `mutex`. An RAII-compliant wrapper, such as `lock_guard`, will help ensure this doesn't happen.

There's more...

While `std::mutex` provides an exclusive mutex suitable for many purposes, the STL does provide a few other choices:

- `shared_mutex` allows more than one thread to simultaneously own a mutex.
- `recursive_mutex` allows one thread to stack multiple locks on a single mutex.
- `timed_mutex` provides a timeout for mutex blocks. Both `shared_mutex` and `recursive_mutex` also have timed versions available.

Share flags and values with std::atomic

The `std::atomic` class encapsulates a single object and guarantees it to be *atomic*. Writing to the *atomic object* is controlled by memory-order policies and reads may occur simultaneously. It's typically used to synchronize access among different threads.

`std::atomic` defines an *atomic type* from its template type. The type must be *trivial*. A type is trivial if it occupies contiguous memory, has no user-defined constructor, and has no virtual member functions. All primitive types are trivial.

While it is possible to construct a trivial type, `std::atomic` is most often used with simple primitive types, such as `bool`, `int`, `long`, `float`, and `double`.

How to do it...

This recipe uses a simple function that loops over a counter to demonstrate sharing atomic objects. We will spawn a swarm of these loops as threads that share atomic values:

- Atomic objects are often placed in a global namespace. They must be accessible to all the threads that need to share its value:

```
std::atomic<bool> ready{};
std::atomic<uint64_t> g_count{};
std::atomic_flag winner{};
```

The `ready` object is a `bool` type that gets set to `true` when all the threads are ready to start counting.

The g_count object is a global counter. It is incremented by each of the threads.

The `winner` object is a special `atomic_flag` type. It is used to indicate which thread finishes first.

- We use a couple of constants to control the number of threads and the number of loops for each thread:

```
constexpr int max_count{1000 * 1000};
constexpr int max_threads{100};
```

I've set it to run 100 threads and count 1,000,000 iterations in each thread.

- The countem() function is spawned for each thread. It loops max_count times and increments g_count for each iteration of the loop. This is where we use our atomic values:

```
void countem (int id) {
    while(!ready) std::this_thread::yield();
    for(int i{}; i < max_count; ++i) ++g_count;
    if(!winner.test_and_set()) {
        std::cout << format("thread {:02} won!\n",
            id);
    }
};
```

The ready atomic value is used to synchronize the threads. Each thread will call yield() until the ready value is set true. The yield() function yields execution to other threads.

Each iteration of the for loop increments the g_count atomic value. The final value should be equal to max_count * max_threads.

After the loop is complete, the test_and_set() method of the winner object is used to report the winning thread. test_and_set() is a method of the atomic_flag class. It sets the flag and returns the bool value from before it is set.

- We've used the make_commas() function before. It displays a number with thousands of separators:

```
string make_commas(const uint64_t& num) {
    string s{ std::to_string(num) };
    for(long l = s.length() - 3; l > 0; l -= 3) {
        s.insert(l, ",");
    }
    return s;
}
```

- The `main()` function spawns the threads and reports the results:

```cpp
int main() {
    vector<std::thread> swarm;
    cout << format("spawn {} threads\n", max_threads);
    for(int i{}; i < max_threads; ++i) {
        swarm.emplace_back(countem, i);
    }
    ready = true;
    for(auto& t : swarm) t.join();
    cout << format("global count: {}\n",
        make_commas(g_count));
    return 0;
}
```

Here, we create a `vector<std::thread>` object to hold the threads.

In the `for` loop, we use `emplace_back()` to create each `thread` in the `vector`.

Once the threads have been spawned, we set the `ready` flag so that the threads may start their loops.

Output:

```
spawn 100 threads
thread 67 won!
global count: 100,000,000
```

Every time you run it, a different thread will win.

How it works...

The `std::atomic` class encapsulates an object to synchronize access among multiple threads.

The encapsulated object must be a *trivial type*, which means it occupies contiguous memory, has no user-defined constructor, and has no virtual member functions. All primitive types are trivial.

It is possible to use a simple struct with `atomic`:

```
struct Trivial {
    int a;
    int b;
};
std::atomic<Trivial> triv1;
```

While this usage is possible, it's not practical. Anything beyond setting and retrieving compound values loses the benefits of the atomicity and ends up requiring a *mutex*. The atomic class is best suited for *scalar* values.

Specializations

There are specializations of the `atomic` class for a few different purposes:

- **Pointers and smart pointers**: The `std::atomic<U*>` specialization includes support for atomic pointer arithmetic operations, including `fetch_add()` for addition and `fetch_sub()` for subtraction.

- **Floating-point types**: When used with the floating-point types `float`, `double`, and `long double`, `std::atomic` includes support for atomic floating-point arithmetic operations, including `fetch_add()` for addition and `fetch_sub()` for subtraction.

- **Integral types**: When used with one of the integral types, `std::atomic` provides support for additional atomic operations, including `fetch_add()`, `fetch_sub()`, `fetch_and()`, `fetch_or()`, and `fetch_xor()`.

Standard aliases

The STL provides type aliases for all the standard scalar integral types. This means that instead of these declarations in our code:

```
std::atomic<bool> ready{};
std::atomic<uint64_t> g_count{};
```

We could use:

```
std::atomic_bool ready{};
std::atomic_uint64_t g_count{};
```

There are 46 standard aliases, one for each of the standard integral types:

`atomic_bool`	`atomic_uint64_t`
`atomic_char`	`atomic_int_least8_t`
`atomic_schar`	`atomic_uint_least8_t`
`atomic_uchar`	`atomic_int_least16_t`
`atomic_short`	`atomic_uint_least16_t`
`atomic_ushort`	`atomic_int_least32_t`
`atomic_int`	`atomic_uint_least32_t`
`atomic_uint`	`atomic_int_least64_t`
`atomic_long`	`atomic_uint_least64_t`
`atomic_ulong`	`atomic_int_fast8_t`
`atomic_llong`	`atomic_uint_fast8_t`
`atomic_ullong`	`atomic_int_fast16_t`
`atomic_char8_t`	`atomic_uint_fast16_t`
`atomic_char16_t`	`atomic_int_fast32_t`
`atomic_char32_t`	`atomic_uint_fast32_t`
`atomic_wchar_t`	`atomic_int_fast64_t`
`atomic_int8_t`	`atomic_uint_fast64_t`
`atomic_uint8_t`	`atomic_intptr_t`
`atomic_int16_t`	`atomic_uintptr_t`
`atomic_uint16_t`	`atomic_size_t`
`atomic_int32_t`	`atomic_ptrdiff_t`
`atomic_uint32_t`	`atomic_intmax_t`
`atomic_int64_t`	`atomic_uintmax_t`

Lock-free variations

Most modern architectures provide *atomic CPU instructions* for performing atomic operations. `std::atomic` should use hardware support for atomic instructions where supported by your hardware. Some atomic types may not be supported on some hardware. `std::atomic` may use a *mutex* to ensure thread-safe operations for those specializations, causing threads to block while waiting for other threads to complete operations. Specializations that use hardware support are said to be *lock-free* because they don't require a mutex.

The `is_lock_free()` method checks whether a specialization is lock-free:

```
cout << format("is g_count lock-free? {}\n",
    g_count.is_lock_free());
```

Output:

is g_count lock-free? true

This result will be `true` for most modern architectures.

There are a few guaranteed lock-free variations of `std::atomic` available. These specializations guarantee the use of the most efficient hardware atomic operations for each purpose:

- `std::atomic_signed_lock_free` is an alias for the most efficient lock-free specialization of a signed integral type.

- `std::atomic_unsigned_lock_free` is an alias for the most efficient lock-free specialization of an unsigned integral type.

- The `std::atomic_flag` class provides a lock-free atomic Boolean type.

> **Important Note**
> Current Windows systems don't support 64-bit hardware integers, even on 64-bit systems. When testing this code on one of these systems in my lab, replacing `std::atomic<uint64_t>` with `std::atomic_unsigned_lock_free` resulted in a *3x* performance improvement. Performance was unchanged on 64-bit Linux and Mac systems.

There's more...

When multiple threads read and write variables simultaneously, one thread may observe the changes in a different order than they were written. `std::memory_order` specifies how memory accesses are ordered around an atomic operation.

`std::atomic` provides methods for accessing and changing its managed value. Unlike the associated operators, these access methods provide arguments for `memory_order` to be specified. For example:

```
g_count.fetch_add(1, std::memory_order_seq_cst);
```

In this case, `memory_order_seq_cst` specifies *sequentially consistent* ordering. So, this call to `fetch_add()` will add 1 to the value of `g_count` with sequentially consistent ordering.

The possible `memory_order` constants are:

- `memory_order_relaxed`: This is a *relaxed operation*. No synchronization or ordering constraints are imposed; only the operation's atomicity is guaranteed.

- `memory_order_consume`: This is a *consume operation*. Access in the current thread that is dependent on the value cannot be reordered before this load. This only affects compiler optimization.

- `memory_order_acquire`: This is an *acquire operation*. Access cannot be reordered before this load.

- `memory_order_release`: This is a *store operation*. Access in the current thread cannot be reordered after this store.

- `memory_order_acq_rel`: This is both *acquire* and *release*. Access in the current thread cannot be reordered before or after this store.

- `memory_order_seq_cst`: This is *sequentially consistent* ordering, either *acquire* or *release*, depending on the context. A load performs acquire, a store performs release, and a read/write/modify performs both. All threads observe all modifications in the same order.

If no `memory_order` is specified, `memory_order_seq_cst` is the default.

Initialize threads with std::call_once

You may need to run the same code in many threads but must initialize that code only once.

One solution would be to call the initialization code before running the threads. This approach can work but has some drawbacks. By separating the initialization, it may be called when unnecessary, or it may be missed when necessary.

The `std::call_once` function provides a more robust solution. `call_once` is in the `<mutex>` header.

How to do it...

In this recipe, we use a print function for the initialization, so we can clearly see when it's called:

- We'll use a constant for the number of threads to spawn:

  ```
  constexpr size_t max_threads{ 25 };
  ```

  We also need a `std::once_flag` to synchronize the `std::call_once` function:

  ```
  std::once_flag init_flag;
  ```

- Our initialization function simply prints a string to let us know it's been called:

  ```
  void do_init(size_t id) {
      cout << format("do_init ({}): ", id);
  }
  ```

- Our worker function, `do_print()`, uses `std::call_once` to call the initialization function then prints its own `id`:

  ```
  void do_print(size_t id) {
      std::call_once(init_flag, do_init, id);
      cout << format("{} ", id);
  }
  ```

- In main(), we use a list container to manage the thread objects:

```
int main() {
    list<thread> spawn;
    for (size_t id{}; id < max_threads; ++id) {
        spawn.emplace_back(do_print, id);
    }
    for (auto& t : spawn) t.join();
    cout << '\n';
}
```

Our output shows the initialization happens first, and only once:

```
do_init (8): 12 0 2 1 9 6 13 10 11 5 16 3 4 17 7 15 8 14
18 19 20 21 22 23 24
```

Notice that it's not always the first spawned thread (0) that ends up calling the initialization function, but it is always called first. If you run this repeatedly, you'll see thread 0 gets the initialization often, but not every time. You'll see thread 0 in the initialization more often on a system with fewer cores.

How it works...

std::call_once is a template function that takes a flag, a *callable* (function or functor), and a parameter pack of arguments:

```
template<class Callable, class... Args>
void call_once(once_flag& flag, Callable&& f, Args&&... args);
```

The callable f is called exactly one time. Even if call_once is called concurrently from several threads, f is still called once and only once.

This requires a std::once_flag object for coordination. The once_flag constructor sets its state to indicate that the callable has not yet been called.

When call_once invokes the callable, any other calls on the same once_flag are blocked until the callable returns. After the callable returns, the once_flag is set, and any subsequent calls to call_once return without invoking f.

Use std::condition_variable to resolve the producer-consumer problem

The simplest version of the *producer-consumer problem* is where you have one process that *produces* data and another that *consumes* data, using one *buffer* or container to hold the data. This requires coordination between the producer and consumer to manage the buffer and prevent unwanted side effects.

How to do it...

In this recipe, we consider a simple solution to the producer-consumer problem using `std::condition_variable` to coordinate the processes:

- We begin with some namespace and alias declarations for convenience:

    ```
    using namespace std::chrono_literals;
    namespace this_thread = std::this_thread;
    using guard_t = std::lock_guard<std::mutex>;
    using lock_t = std::unique_lock<std::mutex>;
    ```

    The `lock_guard` and `unique_lock` aliases make it easier to use these types without error.

- We use a couple of constants:

    ```
    constexpr size_t num_items{ 10 };
    constexpr auto delay_time{ 200ms };
    ```

    Keeping these in one place makes it safer and easier to experiment with different values.

- We're using these global variables for coordinating the data store:

    ```
    std::deque<size_t> q{};
    std::mutex mtx{};
    std::condition_variable cond{};
    bool finished{};
    ```

    We're using `deque` to hold the data as a **First-In-First-Out** (**FIFO**) queue.

    `mutex` is used with the `condition_variable` to coordinate the movement of data from producer to consumer.

    The `finished` flag indicates that there is no more data.

- The producer thread will use this function:

```
void producer() {
    for(size_t i{}; i < num_items; ++i) {
        this_thread::sleep_for(delay_time);
        guard_t x{ mtx };
        q.push_back(i);
        cond.notify_all();
    }
    guard_t x{ mtx };
    finished = true;
    cond.notify_all();
}
```

The producer() function loops num_items iterations and pushes a number onto the deque each time through the loop.

We include a sleep_for() call to simulate a delay in producing each value.

The conditional_variable requires a mutex lock to operate. We use lock_guard (via the guard_t alias) to obtain the lock, then push the value onto the deque, and then call notify_all() on the conditional_variable. This tells the consumer thread that there is a new value available.

When the loop completes, we set the finished flag and notify the consumer thread that the producer is completed.

- The consumer thread waits for each value from the producer, displays it on the console, and waits for the finished flag:

```
void consumer() {
    while(!finished) {
        lock_t lck{ mtx };
        cond.wait(lck, [] { return !q.empty() ||
            finished; });
        while(!q.empty()) {
            cout << format("Got {} from the queue\n",
                q.front());
            q.pop_front();
        }
    }
}
```

The `wait()` method waits to be notified by the producer. It uses the lambda as a predicate to continue waiting until the deque is *not empty* or the `finished` flag is set.

When we get a value, we display it and then pop it from the deque.

- We run this in `main()` with simple `thread` objects:

```
int main() {
    thread t1{ producer };
    thread t2{ consumer };
    t1.join();
    t2.join();
    cout << "finished!\n";
}
```

Output:

```
Got 0 from the queue
Got 1 from the queue
Got 2 from the queue
Got 3 from the queue
Got 4 from the queue
Got 5 from the queue
Got 6 from the queue
Got 7 from the queue
Got 8 from the queue
Got 9 from the queue
finished!
```

Notice that there's a 200 ms delay between each line. This tells us that the producer-consumer coordination is working as expected.

How it works...

The producer-consumer problem requires coordination between writing and reading a buffer or container. In this example, our container is a `deque<size_t>`:

```
std::deque<size_t> q{};
```

The `condition_variable` class can block a thread, or multiple threads, while a shared variable is modified. It may then notify other threads that the value is available.

condition_variable requires a mutex to perform the lock:

```
std::lock_guard x{ mtx };
q.push_back(i);
cond.notify_all();
```

The std::lock_guard acquires a lock, so we can push a value onto our deque.

The wait() method on condition_variable is used to block the current thread until it receives a notification:

```
void wait( std::unique_lock<std::mutex>& lock );
void wait( std::unique_lock<std::mutex>& lock,
    Pred stop_waiting );
```

The predicate form of wait() is equivalent to:

```
while (!stop_waiting()) {
    wait(lock);
}
```

The predicate form is used to prevent spurious waking while waiting for a specific condition. We use it with a lambda in our example:

```
cond.wait(lck, []{ return !q.empty() || finished; });
```

This prevents our consumer from waking until the deque has data or the finished flag is set.

The condition_variable class has two notification methods:

- notify_one() unblocks one waiting thread
- notify_all() unblocks all waiting threads

We used notify_all() in our example. Because there is only one consumer thread, either notification method would work the same.

> **Note**
> Note that unique_lock is the *only* form of lock that supports the wait() method on a condition_variable object.

Implement multiple producers and consumers

The *producer-consumer problem* is really a set of problems. Solutions will differ if the buffer is bounded or unbounded, or if there are multiple producers, multiple consumers, or both.

Let's consider a case with multiple producers, multiple consumers, and a bounded (limited capacity) buffer. This is a common condition.

How to do it...

In this recipe, we'll look at a case with multiple producers and consumers and a *bounded buffer*, using a variety of techniques we've covered in this chapter:

- We'll start with some constants for convenience and reliability:

```
constexpr auto delay_time{ 50ms };
constexpr auto consumer_wait{ 100ms };
constexpr size_t queue_limit{ 5 };
constexpr size_t num_items{ 15 };
constexpr size_t num_producers{ 3 };
constexpr size_t num_consumers{ 5 };
```

  - delay_time is a duration object, used with sleep_for().
  - consumer_wait is a duration object, used with the consumer condition variable.
  - queue_limt is the buffer limit – the maximum number of items in the deque.
  - num_items is the maximum number of items produced per producer.
  - num_producers is the number of spawned producers.
  - num_producers is the number of spawned consumers.

- Now, we need some objects to control the process:

```
deque<string> qs{};
mutex q_mutex{};
condition_variable cv_producer{};
condition_variable cv_consumer{};
bool production_complete{};
```

- qs is a deque of string that holds the produced objects.

- q_mutex controls access to deque.

- cv_producer is a condition variable that coordinates producers.

- cv_consumer is a condition variable that coordinates consumers.

- production_complete is set true when all producer threads have finished.

- The producer() threads run this function:

```
void producer(const size_t id) {
    for(size_t i{}; i < num_items; ++i) {
        this_thread::sleep_for(delay_time * id);
        unique_lock<mutex> lock(q_mutex);
        cv_producer.wait(lock,
            [&]{ return qs.size() < queue_limit; });
        qs.push_back(format("pid {}, qs {},
            item {:02}\n", id, qs.size(), i + 1));
        cv_consumer.notify_all();
    }
}
```

The passed value id is a sequential number used to identify the producer.

The main for loop repeats num_item times. The sleep_for() function is used to simulate some work required to produce an item.

Then we obtain a unique_lock from q_mutex and invoke wait() on cv_producer, using a lambda that checks the size of the deque against the queue_limit constant. If the deque has reached maximum size, the producer waits for consumer threads to reduce the size of the deque. This represents the *bounded buffer* limit on the producer.

Once the condition is satisfied, we push an *item* onto the deque. The item is a formatted string with the producer's id, the size of qs, and an item number (i + 1) from the loop control variable.

Finally, we notify the consumers that new data is available, with notify_all() on the cv_consumer condition variable.

- The `consumer()` threads run this function:

```
void consumer(const size_t id) {
    while(!production_complete) {
        unique_lock<mutex> lock(q_mutex);
        cv_consumer.wait_for(lock, consumer_wait,
            [&]{ return !qs.empty(); });
        if(!qs.empty()){
            cout << format("cid {}: {}", id,
                qs.front());
            qs.pop_front();
        }
        cv_producer.notify_all();
    }
}
```

The passed `id` value is a sequential number used to identify the consumer.

The main `while()` loop continues until `production_complete` is set.

We obtain `unique_lock` from `q_mutex` and invoke `wait_for()` on `cv_consumer`, with a timeout and a lambda that tests if the `deque` is empty. We need the timeout because it's possible for the `producer` threads to finish while some of the `consumer` threads are still running, leaving the `deque` empty.

Once we have a non-empty `deque`, we can print (*consume*) an *item* and pop it off the `deque`.

- In `main()`, we use `async()` to spawn the `producer` and `consumer` threads. `async()` conforms to the RAII pattern, so I'll usually prefer it over `thread`, where possible. `async()` returns a `future` object, so we'll keep a list of `future<void>` objects for process management:

```
int main() {
    list<future<void>> producers;
    list<future<void>> consumers;
    for(size_t i{}; i < num_producers; ++i) {
        producers.emplace_back(async(producer, i));
    }
    for(size_t i{}; i < num_consumers; ++i) {
        consumers.emplace_back(async(consumer, i));
    }
    ...
```

We use `for` loops to create `producer` and `consumer` threads.

- Finally, we use `list` of `future` objects to determine when our `producer` and `consumer` threads are complete:

```
for(auto& f : producers) f.wait();
production_complete = true;
cout << "producers done.\n";

for(auto& f : consumers) f.wait();
cout << "consumers done.\n";
```

We loop through our `producers` container, calling `wait()` to allow the `producer` threads to complete. Then, we can set the `production_complete` flag. We likewise loop through the `consumers` container, calling `wait()` to allow the `consumer` threads to complete. We could perform any final analysis or completion processes here.

- The output is a bit long to show in its entirety:

```
cid 0: pid 0, qs   0, item 01
cid 0: pid 0, qs   1, item 02
cid 0: pid 0, qs   2, item 03
cid 0: pid 0, qs   3, item 04
cid 0: pid 0, qs   4, item 05
...
cid 4: pid 2, qs   0, item 12
cid 4: pid 2, qs   0, item 13
cid 3: pid 2, qs   0, item 14
cid 0: pid 2, qs   0, item 15
producers done.
consumers done.
```

How it works...

The heart of this recipe is in the use of two `condition_variable` objects to control the `producer` and `consumer` threads asynchronously:

```
condition_variable cv_producer{};
condition_variable cv_consumer{};
```

In the `producer()` function, the `cv_producer` object obtains a `unique_lock`, waits for the `deque` to be available, and notifies the `cv_consumer` object when an item has been produced:

```
void producer(const size_t id) {
    for(size_t i{}; i < num_items; ++i) {
        this_thread::sleep_for(delay_time * id);
        unique_lock<mutex> lock(q_mutex);
        cv_producer.wait(lock,
            [&]{ return qs.size() < queue_limit; });
        qs.push_back(format("pid {}, qs  {}, item {:02}\n",
            id, qs.size(), i + 1));
        cv_consumer.notify_all();
    }
}
```

Conversely, in the `consumer()` function, the `cv_consumer` object obtains a `unique_lock`, waits for the `deque` to have items, and notifies the `cv_producer` object when an item has been consumed:

```
void consumer(const size_t id) {
    while(!production_complete) {
        unique_lock<mutex> lock(q_mutex);
        cv_consumer.wait_for(lock, consumer_wait,
            [&]{ return !qs.empty(); });
        if(!qs.empty()) {
            cout << format("cid {}: {}", id, qs.front());
            qs.pop_front();
        }
        cv_producer.notify_all();
    }
}
```

These complementary locks, waits, and notifications constitute the balance of coordination between multiple producers and consumers.

10
Using the File System

The purpose of the STL `filesystem` library is to normalize file system operations across platforms. The `filesystem` library seeks to normalize operations, bridging irregularities between POSIX/Unix, Windows, and other file systems.

The `filesystem` library was adopted from the corresponding *Boost* library and incorporated into the STL with C++17. At the time of writing, there are still gaps in its implementation on some systems, but the recipes in this chapter have been tested on Linux, Windows, and macOS file systems, and compiled with the latest available versions of the GCC, MSVC, and Clang compilers, respectively.

The library uses the `<filesystem>` header, and the `std::filesystem` namespace is commonly aliased as `fs`:

```
namespace fs = std::filesystem;
```

The `fs::path` class is at the core of the `filesystem` library. It provides normalized filename and directory path representation across disparate environments. A `path` object may represent a file, a directory, or any object in a , even a non-existent or impossible object.

In the following recipes, we cover tools for working with files and directories using the filesystem library:

- Specialize std::formatter for the path class
- Use manipulation functions with path
- List files in a directory
- Search directories and files with a grep utility
- Rename files with regex and directory_iterator
- Create a disk usage counter

Technical requirements

You can find the code files for this chapter on GitHub at https://github.com/PacktPublishing/CPP-20-STL-Cookbook/tree/main/chap10.

Specialize std::formatter for the path class

The path class is used throughout the filesystem library to represent a file or directory path. On POSIX-conformant systems, such as macOS and Linux, the path object uses the char type to represent filenames. On Windows, path uses wchar_t. On Windows, cout and format() will not display primitive strings of wchar_t characters. This means there is no simple out-of-the-box way to write code that uses the filesystem library and is portable across POSIX and Windows.

We could use preprocessor directives to write specific versions of code for Windows. That may be a reasonable solution for some code bases, but for this book, it's messy and does not serve the purpose of simple, portable, reusable recipes.

The elegant solution is to write a C++20 formatter specialization for the path class. This allows us to display path objects simply and portably.

How to do it...

In this recipe, we write a formatter specialization for use with the fs::path class:

- We start with a namespace alias for convenience. All the filesystem names are in the std::filesystem namespace:

    ```
    namespace fs = std::filesystem;
    ```

- Our `formatter` specialization for the `path` class is simple and succinct:

```
template<>
struct std::formatter<fs::path>:
std::formatter<std::string> {
    template<typename FormatContext>
    auto format(const fs::path& p, FormatContext& ctx) {
        return format_to(ctx.out(), "{}", p.string());
    }
};
```

Here, we're specializing `formatter` for the `fs::path` type, using its `string()` method to get a printable representation. We cannot use the `c_str()` method because it doesn't work with the `wchar_t` characters on Windows.

There's a more complete explanation of `formatter` specialization in *Chapter 1, New C++20 Features*, of this book.

- In the `main()` function, we use the command line to pass a filename or path:

```
int main(const int argc, const char** argv) {
    if(argc != 2) {
        fs::path fn{ argv[0] };
        cout << format("usage: {} <path>\n",
            fn.filename());
        return 0;
    }

    fs::path dir{ argv[1] };
    if(!fs::exists(dir)) {
        cout << format("path: {} does not exist\n",
            dir);
        return 1;
    }

    cout << format("path: {}\n", dir);
    cout << format("filename: {}\n", dir.filename());
    cout << format("cannonical: {}\n",
        fs::canonical(dir));
}
```

The `argc` and `argv` parameters are the standard command-line arguments.

`argv[0]` is always the full directory path and filename for the executable itself. If we don't have the correct number of arguments, we display the filename part from `argv[0]` as part of our *usage* message.

We've used some `filesystem` functions in this example:

- The `fs::exists()` function checks if a directory or file exists.

- `dir` is a `path` object. We can now pass it directly to `format()`, using our specialization to display the string representation of the path.

- The `filename()` method returns a new `path` object, which we pass directly to `format()` using our specialization.

- The `fs::cannonical()` function takes a `path` object and returns a new `path` object with the canonical absolute directory path. We pass this `path` object directly to `format()` and it displays the directory path returned from `cannonical()`.

Output:

```
$ ./formatter ./formatter.cpp
path: ./formatter.cpp
filename: formatter.cpp
cannonical: /home/billw/working/chap10/formatter.cpp
```

How it works...

The `fs::path` class is used throughout the `filesystem` library to represent directory paths and filenames. By providing a `formatter` specialization, we can easily display `path` objects consistently across platforms.

The `path` class provides some useful methods. We can iterate through a path to see its component parts:

```
fs::path p{ "~/include/bwprint.h" };
cout << format("{}\n", p);
for(auto& x : p) cout << format("[{}] ", x);
cout << '\n';
```

Output:

```
~/include/bwprint.h
[~] [include] [bwprint.h]
```

The iterator returns a `path` object for each element of the path.

We can also get different parts of the path:

```
fs::path p{ "~/include/bwprint.h" };
cout << format("{}\n", p);
cout << format("{}\n", p.stem());
cout << format("{}\n", p.extension());
cout << format("{}\n", p.filename());
cout << format("{}\n", p.parent_path());
```

Output:

```
~/include/bwprint.h
bwprint
.h
bwprint.h
~/include
```

We will continue to use this `formatter` specialization for the `path` class throughout this chapter.

Use manipulation functions with path

The `filesystem` library includes functions for manipulating the contents of `path` objects. In this recipe, we will consider a few of these tools.

How to do it...

In this recipe, we examine some functions that manipulate the contents of `path` objects:

- We start with the `namespace` directive and our `formatter` specialization. We do this in every recipe in this chapter:

```
namespace fs = std::filesystem;
template<>
struct std::formatter<fs::path>:
std::formatter<std::string> {
    template<typename FormatContext>
    auto format(const fs::path& p, FormatContext& ctx) {
```

```
            return format_to(ctx.out(), "{}", p.string());
        }
    };
```

- We can get the current working directory with the `current_path()` function, which returns a `path` object:

```
cout << format("current_path: {}\n", fs::current_path());
```

Output:

current_path: /home/billw/chap10

- The `absolute()` function returns an absolute path from a relative path:

```
cout << format("absolute(p): {}\n", fs::absolute(p));
```

Output:

absolute(p): /home/billw/chap10/testdir/foo.txt

`absolute()` will also dereference symbolic links.

- The `+=` operator *concatenates* a string to the end of the `path` string:

```
cout << format("concatenate: {}\n",
    fs::path{ "testdir" } += "foo.txt");
```

Output:

concatenate: testdirfoo.txt

- The `/=` operator *appends* a string to the end of the `path` string and returns a new `path` object:

```
cout << format("append: {}\n",
    fs::path{ "testdir" } /= "foo.txt");
```

Output:

append: testdir/foo.txt

- The `canonical()` function returns the full canonical directory path:

```
cout << format("canonical: {}\n",
    fs::canonical(fs::path{ "." } /= "testdir"));
```

Output:

canonical: /home/billw/chap10/testdir

- The `equivalent()` function tests if two relative paths resolve to the same file system entity:

```
cout << format("equivalent: {}\n",
    fs::equivalent("testdir/foo.txt",
        "testdir/../testdir/foo.txt"));
```

Output:

```
equivalent: true
```

- The `filesystem` library includes the `filesystem_error` class for exception handling:

```
try {
    fs::path p{ fp };
    cout << format("p: {}\n", p);
    ...
    cout << format("equivalent: {}\n",
        fs::equivalent("testdir/foo.txt",
            "testdir/../testdir/foo.txt"));
} catch (const fs::filesystem_error& e) {
    cout << format("{}\n", e.what());
    cout << format("path1: {}\n", e.path1());
    cout << format("path2: {}\n", e.path2());
}
```

The `filesystem_error` class includes methods for displaying the error message and for getting the path(s) involved in the error.

If we introduce an error into the `equivalent()` call, we can see the results of the `fileystem_error` class:

```
cout << format("equivalent: {}\n",
    fs::equivalent("testdir/foo.txt/x",
        "testdir/../testdir/foo.txt/y"));
```

Output:

```
filesystem error: cannot check file equivalence: No
such file or directory [testdir/foo.txt/x] [testdir/../
testdir/foo.txt/y]
path1: testdir/foo.txt/x
path2: testdir/../testdir/foo.txt/y
```

This is the output on Debian with GCC.

The `filesystem_error` class provides additional detail through its `path1()` and `path2()` methods. These methods return `path` objects.

- You can also use `std::error_code` with some of the `filesystem` functions:

```
fs::path p{ fp };
std::error_code e;
cout << format("canonical: {}\n",
    fs::canonical(p /= "foo", e));
cout << format("error: {}\n", e.message());
```

Output:

```
canonical:
error: Not a directory
```

- Even though Windows uses a very different file system, this code still works as expected, using Windows file naming conventions:

```
p: testdir/foo.txt
current_path: C:\Users\billw\chap10
absolute(p): C:\Users\billw\chap10\testdir\foo.txt
concatenate: testdirfoo.txt
append: testdir\foo.txt
canonical: C:\Users\billw\chap10\testdir
equivalent: true
```

How it works...

Most of these functions take a `path` object, an optional `std::error_code` object, and return a `path` object:

```
path absolute(const path& p);
path absolute(const path& p, std::error_code& ec);
```

The `equivalent()` function takes two `path` objects and returns a `bool`:

```
bool equivalent( const path& p1, const path& p2 );
bool equivalent( const path& p1, const path& p2,
    std::error_code& ec );
```

The `path` class has operators for concatenate and append. Both operators are destructive. They modify the `path` on the left-hand side of the operator:

```
p1 += source; // concatenate
p1 /= source; // append
```

For the right-hand side, these operators take either a `path` object, a `string`, a `string_view`, a C-string, or a pair of iterators.

The concatenate operator adds the string from the right-hand side of the operator to the end of the `p1` path string.

The append operator adds a separator (e.g., / or \), followed by the string from the right-hand side of the operator to the end of the `p1` path string.

List files in a directory

The `filesystem` library provides a `directory_entry` class with directory-related information about a given `path`. We can use this to create useful directory listings.

How to do it...

In this recipe, we create a directory listing utility using the information in the `directory_entry` class:

- We start with our namespace alias and `formatter` specialization for displaying path objects:

```
namespace fs = std::filesystem;
template<>
struct std::formatter<fs::path>:
std::formatter<std::string> {
    template<typename FormatContext>
    auto format(const fs::path& p, FormatContext& ctx) {
        return format_to(ctx.out(), "{}", p.string());
    }
};
```

- The `directory_iterator` class makes it easy to list a directory:

```cpp
int main() {
    constexpr const char* fn{ "." };
    const fs::path fp{fn};
    for(const auto& de : fs::directory_iterator{fp}) {
        cout << format("{} ", de.path().filename());
    }
    cout << '\n';
}
```

Output:

```
chrono Makefile include chrono.cpp working formatter
testdir formatter.cpp working.cpp
```

- We can add command-line options to make this work, like Unix `ls`:

```cpp
int main(const int argc, const char** argv) {
    fs::path fp{ argc > 1 ? argv[1] : "." };
    if(!fs::exists(fp)) {
        const auto cmdname {
          fs::path{argv[0]}.filename() };
        cout << format("{}: {} does not exist\n",
            cmdname, fp);
        return 1;
    }
    if(is_directory(fp)) {
        for(const auto& de :
          fs::directory_iterator{fp}) {
            cout << format("{} ",
                de.path().filename());
        }
    } else {
        cout << format("{} ", fp.filename());
    }
    cout << '\n';
}
```

If there is a command-line argument, we use it to create a `path` object. Otherwise, we use `"."` for the current directory.

We check if the path exists with `if_exists()`. If not, we print an error message and exit. The error message includes `cmdname` from `argv[0]`.

Next, we check `is_directory()`. If we have a directory, we loop through a `directory_iterator` for each entry. `directory_iterator` iterates over `directory_entry` objects. `de.path().filename()` gets the `path` and `filename` from each `directory_entry` object.

Output:

```
$ ./working
chrono Makefile include chrono.cpp working formatter
testdir formatter.cpp working.cpp
$ ./working working.cpp
working.cpp
$ ./working foo.bar
working: foo.bar does not exist
```

- If we want our output sorted, we can store our `directory_entry` objects in a sortable container.

Let's create an alias for `fs::directory_entry`. We'll be using this a lot. This goes at the top of the file:

```
using de = fs::directory_entry;
```

At the top of `main()`, we declare a `vector` of de objects:

```
vector<de> entries{};
```

Inside the `is_directory()` block, we load the `vector`, sort it, and then display it:

```
if(is_directory(fp)) {
    for(const auto& de : fs::directory_iterator{fp}) {
        entries.emplace_back(de);
    }
    std::sort(entries.begin(), entries.end());
    for(const auto& e : entries) {
        cout << format("{} ", e.path().filename());
    }
} else { ...
```

Now our output is sorted:

```
Makefile chrono chrono.cpp formatter formatter.cpp
include testdir working working.cpp
```

Notice that Makefile is sorted first, apparently out of order. This is because capital letters sort before lowercase in ASCII order.

- If we want a case-insensitive sort, we need a comparison function that ignores case. First, we need a function to return a lowercase string:

```
string strlower(string s) {
    auto char_lower = [](const char& c) -> char {
        if(c >= 'A' && c <= 'Z') return c + ('a' - 'A');
        else return c;
    };
    std::transform(s.begin(), s.end(), s.begin(),
        char_lower);
    return s;
}
```

Now we need a function that compares two directory_entry objects, using strlower():

```
bool dircmp_lc(const de& lhs, const de& rhs) {
    const auto lhstr{ lhs.path().string() };
    const auto rhstr{ rhs.path().string() };
    return strlower(lhstr) < strlower(rhstr);
}
```

Now we can use dircmp_lc() in our sort:

```
std::sort(entries.begin(), entries.end(), dircmp_lc);
```

Our output is now sorted ignoring case:

```
chrono chrono.cpp formatter formatter.cpp include
Makefile testdir working working.cpp
```

- At this point, we have a simple directory listing utility.

There's a lot more information available from the `filesystem` library. Let's create a `print_dir()` function to gather more information and format it for display in the style of Unix `ls`:

```cpp
void print_dir(const de& dir) {
    using fs::perms;
    const auto fpath{ dir.path() };
    const auto fstat{ dir.symlink_status() };
    const auto fperm{ fstat.permissions() };
    const uintmax_t fsize{
        is_regular_file(fstat) ? file_size(fpath) : 0 };
    const auto fn{ fpath.filename() };

    string suffix{};
    if(is_directory(fstat)) suffix = "/";
    else if((fperm & perms::owner_exec) != perms::none) {
        suffix = "*";
    }
    cout << format("{}{}\n", fn, suffix);
}
```

The `print_dir()` function takes a `directory_entry` argument. We then retrieve some useful objects from the `directory_entry` object:

- `dir.path()` returns a `path` object.

- `dir.symlink_status()` returns a `file_status` object, without following symbolic links.

- `fstat.permissions()` returns a `perms` object.

- `fsize` is the size of the file and `fn` is the filename `string`. We'll look more closely at each of these as we use them.

Unix `ls` uses trailing characters, after the filename, to indicate a directory or an executable. We test the `fstat` object with `is_directory()` to see if the file is a directory and add a trailing / to the filename. Likewise, we can test if a file is executable with the `fperm` object.

We call `print_dir()` from `main()` in the `for` loop after `sort()`:

```
std::sort(entries.begin(), entries.end(), dircmp_lc);
for(const auto& e : entries) {
    print_dir(e);
}
```

Our output now looks like this:

```
chrono*
chrono.cpp
formatter*
formatter.cpp
include*
Makefile
testdir/
working*
working.cpp
```

- Notice the `include*` entry. That's actually a symbolic link. Let's notate that properly by following the link to get the target path:

```
string suffix{};
if(is_symlink(fstat)) {
    suffix = " -> ";
    suffix += fs::read_symlink(fpath).string();
}
else if(is_directory(fstat)) suffix = "/";
else if((fperm & perms::owner_exec) != perms::none)
suffix = "*";
```

The `read_symlink()` function returns a `path` object. We take the `string()` representation of the returned `path` object and add it to the suffix for this output:

```
chrono*
chrono.cpp
formatter*
formatter.cpp
include -> /Users/billw/include
Makefile
```

```
testdir/
working*
working.cpp
```

- The Unix `ls` command also includes a string of characters to indicate a file's permission bits. It looks something like this: `drwxr-xr-x`.

The first character indicates the type of the file, for example: `d` for directory, `l` for symbolic link, and `-` for a regular file.

The `type_char()` function returns the appropriate character:

```cpp
char type_char(const fs::file_status& fstat) {
         if(is_symlink(fstat))            return 'l';
    else if(is_directory(fstat))          return 'd';
    else if(is_character_file(fstat))     return 'c';
    else if(is_block_file(fstat))         return 'b';
    else if(is_fifo(fstat))               return 'p';
    else if(is_socket(fstat))             return 's';
    else if(is_other(fstat))              return 'o';
    else if(is_regular_file(fstat))       return '-';
    return '?';
}
```

The rest of the string is in three triplets. Each triplet includes positions for the read, write, and execute permission bits, in the form `rwx`. If a bit is not set, its character is replaced by a `-`. There are three triplets for three sets of permissions: owner, group, and other, respectively.

```cpp
string rwx(const fs::perms& p) {
    using fs::perms;
    auto bit2char = [&p](perms bit, char c) {
        return (p & bit) == perms::none ? '-' : c;
    };

    return { bit2char(perms::owner_read,   'r'),
             bit2char(perms::owner_write,  'w'),
             bit2char(perms::owner_exec,   'x'),
             bit2char(perms::group_read,   'r'),
             bit2char(perms::group_write,  'w'),
             bit2char(perms::group_exec,   'x'),
```

```
        bit2char(perms::others_read,    'r'),
        bit2char(perms::others_write,   'w'),
        bit2char(perms::others_exec,    'x') };
}
```

The perms object represents the POSIX permissions bitmap, but it's not necessarily implemented as bits. Each entry must be compared to the perms::none value. Our lambda function fulfills this requirement.

We add this definition to the top of our print_dir() function:

```
const auto permstr{ type_char(fstat) + rwx(fperm) };
```

We update our format() string:

```
cout << format("{} {}{}\n", permstr, fn, suffix);
```

And we get this output:

```
-rwxr-xr-x chrono*
-rw-r--r-- chrono.cpp
-rwxr-xr-x formatter*
-rw-r--r-- formatter.cpp
lrwxr-xr-x include -> /Users/billw/include
-rw-r--r-- Makefile
drwxr-xr-x testdir/
-rwxr-xr-x working*
-rw-r--r-- working.cpp
```

- Now, let's add a size string. The fsize value is from the file_size() function, which returns a std::uintmax_t type. This represents the maximum size natural integer on the target system. uintmax_t is not always the same as size_t and does not always convert easily. Notably, uintmax_t is 32 bits on Windows, where size_t is 64 bits:

```
string size_string(const uintmax_t fsize) {
    constexpr const uintmax_t kilo{ 1024 };
    constexpr const uintmax_t mega{ kilo * kilo };
    constexpr const uintmax_t giga{ mega * kilo };
    string s;
```

```
    if(fsize >= giga ) return
        format("{}{}", (fsize + giga / 2) / giga, 'G');
    else if (fsize >= mega) return
        format("{}{}", (fsize + mega / 2) / mega, 'M');
    else if (fsize >= kilo) return
        format("{}{}", (fsize + kilo / 2) / kilo, 'K');
    else return format("{}B", fsize);
}
```

I chose to use 1,024 as 1K in this function, as that appears to be the default on both Linux and BSD Unix. In production, this could be a command-line option.

We update our `format()` string in `main()`:

```
cout << format("{} {:>6} {}{}\n",
    permstr, size_string(fsize), fn, suffix);
```

Now, we get this output:

```
-rwxr-xr-x    284K chrono*
-rw-r--r--      2K chrono.cpp
-rwxr-xr-x    178K formatter*
-rw-r--r--    906B formatter.cpp
lrwxr-xr-x      0B include -> /Users/billw/include
-rw-r--r--    642B Makefile
drwxr-xr-x      0B testdir/
-rwxr-xr-x    197K working*
-rw-r--r--      5K working.cpp
```

> **Note**
> This utility is designed for POSIX systems, such as Linux and macOS. It works
> on a Windows system, but the Windows permissions system is different from the
> POSIX system. On Windows, the permissions bits will always appear fully set.

How it works...

The `filesystem` library carries a rich set of information through its `directory_entry` and related classes. The major classes we used in this recipe include:

- The `path` class represents a file system path, according to the rules of the target system. A `path` object is constructed from a string or another path. It need not represent an existing path, or even a possible path. The path string is parsed to component parts, including a root name, root directory, and an optional series of filenames and directory separators.

- The `directory_entry` class carries a `path` object as a member, and may also store additional attributes, including hard link count, status, symbolic link, file size, and last write time.

- The `file_status` class carries information about the type and permissions of a file. A `perms` object may be a member of `file_status`, representing the permissions structure of a file.

There are two functions for retrieving a `perms` object from `file_status`. The `status()` function and the `symlink_status()` function both return a `perms` object. The difference is in how they handle a symbolic link. The `status()` function will follow a symbolic link and return the `perms` from the target file. `symlink_status()` will return the `perms` from the symbolic link itself.

There's more...

I had intended to include the last-write time of each file in the directory listing.

The `directory_entry` class has a member function, `last_write_time()`, which returns a `file_time_type` object representing the timestamp of the last time the file was written.

Unfortunately, at the time of writing, the available implementations lack a portable way to convert a `file_time_type` object to a standard `chrono::sys_time`, suitable for use with `cout` or `format()`.

For now, here's a solution that works with GCC:

```cpp
string time_string(const fs::directory_entry& dir) {
    using std::chrono::file_clock;
    auto file_time{ dir.last_write_time() };
    return format("{:%F %T}",
        file_clock::to_sys(dir.last_write_time()));
}
```

It's recommended that user code should use `std::chrono::clock_cast` instead of `file::clock::to_sys` to convert time points between clocks. Unfortunately, none of the currently available implementations have a working `std::chrono::clock_cast` specialization for this purpose.

Using this `time_string()` function, we can add to `print_dir()`:

```
const string timestr{ time_string(dir) };
```

We can then change the `format()` string:

```
cout << format("{} {:>6} {} {}{}\n",
    permstr, sizestr, timestr, fn, suffix);
```

And we get this output:

```
-rwxr-xr-x    248K 2022-03-09 09:39:49 chrono*
-rw-r--r--      2K 2022-03-09 09:33:56 chrono.cpp
-rwxr-xr-x    178K 2022-03-09 09:39:49 formatter*
-rw-r--r--    906B 2022-03-09 09:33:56 formatter.cpp
lrwxrwxrwx      0B 2022-02-04 11:39:53 include -> /home/billw/
include
-rw-r--r--    642B 2022-03-09 14:08:37 Makefile
drwxr-xr-x      0B 2022-03-09 10:38:39 testdir/
-rwxr-xr-x    197K 2022-03-12 17:13:46 working*
-rw-r--r--      5K 2022-03-12 17:13:40 working.cpp
```

This works on Debian with GCC-11. Do not expect it to work without modification on any other systems.

Search directories and files with a grep utility

To demonstrate traversing and searching directory structures, we create a simple utility that works like Unix *grep*. This utility uses `recursive_directory_iterator` to traverse nested directories and searches files for matches with a regular expression.

How to do it...

In this recipe, we write a simple *grep* utility that traverses directories to search files with a regular expression:

- We start with some convenience aliases:

```
namespace fs = std::filesystem;
using de = fs::directory_entry;
using rdit = fs::recursive_directory_iterator;
using match_v = vector<std::pair<size_t, std::string>>;
```

match_v is a vector of regular expression match results.

- We continue using our formatter specialization for path objects:

```
template<>
struct std::formatter<fs::path>:
std::formatter<std::string> {
    template<typename FormatContext>
    auto format(const fs::path& p, FormatContext& ctx) {
        return format_to(ctx.out(), "{}", p.string());
    }
};
```

- We have a simple function for getting regular expression matches from a file:

```
match_v matches(const fs::path& fpath, const regex& re) {
    match_v matches{};
    std::ifstream instrm(fpath.string(),
        std::ios_base::in);
    string s;
    for(size_t lineno{1}; getline(instrm, s); ++lineno) {
        if(std::regex_search(s.begin(), s.end(), re)) {
            matches.emplace_back(lineno, move(s));
        }
    }
    return matches;
}
```

In this function, we open the file with `ifstream`, read lines from the file with `getline()`, and match the regular expression with `regex_search()`. Results are collected in the `vector` and returned.

* We can now call this function from `main()`:

```
int main() {
    constexpr const char * fn{ "working.cpp" };
    constexpr const char * pattern{ "path" };

    fs::path fpath{ fn };
    regex re{ pattern };
    auto regmatches{ matches(fpath, re) };
    for(const auto& [lineno, line] : regmatches) {
        cout << format("{}: {}\n", lineno, line);
    }
    cout << format("found {} matches\n", regmatches.size());
}
```

In this example, we use constants for the filename and the regular expression pattern. We create `path` and `regex` objects, call the `matches()` function, and print the results.

Our output has line numbers and strings for the matching lines:

```
25: struct std::formatter<fs::path>:
std::formatter<std::string> {
27:     auto format(const fs::path& p, FormatContext&
ctx) {
32: match_v matches(const fs::path& fpath, const regex&
re) {
34:     std::ifstream instrm(fpath.string(), std::ios_
base::in);
62:     constexpr const char * pattern{ "path" };
64:     fs::path fpath{ fn };
66:     auto regmatches{ matches(fpath, re) };
```

- Our utility needs to take command-line arguments for the `regex` pattern and filenames. It should be able to traverse directories or take a list of filenames (which may be the result of command-line wildcard expansion). This requires a bit of logic in the `main()` function.

First, we need one more helper function:

```
size_t pmatches(const regex& re, const fs::path& epath,
        const fs::path& search_path) {
    fs::path target{epath};
    auto regmatches{ matches(epath, re) };
    auto matchcount{ regmatches.size() };
    if(!matchcount) return 0;

    if(!(search_path == epath)) {
        target =
            epath.lexically_relative(search_path);
    }
    for (const auto& [lineno, line] : regmatches) {
        cout << format("{} {}: {}\n", target, lineno,
            line);
    }
    return regmatches.size();
}
```

This function calls our `matches()` function and prints the results. It takes a `regex` object and two `path` objects. `epath` is the result of a directory search, and `search_path` is the search directory itself. We'll set these in `main()`.

- In `main()`, we use the `argc` and `argv` command-line arguments and we declare a few variables:

```
int main(const int argc, const char** argv) {
    const char * arg_pat{};
    regex re{};
    fs::path search_path{};
    size_t matchcount{};
    ...
```

The variables declared here are:

- `arg_pat` is for the regular expression pattern from the command line
- `re` is the `regex` object
- `search_path` is the command-line search path argument
- `matchcount` is for counting the matched lines

- Continuing in `main()`, if we have no arguments, then we print a short usage string:

```
if(argc < 2) {
    auto cmdname{ fs::path(argv[0]).filename() };
    cout << format("usage: {} pattern [path/file]\n",
        cmdname);
    return 1;
}
```

`argv[1]` is always the invoking command from the command line. `cmdname` uses the `filename()` method to return a `path` with just the filename part of the invoking command path.

- Next, we parse the regular expression. We use a `try-catch` block to capture any error from the `regex` parser:

```
arg_pat = argv[1];
try {
    re = regex(arg_pat, std::regex_constants::icase);
} catch(const std::regex_error& e) {
    cout << format("{}: {}\n", e.what(), arg_pat);
    return 1;
}
```

We use the `icase` flag to tell the `regex` parser to ignore case.

- If `argc == 2`, we have just one argument, which we treat as the regular expression pattern, and we use the current directory for the search path:

```
if(argc == 2) {
    search_path = ".";
        for (const auto& entry : rdit{ search_path }) {
        const auto epath{ entry.path() };
        matchcount += pmatches(re, epath,
```

```
                    search_path);
        }
    }
```

rdit is an alias for the `recursive_directory_iterator` class, which traverses the directory tree from the starting path, returning a `directory_entry` object for each file it encounters. We then create a `path` object and call `pmatches()` to go through the file and print any regular expression matches.

- At this point in `main()`, we know that `argc` is `>=2`. Now, we handle cases where we have one or more file paths on the command line:

```
int count{ argc - 2 };
while(count-- > 0) {
    fs::path p{ argv[count + 2] };
    if(!exists(p)) {
        cout << format("not found: {}\n", p);
        continue;
    }
    if(is_directory(p)) {
        for (const auto& entry : rdit{ p }) {
            const auto epath{ entry.path() };
            matchcount += pmatches(re, epath, p);
        }
    } else {
        matchcount += pmatches(re, p, p);
    }
}
```

The `while` loop handles one or more arguments past the search pattern on the command line. It checks each filename to ensure it exists. Then, if it's a directory, it uses the `rdit` alias for the `recursive_directory_iterator` class to traverse the directory and call `pmatches()` to print any pattern matches in the files.

If it's a single file, it calls `pmatches()` on that file.

- We can run our `grep` clone with one argument as the search pattern:

```
$ ./bwgrep using
dir.cpp 12: using std::format;
dir.cpp 13: using std::cout;
dir.cpp 14: using std::string;

...

formatter.cpp 10: using std::cout;
formatter.cpp 11: using std::string;
formatter.cpp 13: using namespace std::filesystem;
found 33 matches
```

We can run it with a second argument as a directory to search:

```
$ ./bwgrep using ..
chap04/iterator-adapters.cpp 12: using std::format;
chap04/iterator-adapters.cpp 13: using std::cout;
chap04/iterator-adapters.cpp 14: using std::cin;

...

chap01/hello-version.cpp 24: using std::print;
chap01/chrono.cpp 8: using namespace std::chrono_
literals;
chap01/working.cpp 15: using std::cout;
chap01/working.cpp 34:      using std::vector;
found 529 matches
```

Notice that it *traverses the directory tree* to find files in sub-directories.

Or we can run it with a single file argument:

```
$ ./bwgrep using bwgrep.cpp
bwgrep.cpp 13: using std::format;
bwgrep.cpp 14: using std::cout;
bwgrep.cpp 15: using std::string;

...

bwgrep.cpp 22: using rdit = fs::recursive_directory_
iterator;
bwgrep.cpp 23: using match_v = vector<std::pair<size_t,
std::string>>;
found 9 matches
```

How it works...

While the main task of this utility is the regular expression matching, we're concentrating on the technique of recursively processing directories of files.

The `recursive_directory_iterator` object is interchangeable with `directory_iterator`, except `recursive_directory_iterator` operates recursively over all the entries of each sub-directory.

See also...

For more about regular expressions, see the recipe *Parse strings with Regular Expressions* in *Chapter 7, Strings, Streams, and Formatting.*

Rename files with regex and directory_iterator

This is a simple utility that renames files using regular expressions. It uses `directory_iterator` to find the files in a directory and `fs::rename()` to rename them.

How to do it...

In this recipe, we create a file rename utility that uses regular expressions:

- We start by defining a few convenience aliases:

```
namespace fs = std::filesystem;
using dit = fs::directory_iterator;
using pat_v = vector<std::pair<regex, string>>;
```

The pat_v alias is a vector for use with our regular expressions.

- We also continue to use the `formatter` specialization for `path` objects:

```
template<>
struct std::formatter<fs::path>:
std::formatter<std::string> {
    template<typename FormatContext>
    auto format(const fs::path& p, FormatContext& ctx) {
        return format_to(ctx.out(), "{}", p.string());
    }
};
```

- We have a function for applying the regular expression replacement to filename strings:

```
string replace_str(string s, const pat_v& replacements) {
    for(const auto& [pattern, repl] : replacements) {
        s = regex_replace(s, pattern, repl);
    }
    return s;
}
```

Notice that we loop through a `vector` of pattern/replacement pairs, applying the regular expressions successively. This allows us to stack our replacements.

- In `main()`, we first check the command-line arguments:

```
int main(const int argc, const char** argv) {
    pat_v patterns{};

    if(argc < 3 || argc % 2 != 1) {
        fs::path cmdname{ fs::path{argv[0]}.filename() };
        cout << format(
            "usage: {} [regex replacement] ...\n",
            cmdname);
        return 1;
    }
```

The command line accepts one or more *pairs of strings*. Each pair of strings includes a *regex* (regular expression) followed by a *replacement*.

- Now we populate the `vector` with `regex` and `string` objects:

```
for(int i{ 1 }; i < argc; i += 2) {
    patterns.emplace_back(argv[i], argv[i + 1]);
}
```

The `pair` constructor constructs the `regex` and `string` objects in place, from the C-strings passed on the command line. These are added to the `vector` with the `emplace_back()` method.

- We search the current directory using a `directory_iterator` object:

```cpp
for(const auto& entry : dit{fs::current_path()}) {
    fs::path fpath{ entry.path() };
    string rname{
        replace_str(fpath.filename().string(),
            patterns) };

    if(fpath.filename().string() != rname) {
        fs::path rpath{ fpath };
        rpath.replace_filename(rname);

        if(exists(rpath)) {
            cout << "Error: cannot rename - destination
file exists.\n";
        } else {
            fs::rename(fpath, rpath);
            cout << format(
                "{} -> {}\n",
                fpath.filename(),
                rpath.filename());
        }
    }
}
```

In this `for` loop, we call `replace_str()` to get the replacement filename and then check that the new name is not a duplicate of a file in the directory. We use the `replace_filename()` method on a `path` object to create a `path` with the new filename and use `fs::rename()` to rename the file.

- To test the utility, I've created a directory with a few files in it for renaming:

```
$ ls
bwfoo.txt bwgrep.cpp chrono.cpp dir.cpp formatter.cpp
path-ops.cpp working.cpp
```

- We can do something simple, like change `.cpp` to `.Cpp`:

```
$ ../rerename .cpp .Cpp
dir.cpp -> dir.Cpp
path-ops.cpp -> path-ops.Cpp
bwgrep.cpp -> bwgrep.Cpp
working.cpp -> working.Cpp
formatter.cpp -> formatter.Cpp
```

Let's change them back again:

```
$ ../rerename .Cpp .cpp
formatter.Cpp -> formatter.cpp
bwgrep.Cpp -> bwgrep.cpp
dir.Cpp -> dir.cpp
working.Cpp -> working.cpp
path-ops.Cpp -> path-ops.cpp
```

- Using standard regular expression syntax, I can add "bw" to the beginning of each of the filenames:

```
$ ../rerename '^' bw
bwgrep.cpp -> bwbwgrep.cpp
chrono.cpp -> bwchrono.cpp
formatter.cpp -> bwformatter.cpp
bwfoo.txt -> bwbwfoo.txt
working.cpp -> bwworking.cpp
```

Notice that it even renamed the files that already had "bw" at the beginning. Let's have it not do that. First, we restore the filenames:

```
$ ../rerename '^bw' ''
bwbwgrep.cpp -> bwgrep.cpp
bwworking.cpp -> working.cpp
bwformatter.cpp -> formatter.cpp
bwchrono.cpp -> chrono.cpp
bwbwfoo.txt -> bwfoo.txt
```

Now we use a *regex* that checks if the filename already begins with "bw":

```
$ ../rerename '^(?!bw)' bw
chrono.cpp -> bwchrono.cpp
formatter.cpp -> bwformatter.cpp
working.cpp -> bwworking.cpp
```

Because we use a `vector` of regex/replacement strings, we can stack several replacements:

```
$ ../rerename foo bar '\.cpp$' '.xpp' grep grok
bwgrep.cpp -> bwgrok.xpp
bwworking.cpp -> bwworking.xpp
bwformatter.cpp -> bwformatter.xpp
bwchrono.cpp -> bwchrono.xpp
bwfoo.txt -> bwbar.txt
```

How it works...

The `filesystem` part of this recipe uses `directory_iterator` to return a `directory_entry` object for each file in the current directory:

```
for(const auto& entry : dit{fs::current_path()}) {
    fs::path fpath{ entry.path() };
    ...
}
```

We then construct a `path` object from the `directory_entry` object to process the file.

We use the `replace_filename()` method on a `path` object to create the destination for the rename operation:

```
fs::path rpath{ fpath };
rpath.replace_filename(rname);
```

Here, we create a duplicate and change its name, giving us both sides for the rename operation:

```
fs::rename(fpath, rpath);
```

On the regular expression side of the recipe, we use `regex_replace()`, which uses regular expression syntax to perform substitutions in a string:

```
s = regex_replace(s, pattern, repl);
```

Regular expression syntax is extremely powerful. It even allows replacements to include sections of the search string:

```
$ ../rerename '(bw)(.*\.)(.*)$' '$3$2$1'
bwgrep.cpp -> cppgrep.bw
bwfoo.txt -> txtfoo.bw
```

By using parentheses in the search pattern, I can easily rearrange parts of a filename.

See also...

For more about regular expressions, see the recipe *Parse strings with Regular Expressions* in *Chapter 7, Strings, Streams, and Formatting.*

Create a disk usage counter

This is a simple utility that totals the size of every file in a directory and its sub-directories. It runs on both POSIX/Unix and Windows file systems.

How to do it...

This recipe is a utility to report the size of every file in a directory and its sub-directories, along with a total. We'll re-use some of the functions we've used elsewhere in this chapter:

- We start with a few convenience aliases:

```
namespace fs = std::filesystem;
using dit = fs::directory_iterator;
using de = fs::directory_entry;
```

- We also use our format specialization for fs::path objects:

```
template<>
struct std::formatter<fs::path>:
std::formatter<std::string> {
    template<typename FormatContext>
    auto format(const fs::path& p, FormatContext& ctx) {
```

```
        return format_to(ctx.out(), "{}", p.string());
    }
};
```

- For reporting the size of the directory, we'll use this make_commas() function:

```
string make_commas(const uintmax_t& num) {
    string s{ std::to_string(num) };
    for(long l = s.length() - 3; l > 0; l -= 3) {
        s.insert(l, ",");
    }
    return s;
}
```

We've used this before. It inserts a comma before every third character from the end.

- To sort our directory, we'll need a lowercase string function:

```
string strlower(string s) {
    auto char_lower = [] (const char& c) -> char {
        if(c >= 'A' && c <= 'Z') return c + ('a' -
          'A');
        else return c;
    };
    std::transform(s.begin(), s.end(), s.begin(),
      char_lower);
    return s;
}
```

- We need a comparison predicate for sorting directory_entry objects by the lowercase of the path name:

```
bool dircmp_lc(const de& lhs, const de& rhs) {
    const auto lhstr{ lhs.path().string() };
    const auto rhstr{ rhs.path().string() };
    return strlower(lhstr) < strlower(rhstr);
}
```

- `size_string()` returns abbreviated values for reporting file size in gigabytes, megabytes, kilobytes, or bytes:

```
string size_string(const uintmax_t fsize) {
    constexpr const uintmax_t kilo{ 1024 };
    constexpr const uintmax_t mega{ kilo * kilo };
    constexpr const uintmax_t giga{ mega * kilo };

    if(fsize >= giga ) return format("{}{}",
        (fsize + giga / 2) / giga, 'G');
    else if (fsize >= mega) return format("{}{}",
        (fsize + mega / 2) / mega, 'M');
    else if (fsize >= kilo) return format("{}{}",
        (fsize + kilo / 2) / kilo, 'K');
    else return format("{}B", fsize);
}
```

- `entry_size()` returns the size of a file or, if it's a directory, the recursive size of the directory:

```
uintmax_t entry_size(const fs::path& p) {
    if(fs::is_regular_file(p)) return
        fs::file_size(p);
    uintmax_t accum{};
    if(fs::is_directory(p) && ! fs::is_symlink(p)) {
        for(auto& e : dit{ p }) {
            accum += entry_size(e.path());
        }
    }
    return accum;
}
```

- In `main()`, we start with declarations and test if we have a valid directory to search:

```
int main(const int argc, const char** argv) {
    auto dir{ argc > 1 ?
        fs::path(argv[1]) : fs::current_path() };
    vector<de> entries{};
    uintmax_t accum{};
```

```
    if (!exists(dir)) {
        cout << format("path {} does not exist\n",
          dir);
        return 1;
    }
    if(!is_directory(dir)) {
        cout << format("{} is not a directory\n",
          dir);
        return 1;
    }
    cout << format("{}:\n", absolute(dir));
```

For our directory path, dir, we use argv[1] if we have an argument; otherwise, we use current_path() for the current directory. Then we set up an environment for our usage counter:

- The vector of directory_entry objects is used for sorting our response.

- accum is used to accumulate values for our final size total.

- We make sure dir exists and is a directory before proceeding to examine the directory.

- Next, a simple loop to populate the vector. Once populated, we sort entries using our dircmp_lc() function as a comparison predicate:

```
    for (const auto& e : dit{ dir }) {
        entries.emplace_back(e.path());
    }
    std::sort(entries.begin(), entries.end(), dircmp_lc);
```

- Now that everything is set up, we can accumulate results from the sorted vector of directory_entry objects:

```
    for (const auto& e : entries) {
        fs::path p{ e };
        uintmax_t esize{ entry_size(p) };
        string dir_flag{};

        accum += esize;
        if(is_directory(p) && !is_symlink(p)) dir_flag =
```

```
        " ▽";
    cout << format("{:>5} {}{}\n",
        size_string(esize), p.filename(), dir_flag);
}

cout << format("{:->25}\n", "");
cout << format("total bytes: {} ({})\n",
    make_commas(accum), size_string(accum));
```

The call to `entry_size()` returns the size of the file or directory represented in the `directory_entry` object.

If the current entry is a directory (and not a *symbolic link*), we add a symbol to indicate it's a directory. I chose an inverted triangle. You may use anything here.

After the loop is complete, we display the accumulated size in both bytes with commas, and the abbreviated notation from `size_string()`.

Our output:

```
/home/billw/working/cpp-stl-wkbk/chap10:
327K bwgrep
  3K bwgrep.cpp
199K dir
  4K dir.cpp
176K formatter
905B formatter.cpp
  0B include
  1K Makefile
181K path-ops
  1K path-ops.cpp
327K rerename
  2K rerename.cpp
 11K testdir ▽
 11K testdir-backup ▽
203K working
  3K working.cpp
-------------------------
total bytes: 1,484,398 (1M)
```

How it works...

The `fs::file_size()` function returns a `uintmax_t` value that represents the size of the file as the largest natural unsigned integer on a given platform. While this is normally a 64-bit integer on most 64-bit systems, a notable exception is Windows, which uses a 32-bit integer. This means that while `size_t` may work for this value on some systems, it fails to compile on Windows because it may try to promote a 64-bit value to a 32-bit value.

The `entry_size()` function takes a `path` object and returns a `uintmax_t` value:

```
uintmax_t entry_size(const fs::path& p) {
    if(fs::is_regular_file(p)) return fs::file_size(p);

    uintmax_t accum{};
    if(fs::is_directory(p) && !fs::is_symlink(p)) {
        for(auto& e : dit{ p }) {
            accum += entry_size(e.path());
        }
    }
    return accum;
}
```

The function checks for a regular file and returns the size of the file. Otherwise, it checks for a directory that is not also a symbolic link. We just want the size of the files in a directory, so we don't want to follow symbolic links. (Symbolic links may also cause reference loops, leading to a runaway condition.)

If we find a directory, we loop through it, calling `entry_size()` for each file we encounter. This is a recursive loop, so we eventually end up with the size of the directory.

11
A Few More Ideas

We've learned some useful techniques in this book, including optional values, containers, iterators, algorithms, smart pointers, and more. We've seen examples of these concepts in use, and we've had the opportunity to experiment and apply them to some small projects. Let's now apply these techniques to a few more practical ideas.

In this chapter, we cover the following recipes:

- Create a trie class for search suggestions
- Calculate the error sum of two vectors
- Build your own algorithm: `split`
- Leverage existing algorithms: `gather`
- Remove consecutive whitespace
- Convert numbers to words

Technical requirement

You can find the code files for this chapter on GitHub at `https://github.com/PacktPublishing/CPP-20-STL-Cookbook/tree/main/chap11`.

Create a trie class for search suggestions

A *trie*, sometimes called a *prefix tree*, is a type of search tree, commonly used for predictive text and other search applications. A trie is a recursive structure designed for depth-first searches, where each *node* is both a key and another trie.

A common use case is a *trie of strings*, where each node is a string in a sentence. For example:

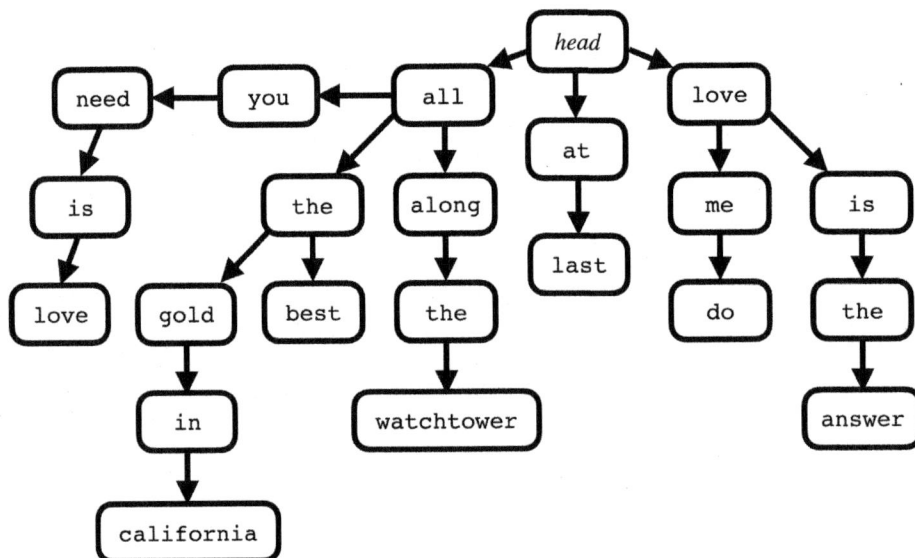

Figure 11.1 – A trie of strings

We often start a search at the *head* of a trie, looking for sentences that begin with a specific word. In this example, when I search for `all`, I get three nodes: `you`, `the`, and `along`. If I search for `love`, I get `me` and `is`.

A string trie is commonly used for creating search suggestions. Here we will implement a string trie using `std::map` for the trie structure.

How to do it...

In this recipe, we create a recursive `trie` class that stores nodes in a `std::map` container. It's a simple solution for a small in-memory trie. This is a rather large class, so we'll only show the important parts here.

For the full class, please see the source code at `https://github.com/PacktPublishing/CPP-20-STL-Cookbook/blob/main/chap11/trie.cpp`.

- We have one convenience alias:

```
using ilcstr = initializer_list<const char *>;
```

We use `ilcstr` in for searching the `trie`.

- We'll put this class in a private namespace to avoid collisions:

```
namespace bw {
    using std::map;
    using std::deque;
    using std::initializer_list;
```

We have a few `using` statements in this namespace for convenience.

- The class itself is called `trie`. It has three data members:

```
class trie {
    using get_t = deque<deque<string>>;
    using nodes_t = map<string, trie>;
    using result_t = std::optional<const trie*>;

    nodes_t nodes{};
    mutable get_t result_dq{};
    mutable deque<string> prefix_dq{};
```

The `trie` class has a few local type aliases:

- `get_t` is a deque of deque of `string`, used for string results.

- `nodes_t` is a map of `trie` classes with `string` keys.

- `result_t` is an `optional` of a pointer to a `trie`, for returning search results. An empty `trie` is a valid result, so we use an `optional` value.

The `nodes` object is used for holding a recursive map of nodes, where each node on a `trie` is another `trie`.

- The public interface often calls utility functions in the private interface. For example, the `insert()` method takes an `initializer_list` object and calls the private function `_insert()`:

```
void insert(const ilcstr& il) {
    _insert(il.begin(), il.end());
}
```

The private _insert() function does the work of inserting elements:

```
template <typename It>
void _insert(It it, It end_it) {
    if(it == end_it) return;
    nodes[*it]._insert(++it, end_it);
}
```

This facilitates the recursive function calls necessary to navigate the trie. Note that referencing a key that does not appear in a map creates an empty element with that key. So, the line that calls _insert() on a nodes element creates an empty trie object if the element doesn't already exist.

- The get() method returns a get_t object, which is an alias for a deque of deque of string. This allows us to return multiple sets of results:

```
get_t& get() const {
    result_dq.clear();
    deque<string> dq{};
    _get(dq, result_dq);
    return result_dq;
}
```

The get() method calls the private _get() function, which recursively traverses the trie:

```
void _get(deque<string>& dq, get_t& r_dq) const {
    if(empty()) {
        r_dq.emplace_back(dq);
        dq.clear();
    }
    for(const auto& p : nodes) {
        dq.emplace_back(p.first);
        p.second._get(dq, r_dq);
    }
}
```

- The `find_prefix()` function returns a deque with all matches to a partial string.

```
deque<string>& find_prefix(const char * s) const {
    _find_prefix(s, prefix_dq);
    return prefix_dq;
}
```

The public interface calls the private function `_find_prefix()`:

```
void _find_prefix(const string& s, auto& pre_dq) const {
    if(empty()) return;
    for(const auto& [k, v] : nodes) {
        if(k.starts_with(s)) {
            pre_dq.emplace_back(k);
            v._find_prefix(k, pre_dq);
        }
    }
}
```

The private `_find_prefix()` function traverses the `trie` recursively, comparing the prefix with beginning of each key. The `starts_with()` method is new with C++20. With an older STL, you could use the `find()` method and check the return value for 0:

```
if(k.find(s) == 0) {
    . . .
```

- The `search()` function returns an `optional<const trie*>`, aliased as `result_t`. It has two overloads:

```
result_t search(const ilcstr& il) const {
    return _search(il.begin(), il.end());
}
result_t search(const string& s) const {
    const ilcstr il{s.c_str()};
    return _search(il.begin(), il.end());
}
```

These methods pass iterators to the private member function _search(), which does the work of the search:

```
template <typename It>
result_t _search(It it, It end_it) const {
    if(it == end_it) return {this};
    auto found_it = nodes.find(*it);
    if(found_it == nodes.end()) return {};
    return found_it->second._search(++it, end_it);
}
```

The _search() function searches recursively until it finds a match, then returns a node in the result_t object. If it finds no match, it returns the non-value optional.

- We also have two overloads of a print_trie_prefix() function. This function prints the contents of a trie from a prefix, used as a search key. One version uses a string for the prefix, the other uses an initializer_list of C-strings:

```
void print_trie_prefix(const bw::trie& t,
        const string& prefix) {
    auto& trie_strings = t.get();
    cout << format("results for \"{}...\":\n", prefix);
    for(auto& dq : trie_strings) {
        cout << format("{} ", prefix);
        for(const auto& s : dq) cout << format("{} ", s);
        cout << '\n';
    }
}

void print_trie_prefix(const bw::trie& t,
        const ilcstr & prefix) {
    string sprefix{};
    for(const auto& s : prefix) sprefix +=
        format("{} ", s);
    print_trie_prefix(t, sprefix);
}
```

These functions call the `get()` member function to retrieve the results from the `trie`.

- Now we can test the `trie` class in the `main()` function. First, we declare a `trie` and insert some sentences:

```
int main() {
    bw::trie ts;
    ts.insert({ "all", "along", "the", "watchtower" });
    ts.insert({ "all", "you", "need", "is", "love" });
    ts.insert({ "all", "shook", "up" });
    ts.insert({ "all", "the", "best" });
    ts.insert({ "all", "the", "gold", "in",
        "california" });
    ts.insert({ "at", "last" });
    ts.insert({ "love", "the", "one", "you're",
        "with" });
    ts.insert({ "love", "me", "do" });
    ts.insert({ "love", "is", "the", "answer" });
    ts.insert({ "loving", "you" });
    ts.insert({ "long", "tall", "sally" });
    ...
```

The `insert()` calls pass an `initializer_list` with all the strings of a sentence. Each of the strings of a sentence are inserted into the hierarchy of the `trie`.

- Now we can search the trie. Here's a simple search for the single string `"love"`.

```
const auto prefix = {"love"};
if (auto st = ts.search(prefix); st.have_result) {
    print_trie_prefix(*st.t, prefix);
}
cout << '\n';
```

This calls `ts.search()` with an `initializer_list` of one C-string, called `prefix`. The result, along with the `prefix`, is then passed to the `print_trie_prefix()` function.

The output is:

```
results for "love...":
love is the answer
love me do
love the one you're with
```

- Here's a search for a two-string prefix:

```
const auto prefix = {"all", "the"};
if (auto st = ts.search(prefix); st.have_result) {
    print_trie_prefix(*st.t, prefix);
}
cout << '\n';
```

Output:

```
results for "all the ...":
all the   best
all the   gold in california
```

- And here's a search for a partial prefix, using the find_prefix() function:

```
const char * prefix{ "lo" };
auto prefix_dq = ts.find_prefix(prefix);
for(const auto& s : prefix_dq) {
    cout << format("match: {} -> {}\n", prefix, s);
    if (auto st = ts.search(s); st.have_result) {
        print_trie_prefix(*st.t, s);
    }
}
cout << '\n';
```

Output:

```
match: lo -> long
results for "long...":
long tall sally
match: lo -> love
results for "love...":
love is the answer
love me do
```

```
love the one you're with
match: lo -> loving
results for "loving...":
loving you
```

The find_prefix() search returned several results, each of which we passed to a search of its own, resulting in several results for each result.

How it works...

The data for the trie class is stored in recursive map containers. Each node in the map contains another trie object, which in turn has its own map node.

```
using nodes_t = map<string, trie>
```

The _insert() function takes begin and end iterators, and uses them to recursively call _insert() on new nodes:

```
template <typename It>
void _insert(It it, It end_it) {
    if(it == end_it) return;
    nodes[*it]._insert(++it, end_it);
}
```

Likewise, the _search() function recursively calls _search() on the nodes it finds:

```
template <typename It>
result_t _search(It it, It end_it) const {
    if(it == end_it) return {this};
    auto found_it = nodes.find(*it);
    if(found_it == nodes.end()) return {};
    return found_it->second._search(++it, end_it);
}
```

This recursive approach using std::map allows us to implement a trie class concisely and efficiently.

Calculate the error sum of two vectors

Given two similar vectors that differ only by quantization or resolution, we can use the `inner_product()` algorithm to calculate an *error sum*, defined as:

$$e = \sum_{i=1}^{n} (a_i - b_i)^2$$

Figure 11.2 – Error sum definition

Where *e* is the error sum, the sum of the square of the difference between a series of points in two vectors.

We can use the `inner_product()` algorithm, from the `<numeric>` header, to calculate the error sum between two vectors.

How to do it...

In this recipe we define two vectors, each with a *sine wave*. One `vector` has values of type `double` and the other has type `int`. This gives us vectors that differ in quantization, because the `int` type cannot represent fractional values. We then use `inner_product()` to calculate the error sum between the two vectors:

- In our `main()` function we define our vectors and a handy `index` variable:

```
int main() {
    constexpr size_t vlen{ 100 };
    vector<double> ds(vlen);
    vector<int> is(vlen);
    size_t index{};
    ...
```

ds is the vector of double sine waves and is is the vector of int sine waves. Each vector has 100 elements to hold a sine wave. The index variable is used to initialize the vector objects.

- We generate the sine wave in the vector of double, using a loop and a lambda:

```
auto sin_gen = [&index] {
    return 5.0 * sin(index++ * 2 * pi / 100);
};
for(auto& v : ds) v = sin_gen();
```

The lambda captures a reference to the index variable so it can be incremented.

The pi constant is from the std::numbers library.

- We now have a double sine wave and we can use it to derive the int version:

```
index = 0;
for(auto& v : is) {
    v = static_cast<int>(round(ds.at(index++)));
}
```

This takes each point from ds, rounds it, casts it to an int, and updates it in position in the is container.

- We display our sine waves with a simple loop:

```
for(const auto& v : ds) cout << format("{:-5.2f} ", v);
cout << "\n\n";
for(const auto& v : is) cout << format("{:-3d} ", v);
cout << "\n\n";
```

Our output is the sine waves as data points in the two containers:

```
0.00   0.31   0.63   0.94   1.24   1.55   1.84   2.13   2.41
2.68   2.94   3.19   3.42   3.64   3.85   4.05   4.22   4.38
4.52   4.65   4.76   4.84   4.91   4.96   4.99   5.00   4.99
4.96   4.91   4.84   4.76   4.65   4.52   4.38   4.22   4.05
3.85   3.64   3.42   3.19   2.94   2.68   2.41   2.13   1.84
1.55   1.24   0.94   0.63   0.31   0.00  -0.31  -0.63  -0.94
-1.24  -1.55  -1.84  -2.13  -2.41  -2.68  -2.94  -3.19  -3.42
-3.64  -3.85  -4.05  -4.22  -4.38  -4.52  -4.65  -4.76  -4.84
-4.91  -4.96  -4.99  -5.00  -4.99  -4.96  -4.91  -4.84  -4.76
-4.65  -4.52  -4.38  -4.22  -4.05  -3.85  -3.64  -3.42  -3.19
-2.94  -2.68  -2.41  -2.13  -1.84  -1.55  -1.24  -0.94  -0.63
-0.31

0    0    1    1    1    2    2    2    2    3    3    3    3    4    4
4    4    4    5    5    5    5    5    5    5    5    5    5    5    5
5    5    5    4    4    4    4    4    3    3    3    3    2    2    2
2    1    1    1    0    0    0   -1   -1   -1   -2   -2   -2   -2   -3
-3   -3   -3   -4   -4   -4   -4   -4   -5   -5   -5   -5   -5   -5
-5   -5   -5   -5   -5   -5   -5   -5   -5   -4   -4   -4   -4   -4
-3   -3   -3   -3   -2   -2   -2   -2   -1   -1   -1    0
```

- Now we calculate the error sum using `inner_product()`:

```
double errsum = inner_product(ds.begin(), ds.end(),
    is.begin(), 0.0, std::plus<double>(),
    [](double a, double b){ return pow(a - b, 2); });
cout << format("error sum: {:.3f}\n\n", errsum);
```

The lambda expression returns the $(a_i - b_i)^2$ part of the formula. The `std::plus()` algorithm performs the sum operation.

Output:

```
error sum: 7.304
```

How it works...

The `inner_product()` algorithm computes a sum of products on the first input range. Its signature is:

```
T inner_product(InputIt1 first1, InputIt1 last1,
    InputIt2 first2, T init, BinaryOperator1 op1,
    BinaryOperator2 op2)
```

The function takes two binary operator functors, op1 and op2. The first op1 is for the *sum* and the second op2 is for the *product*. We use `std::plus()` as the sum operator, and a lambda as the product operator.

The init parameter can be used as a starting value or bias. We pass it the literal value, `0.0`.

The return value is the accumulated sum of the products.

There's more...

We can calculate an accumulated error sum by putting `inner_product()` in a loop:

```
cout << "accumulated error:\n";
for (auto it{ds.begin()}; it != ds.end(); ++it) {
    double accumsum = inner_product(ds.begin(), it,
        is.begin(), 0.0, std::plus<double>(),
        [](double a, double b){ return pow(a - b, 2); });
    cout << format("{:-5.2f} ", accumsum);
}
cout << '\n';
```

Output:

```
accumulated error:
0.00  0.00  0.10  0.24  0.24  0.30  0.51  0.53  0.55  0.72
0.82  0.82  0.86  1.04  1.16  1.19  1.19  1.24  1.38  1.61
1.73  1.79  1.82  1.82  1.83  1.83  1.83  1.83  1.83  1.84
1.86  1.92  2.04  2.27  2.42  2.46  2.47  2.49  2.61  2.79
2.83  2.83  2.93  3.10  3.12  3.14  3.35  3.41  3.41  3.55
3.65  3.65  3.75  3.89  3.89  3.95  4.16  4.19  4.20  4.37
4.47  4.48  4.51  4.69  4.82  4.84  4.84  4.89  5.03  5.26
5.38  5.44  5.47  5.48  5.48  5.48  5.48  5.48  5.48  5.49
5.51  5.57  5.70  5.92  6.07  6.12  6.12  6.14  6.27  6.45
6.48  6.48  6.59  6.75  6.77  6.80  7.00  7.06  7.07  7.21
```

This may be useful in some statistical applications.

Build your own algorithm: split

The STL has a rich `algorithm` library. Yet, on occasion you may find it missing something you need. One common need is a `split` function.

A `split` function splits a string on a character separator. For example, here's a Unix `/etc/passwd` file from a standard Debian installation:

```
root:x:0:0:root:/root:/bin/bash
daemon:x:1:1:daemon:/usr/sbin:/usr/sbin/nologin
bin:x:2:2:bin:/bin:/usr/sbin/nologin
sys:x:3:3:sys:/dev:/usr/sbin/nologin
sync:x:4:65534:sync:/bin:/bin/sync
```

Each field is separated by a colon : character, where the fields are:

1. Login name

2. Optional encrypted password

3. User ID

4. Group ID

5. Username or comment

6. Home directory

7. Optional command interpreter

This is a standard file in POSIX-based operating systems, and there are others like it. Most scripting languages include a built-in function for splitting a string on a separator. There are simple ways to do this in C++. Still, `std::string` is just another container in the STL, and a generic algorithm that splits a container on a separator could be a useful addition to the toolbox. So, let's build one.

How to do it...

In this recipe, we build a generic algorithm that splits a container on a separator and puts the results in a target container.

- Our algorithm is in the bw namespace, to avoid collisions with `std`:

```cpp
namespace bw {
    template<typename It, typename Oc, typename V,
        typename Pred>
    It split(It it, It end_it, Oc& dest,
            const V& sep, Pred& f) {
        using SliceContainer = typename
          Oc::value_type;
        while(it != end_it) {
            SliceContainer dest_elm{};
            auto slice{ it };
            while(slice != end_it) {
                if(f(*slice, sep)) break;
                dest_elm.push_back(*slice++);
            }
            dest.push_back(dest_elm);
            if(slice == end_it) return end_it;
            it = ++slice;
        }
        return it;
    }
};
```

The `split()` algorithm searches a container for separators and collects the separated slices into a new output container, where each slice is a container within the output container.

We want the `split()` algorithm to be as generic as possible, just like those in the `algorithm` library. This means that all the parameters are templated, and the code will work with a comprehensive variety of parameter types.

First, let's look at the template parameters:

- `It` is the input iterator type for the source container.
- `Oc` is the output container type. This is a container of containers.
- `V` is the separator type.
- `Pred` is for the predicate functor.

Our output type is a container of containers. It needs to hold containers of slices. It could be `vector<string>`, where the string values are slices, or `vector<vector<int>>`, where the inner `vector<int>` contains the slices. This means we need to derive the type of the inner container from the output container type. We do that with the `using` declaration in the body of the function.

```
using SliceContainer = typename Oc::value_type;
```

This is also why we cannot use an output iterator for the output parameter. By definition, an output iterator cannot determine the type of its contents and its `value_type` is set to `void`.

We use `SliceContainer` to define a temporary container that is added to the output container with the statement:

```
dest.push_back(dest_elm);
```

- The predicate is a binary operator that compares an input element with the separator. We include a default equality operator in the `bw` namespace:

```
constexpr auto eq = [](const auto& el, const auto& sep) {
    return el == sep;
};
```

- We also include a specialization of `split()` that uses the `eq` operator by default:

```
template<typename It, typename Oc, typename V>
It split(It it, const It end_it, Oc& dest, const V& sep)
{
    return split(it, end_it, dest, sep, eq);
}
```

- Because splitting `string` objects is a common use case for this algorithm, we include a helper function for that specific purpose:

```
template<typename Cin, typename Cout, typename V>
Cout& strsplit(const Cin& str, Cout& dest, const V& sep)
{
    split(str.begin(), str.end(), dest, sep, eq);
    return dest;
}
```

- We test our split algorithm `main()`, starting with a `string` object:

```
int main() {
    constexpr char strsep{ ':' };
    const string str
        { "sync:x:4:65534:sync:/bin:/bin/sync" };
    vector<string> dest_vs{};
    bw::split(str.begin(), str.end(), dest_vs, strsep,
        bw::eq);
    for(const auto& e : dest_vs) cout <<
        format("[{}] ", e);
    cout << '\n';
}
```

We use a string from the `/etc/passwd` file to test our algorithm, with this result:

```
[sync] [x] [4] [65534] [sync] [/bin] [/bin/sync]
```

- It's even simpler using our `strsplit()` helper function:

```
vector<string> dest_vs2{};
bw::strsplit(str, dest_vs2, strsep);
for(const auto& e : dest_vs2) cout << format("[{}] ", e);
cout << '\n';
```

Output:

```
[sync] [x] [4] [65534] [sync] [/bin] [/bin/sync]
```

This would make it easy to parse the `/etc/passwd` file.

- Of course, we can use the same algorithm with any container:

```
constexpr int intsep{ -1 };
vector<int> vi{ 1, 2, 3, 4, intsep, 5, 6, 7, 8, intsep,
     9, 10, 11, 12 };
vector<vector<int>> dest_vi{};
bw::split(vi.begin(), vi.end(), dest_vi, intsep);
for(const auto& v : dest_vi) {
    string s;
    for(const auto& e : v) s += format("{}", e);
    cout << format("[{}] ", s);
}
cout << '\n';
```

Output:

```
[1234] [5678] [9101112]
```

How it works...

The split algorithm itself is relatively simple. The magic in this recipe is in the use of templates to make it as generic as possible.

The derived type in the using declaration allows us to create a container for use with the output container:

```
using SliceContainer = typename Oc::value_type;
```

This gives us a SliceContainer type that we can use to create a container for the slices:

```
SliceContainer dest_elm{};
```

This is a temporary container that is added to the output container for each slice:

```
dest.push_back(dest_elm);
```

Leverage existing algorithms: gather

gather() is an example of an algorithm that leverages existing algorithms.

The gather() algorithm takes a pair of container iterators and moves the elements that satisfy a predicate toward a *pivot* position within the sequence, returning a pair of iterators that contains the elements that satisfy the predicate.

For example, we could use a `gather` algorithm to sort all the even numbers to the mid-point of a `vector`:

```
vector<int> vint{ 0, 1, 2, 3, 4, 5, 6, 7, 8, 9 };
gather(vint.begin(), vint.end(), mid(vint), is_even);
for(const auto& el : vint) cout << el;
```

Our output is:

```
1302468579
```

Notice that the even numbers are all in the middle of the output.

In this recipe, we will implement a `gather` algorithm using standard STL algorithms.

How to do it...

Our `gather` algorithm uses the `std::stable_partition()` algorithm to move items before the pivot iterator and again to move items past the pivot.

- We put the algorithm in the bw namespace to avoid collisions.

```
namespace bw {
using std::stable_partition;
using std::pair;
using std::not_fn;

template <typename It, typename Pred>
pair<It, It> gather(It first, It last, It pivot,
        Pred pred) {
    return {stable_partition(first, pivot, not_fn(pred)),
        stable_partition(pivot, last, pred)};
}
};
```

The `gather()` algorithm returns a `pair` of iterators, returned from two calls to `stable_partition()`.

- We also include some helper lambdas:

```
constexpr auto midit = [] (auto& v) {
    return v.begin() + (v.end() - v.begin()) / 2;
};
constexpr auto is_even = [] (auto i) {
    return i % 2 == 0;
};
constexpr auto is_even_char = [] (auto c) {
    if(c >= '0' && c <= '9') return (c - '0') % 2 == 0;
    else return false;
};
```

These three lambdas are as follows:

- midit returns an iterator at the midpoint of a container, for use as a pivot point.

- is_even returns Boolean true if the value is even, for use as a predicate.

- is_even_char returns Boolean true if the value is a character between '0' and '9' and is even, for use as a predicate.

- We call gather() from the main() function with a vector of int like this:

```
int main() {
    vector<int> vint{ 0, 1, 2, 3, 4, 5, 6, 7, 8, 9 };
    auto gathered_even = bw::gather(vint.begin(),
        vint.end(), bw::midit(vint), bw::is_even);
    for(const auto& el : vint) cout << el;
    cout << '\n';
}
```

Our output shows that the even numbers have been gathered in the middle:

```
1302468579
```

The gather() function returns a pair of iterators that contain just the even values:

```
auto& [it1, it2] = gathered_even;
for(auto it{ it1 }; it < it2; ++it) cout << *it;
cout << '\n';
```

Output:

```
02468
```

- We can set the pivot point to the begin() or end() iterators:

```
bw::gather(vint.begin(), vint.end(), vint.begin(),
    bw::is_even);
for(const auto& el : vint) cout << el;
cout << '\n';
bw::gather(vint.begin(), vint.end(), vint.end(),
    bw::is_even);
for(const auto& el : vint) cout << el;
cout << '\n';
```

Output:

```
0246813579
1357902468
```

- Because gather() is iterator-based, we can use it with any container. Here's a string of character digits:

```
string jenny{ "867-5309" };
bw::gather(jenny.begin(), jenny.end(), jenny.end(),
    bw::is_even_char);
for(const auto& el : jenny) cout << el;
cout << '\n';
```

This moves all the even digits to the end of the string:

Output:

```
7-539860
```

How it works...

The gather() function uses the std::stable_partition() algorithm to move the elements that match the predicate to the pivot point.

gather() has two calls to stable_partition(), one with the predicate, and one with the predicate negated:

```
template <typename It, typename Pred>
pair<It, It> gather(It first, It last, It pivot, Pred pred) {
    return { stable_partition(first, pivot, not_fn(pred)),
             stable_partition(pivot, last, pred) };
}
```

The iterators returned from the two stable_partition() calls are returned in the pair.

Remove consecutive whitespace

When receiving input from users, it's common to end up with excessive consecutive whitespace characters in your strings. This recipe presents a function for removing consecutive spaces, even when it includes tabs or other whitespace characters.

How to do it...

This function leverages the std::unique() algorithm to remove consecutive whitespace characters from a string.

- In the bw namespace, we start with a function to detect whitespace:

```
template<typename T>
bool isws(const T& c) {
    constexpr const T whitespace[]{ " \t\r\n\v\f" };
    for(const T& wsc : whitespace) {
        if(c == wsc) return true;
    }
    return false;
}
```

This templated isws() function should work with any character type.

- The `delws()` function uses `std::unique()` to erase consecutive whitespace in a `string`:

```
string delws(const string& s) {
    string outstr{s};
    auto its = unique(outstr.begin(), outstr.end(),
        [](const auto &a, const auto &b) {
            return isws(a) && isws(b);
        });
    outstr.erase(its, outstr.end());
    outstr.shrink_to_fit();
    return outstr;
}
```

`delws()` makes a copy of the input string, removes consecutive whitespace, and returns the new string.

- We call it with a `string` from `main()`:

```
int main() {
    const string s{ "big      bad    \t   wolf" };
    const string s2{ bw::delws(s) };
    cout << format("[{}]\n", s);
    cout << format("[{}]\n", s2);
    return 0;
}
```

Output:

```
[big      bad          wolf]
[big bad wolf]
```

How it works...

This function uses the `std::unique()` algorithm with a comparison lambda to find consecutive whitespace in a `string` object.

The comparison lambda calls our own `isws()` function to determine if we have found consecutive whitespace:

```cpp
auto its = unique(outstr.begin(), outstr.end(),
    [](const auto &a, const auto &b) {
        return isws(a) && isws(b);
    });
```

We could use the `isspace()` function from the standard library, but it's a standard C function that depends on a narrowing type conversion from `int` to `char`. This may issue warnings on some modern C++ compilers and is not guaranteed to work without an explicit cast. Our `isws()` function uses a templated type and should work on any system, and with any specialization of `std::string`.

Convert numbers to words

Over the course of my career, I've used a lot of programming languages. When learning a new language, I like to have a project to work on that exposes me to the nuances of the language. The numwords class is one of my favorite exercises for this purpose. I have written it in dozens of languages over the years, including several times in C and C++.

numwords is a class that spells out a number in words. It can be useful for banking and accounting applications. It looks like this in use:

```cpp
int main() {
    bw::numword nw{};
    uint64_t n;
    nw = 3; bw::print("n is {}, {}\n", nw.getnum(), nw);
    nw = 47; bw::print("n is {}, {}\n", nw.getnum(), nw);
    n = 100073; bw::print("n is {}, {}\n", n,
        bw::numword{n});
    n = 1000000001; bw::print("n is {}, {}\n", n,
        bw::numword{n});
    n = 123000000000; bw::print("n is {}, {}\n", n,
        bw::numword{n});
    n = 1474142398007; bw::print("n is {}, {}\n", n,
        nw.words(n));
    n = 999999999999999999; bw::print("n is {}, {}\n", n,
        nw.words(n));
```

```
n = 1000000000000000000; bw::print("n is {}, {}\n", n,
    nw.words(n));
}
```

Output:

```
n is 3, three
n is 47, forty-seven
n is 100073, one hundred thousand seventy-three
n is 1000000001, one billion one
n is 123000000000, one hundred twenty-three billion
n is 1474142398007, one trillion four hundred seventy-four
billion one hundred forty-two million three hundred ninety-
eight thousand seven
n is 999999999999999999, nine hundred ninety-nine quadrillion
nine hundred ninety-nine trillion nine hundred ninety-nine
billion nine hundred ninety-nine million nine hundred ninety-
nine thousand nine hundred ninety-nine
n is 1000000000000000000, error
```

How to do it...

This recipe originated as an exercise in creating production-ready code. For that reason, it's in three different files:

- numword.h is the header/interface file for the numwords class.

- numword.cpp is the implementation file for the numwords class.

- numword-test.cpp is the application file for testing the numword class.

The class itself is about 180 lines of code so we'll just cover the highlights here. You can find the full source code at https://github.com/PacktPublishing/CPP-20-STL-Cookbook/tree/main/chap11/numword.

- In the numword.h file, we put the class in the bw namespace and start with some using statements:

```
namespace bw {
    using std::string;
    using std::string_view;
    using numnum = uint64_t;
    using bufstr = std::unique_ptr<string>;
```

We use `string` and `string_view` objects throughout the code.

`uint64_t` is our primary integer type because it will hold very large numbers. Because the class is called `numword`, I like `numnum` for the integer type.

`_bufstr` is the main output buffer. It's a `string` wrapped in a `unique_ptr`, which handles the memory management for automatic RAII compliance.

- We also have a few constants for various purposes:

```
constexpr numnum maxnum = 999'999'999'999'999'999;
constexpr int zero_i{ 0 };
constexpr int five_i{ 5 };
constexpr numnum zero{ 0 };
constexpr numnum ten{ 10 };
constexpr numnum twenty{ 20 };
constexpr numnum hundred{ 100 };
constexpr numnum thousand{ 1000 };
```

The `maxnum` constant translates to "nine hundred ninety-nine quadrillion nine hundred ninety-nine trillion nine hundred ninety-nine billion nine hundred ninety-nine million nine hundred ninety-nine thousand nine hundred ninety-nine," which should be sufficient for most purposes.

The rest of the `numnum` constants are used to avoid literals in the code.

- The main data structures are `constexpr` arrays of `string_view` objects, representing the words used in the output. The `string_view` class is perfect for these constants, as it provides encapsulation with minimum overhead:

```
constexpr string_view errnum{ "error" };
constexpr string_view _singles[] {
    "zero", "one", "two", "three", "four", "five",
    "six", "seven", "eight", "nine"
};
constexpr string_view _teens[] {
    "ten", "eleven", "twelve", "thirteen", "fourteen",
    "fifteen", "sixteen", "seventeen", "eighteen",
    "nineteen"
};
constexpr string_view _tens[] {
    errnum, errnum, "twenty", "thirty", "forty",
```

```
        "fifty", "sixty", "seventy", "eighty", "ninety",
    };
    constexpr string_view _hundred_string = "hundred";
    constexpr string_view _powers[] {
        errnum, "thousand", "million", "billion",
        "trillion", "quadrillion"
    };
```

The words are grouped into sections, useful in translating numbers to words. Many languages use a similar breakdown so this structure should translate easily to those languages.

- The numword class has a few private members:

```
    class numword {
        bufstr _buf{ std::make_unique<string>(string{}) };
        numnum _num{};
        bool _hyphen_flag{ false };
```

- _buf is the output string buffer. Its memory is managed by a unique_ptr.

- _num holds the current numeric value.

- _hyphen_flag is used during the translation process to insert a hyphen between words, rather than a space character.

- These private methods are used to manipulate the output buffer.

```
    void clearbuf();
    size_t bufsize();
    void appendbuf(const string& s);
    void appendbuf(const string_view& s);
    void appendbuf(const char c);
    void appendspace();
```

There is also a pow_i() private method used to calculate x^y with numnum types:

```
    numnum pow_i(const numnum n, const numnum p);
```

pow_i() is used to discriminate parts of the numeric value for word output.

- The public interface includes constructors and various ways to call the `words()` method, which does the work of translating a numnum to a `string` of words:

```cpp
numword(const numnum& num = 0) : _num(num) {}
numword(const numword& nw) : _num(nw.getnum()) {}
const char * version() const { return _version; }
void setnum(const numnum& num) { _num = num; }
numnum getnum() const { return _num; }
numnum operator= (const numnum& num);
const string& words();
const string& words(const numnum& num);
const string& operator() (const numnum& num) {
    return words(num); };
```

- In the implementation file, numword.cpp, the bulk of the work is handled in the `words()` member function:

```cpp
const string& numword::words( const numnum& num ) {
    numnum n{ num };
    clearbuf();
    if(n > maxnum) {
        appendbuf(errnum);
        return *_buf;
    }
    if (n == 0) {
        appendbuf(_singles[n]);
        return *_buf;
    }
    // powers of 1000
    if (n >= thousand) {
        for(int i{ five_i }; i > zero_i; --i) {
            numnum power{ pow_i(thousand, i) };
            numnum _n{ ( n - ( n % power ) ) / power };
            if (_n) {
                int index = i;
                numword _nw{ _n };
                appendbuf(_nw.words());
                appendbuf(_powers[index]);
```

```
                    n -= _n * power;
                }
            }
        }
        // hundreds
        if (n >= hundred && n < thousand) {
            numnum _n{ ( n - ( n % hundred ) ) / hundred };
            numword _nw{ _n };
            appendbuf(_nw.words());
            appendbuf(_hundred_string);
            n -= _n * hundred;
        }
        // tens
        if (n >= twenty && n < hundred) {
            numnum _n{ ( n - ( n % ten ) ) / ten };
            appendbuf(_tens[_n]);
            n -= _n * ten;
            _hyphen_flag = true;
        }
        // teens
        if (n >= ten && n < twenty) {
            appendbuf(_teens[n - ten]);
            n = zero;
        }
        // singles
        if (n > zero && n < ten) {
            appendbuf(_singles[n]);
        }
        return *_buf;
    }
```

Each part of the function peels off part of the number with a *modulus of a power of ten*, recursively in the case of the thousands, and appends strings from the `string_view` constant arrays.

- There are three overloads of appendbuf(). One appends a string:

```
void numword::appendbuf(const string& s) {
    appendspace();
    _buf->append(s);
}
```

Another appends a string_view:

```
void numword::appendbuf(const string_view& s) {
    appendspace();
    _buf->append(s.data());
}
```

And the third appends a single character:

```
void numword::appendbuf(const char c) {
    _buf->append(1, c);
}
```

The appendspace() method appends a space character or a hyphen, depending on the context:

```
void numword::appendspace() {
    if(bufsize()) {
        appendbuf( _hyphen_flag ? _hyphen : _space);
        _hyphen_flag = false;
    }
}
```

- The numword-test.cpp file is the testing environment for bw::numword. It includes a formatter specialization:

```
template<>
struct std::formatter<bw::numword>:
std::formatter<unsigned> {
    template<typename FormatContext>
    auto format(const bw::numword& nw,
        FormatContext& ctx) {
        bw::numword _nw{nw};
        return format_to(ctx.out(), "{}",
```

```
        _nw.words());
    }
};
```

This allows us to pass a `bw::numword` object directly to `format()`.

- There's also a `print()` function that sends `formatter` output directly to `stdout`, bypassing `cout` and the `iostream` library entirely:

```
namespace bw {
    template<typename... Args> constexpr void print(
            const std::string_view str_fmt, Args&&...
        args) {
        fputs(std::vformat(str_fmt,
            std::make_format_args(args...)).c_str(),
            stdout);
    }
};
```

This allows us to use `print("{}\n", nw)` instead of piping `format()` through `cout`. A function like this will be included in the C++23 standard. It's simple enough to include it like this for now.

- In `main()`, we declare a `bw::numword` object and a `uint64_t` for use in testing:

```
int main() {
    bw::numword nw{};
    uint64_t n{};

    bw::print("n is {}, {}\n", nw.getnum(), nw);
    ...
```

The numword object is initialized to zero, giving us this output from our `print()` statement:

n is 0, zero

- We test a variety of ways to call numword:

```
nw = 3; bw::print("n is {}, {}\n", nw.getnum(), nw);
nw = 47; bw::print("n is {}, {}\n", nw.getnum(), nw);
...
n = 100073; bw::print("n is {}, {}\n", n,
bw::numword{n});
n = 1000000001; bw::print("n is {}, {}\n", n,
bw::numword{n});
...
n = 474142398123; bw::print("n is {}, {}\n", n, nw(n));
n = 1474142398007; bw::print("n is {}, {}\n", n, nw(n));
...
n = 999999999999999999; bw::print("n is {}, {}\n", n,
nw(n));
n = 1000000000000000000; bw::print("n is {}, {}\n", n,
nw(n));
```

Output:

```
n is 3, three
n is 47, forty-seven
...
n is 100073, one hundred thousand seventy-three
n is 1000000001, one billion one
...
n is 474142398123, four hundred seventy-four billion
one hundred forty-two million three hundred ninety-eight
thousand one hundred twenty-three
n is 1474142398007, one trillion four hundred seventy-
four billion one hundred forty-two million three hundred
ninety-eight thousand seven
...
n is 999999999999999999, nine hundred ninety-nine
quadrillion nine hundred ninety-nine trillion nine
hundred ninety-nine billion nine hundred ninety-nine
million nine hundred ninety-nine thousand nine hundred
ninety-nine
n is 1000000000000000000, error
```

How it works...

This class is significantly driven by the data structures. By organizing `string_view` objects into arrays, we can easily translate scalar values into corresponding words:

```
appendbuf(_tens[_n]);  // e.g., _tens[5] = "fifty"
```

The rest of it is mostly the math:

```
numnum power{ pow_i(thousand, i) };
numnum _n{ ( n - ( n % power ) ) / power };
if (_n) {
    int index = i;
    numword _nw{ _n };
    appendbuf(_nw.words());
    appendbuf(_powers[index]);
    n -= _n * power;
}
```

There's more...

I also have a utility that uses the `numwords` class to tell time in words. Its output looks like this:

```
$ ./saytime
three past five
```

In test mode, it gives this output:

```
$ ./saytime test
00:00 midnight
00:01 one past midnight
11:00 eleven o'clock
12:00 noon
13:00 one o'clock
12:29 twenty-nine past noon
12:30 half past noon
12:31 twenty-nine til one
12:15 quarter past noon
12:30 half past noon
```

```
12:45 quarter til one
11:59 one til noon
23:15 quarter past eleven
23:59 one til midnight
12:59 one til one
13:59 one til two
01:60 OOR
24:00 OOR
```

I leave its implementation as an exercise for the reader.

Index

Symbols

\<version\> header
feature test macros, searching
with 16, 17

A

absolute() function 348
accumulated error sum
calculating, by putting inner_
product() in loop 390, 391
algorithm library
lambdas, using as predicates 155-158
algorithms: gather
leveraging 395-399
algorithm: split
building 391-395
algorithms, working with ranges
reference link 34
allocated memory
manging, with std::unique_ptr 270-275
array 53

assign() member function
overriding 240, 241
associative containers, STL
about 54
map 54
multimap 54
multiset 54
set 54
unordered_map 54
unordered_multimap 54
unordered_multiset 54
unordered_set 54
atomic constraint 22
automatic type deduction 41

B

backward iteration
performing, with reverse
iterator adapter 127-130
bidirectional iterator 127
bounded buffer 337, 338
Byte Order Mark (BOM) 235, 236

C

C++20's format library
    used, for formatting text 218-224
canonical() function 348
captures 148
char_traits
    string class, customizing with 237-240
clock classes 264
closure 148, 149
compiled module 25
compile-time decisions
    simplifying, with if constexpr 51, 52
compile-time vectors
    using, with constexpr 7-9
complex structures
    initializing, from file input 232-235
concepts and constraints
    templates, creating with 17-21
concurrency
    about 297
    std::async(), using for 306-312
    std::thread, using for 300-304
consecutive whitespace characters
    removing 399-401
constexpr
    compile-time vectors, using 7-9
    strings, using 7-9
constraint conjunction 21, 22
container adapters, STL
    about 55
    priority_queue 55
    queue 55
    stack 55
container elements
    joining, into string 176-179

containers
    items, deleting with uniform
        erasure functions 56-61
    items, finding 188-190
    merge sort 200-202
    modifying, with std::transform()
        185-187
    sorting 180-185
    values, limiting to range with
        std::clamp() 191-194
copy algorithms
    used, for copying from one
        iterator to another 172-176
copy() member function
    overriding 240, 241
cppreference
    reference link 17
C-string
    about 130
    using 130
custom keys
    unordered_map, using with 79-82

D

data
    sharing, safely with locks 315-323
    sharing, safely with mutex 315-323
data sequences
    permutations, generating of 197-199
data sets
    sampling, with std::sample() 194-197
deduction guide 50
deque
    about 54
    RPN calculator with 84-91

directories
    searching, with grep utility 361-368
directory
    files, listing in 351-360
directory_iterator
    using 368-373
disk usage counter
    creating 373-378

E

elements
    inserting, into map 70-74
elements, from unsorted vector
    deleting, in constant time 61-64
emplace() function 70
equivalent() function 349
error sum
    calculating, of two vectors 388-390
execution policies
    used, for running STL algorithms
        in parallel 312-314

F

feature test macros
    searching, with <version> header 16, 17
Fibonacci sequence 122
file input
    complex structures, initializing
        from 232-235
files
    listing, in directory 351-360
    renaming, with regex 368-373
    searching, with grep utility 361-368
    words, counting 231, 232

filesystem library 343
filter() function 191
find() algorithm 188
find() function 191
first-in, first-out (FIFO) 55, 333
flags
    sharing, with std::atomic 324-326
fold expressions
    about 265, 266
    using, for variadic tuples 265-268
format library
    customization 6, 7
    text, formatting with 2-5
formatter specialization
    writing, for fs::path class 344-347
forward iterators 180
fs::path class
    about 343, 344
    formatter specialization,
        writing for 344-347

G

generator
    about 122
    creating, as iterators 122-126
grep utility
    used, for searching directories
        and files 361-368

I

if constexpr
    about 51
    using, to simplify compile-
        time decisions 51, 52

if statement
    variables, initializing within 43, 44
insert iterators 118
integers
    comparing 9-11
items
    finding, in container 188-190
iterable range
    creating 112-115
iterator adapters
    about 118
    used, for filling STL containers 118-121
iterators
    about 105
    begin() iterator 105
    bidirectional iterator 108
    categories 108
    concepts 108-111
    end() iterator 106
    forward iterator 108
    generator, creating as 122-126
    input iterator 108
    making, compatible with STL
        iterator traits 115-117
    mutable iterator 108
    output iterator 108
    using 105-107

J

join() function 180
jump table
    mapped lambdas, using for 168-170

K

keys, of map items
    modifying 75-79

L

lambda expressions
    about 147, 149
    capture-list 153
    constexpr specifier 154
    exception attribute 155
    mutable modifier 154
    parameters 154
    trailing return type 155
lambdas
    concatenating, with recursion 162, 163
    using, as predicates with
        algorithm library 155-158
    using, for scoped reusable code 150-153
last-in, first-out (LIFO) interface 55
lightweight string object
    string_view class, using as 205-208
list 54
Little Endian (LE) 254
lock-free variations 329
lock_guard 45
locks
    about 315
    used, for sharing data 315-323
logical conjunction
    used, for combining predicates 164-166

M

managed object
    members, sharing of 284-286
manipulation functions
    using, with path 347-351
map
    about 54
    elements, inserting 70-74
    keys, modifying 75-79
    using, for word frequency counter 92-96

mapped lambdas
  using, for jump table 168-170
memory_order_acq_rel 330
memory_order_acquire 330
memory_order_consume 330
memory_order_relaxed 330
memory_order_release 330
memory_order_seq_cst 330
modules
  implementations 26, 27
  used, for avoiding template libraries
    recompilation 23-28
multimap
  about 54
  using, for ToDo list 101-103
multiple consumers
  implementing 337-341
multiple lambdas
  calling, with same input 166, 167
multiple producers
  implementing 337-341
multiple values
  returning, by using structured
    binding 38-43
multiset 54
mutex
  about 315
  used, for sharing data 315-323

N

numbers
  converting, to words 401-411

O

objects
  sharing, with std::shared_ptr
    class 275-279
objects, of unknown length
  iterating, with sentinel 130-133
optional values
  managing, with std::optional 246-249
ostream << operator
  overloading 224, 225

P

parallelism 297
path
  manipulation functions,
    using with 347-351
permutations
  generating, of data sequences 197, 199
polymorphic wrapper
  std::function, using 158-161
predicates
  combining, with logical
    conjunction 164-166
prefix tree 380
primitive union structure
  versus std::variant class 253, 254
priority_queue 55
producer-consumer problem
  about 337
  resolving, with std::condition_
    variable 333-336

Q

queue 55

R

random-access iterator
  creating 140-142
  operator overloads 143, 144
  validation code 144, 145
  working 146
random number distribution generators
  comparing 292-295
random number engines
  comparing 287-291
  methodologies 291
Random Number Generator (RNG) 291
range
  about 28
  reference link 33
  used, for creating views in
    containers 28-34
recursion 123
recursive function
  used, for concatenating
    lambdas 162, 163
recursive_mutex 323
Regular Expressions (regex)
  files, renaming with 368-373
  used, for parsing strings 241-244
Resource Acquisition Is Initialization
    (RAII) 270, 321
reverse adapters 121
reverse iterator adapter
  about 127
  using, for backward iteration 127-130
reverse iterators 118
Reverse Polish Notation (RPN) calculator
  with deque 84-91

S

search suggestions
  trie class, creating for 380-387
sentinel
  about 131
  used, for iterating objects of
    unknown length 130-133
sequential containers, STL
  about 53
  array 53
  deque 54
  list 54
  vector 53
set container
  about 54
  used, for filtering user input 82-84
  used, for sorting user input 82-84
shared_mutex 323
shared objects
  weak pointers, using with 280-282
share members
  of managed object 284-286
sleep_for() function
  usage, exploring 298, 299
sleep() function 300
sleep_until() function
  usage, exploring 298, 299
spaceship operator
  using 11-14
  working 14-16
span class
  using, to make C-arrays safer 36-38
stack 55
std::bind 161
std::function
  about 161
  using, as polymorphic wrapper 158-161

std::sort() algorithm 180
std::any class
  using, for type safety 250-253
std::async()
  using, for concurrency 306-312
std::atomic
  lock-free variations 329
  specializations 327
  standard aliases 327
  used, for sharing flags 324-326
  used, for sharing values 324-326
std::call_once
  used, for initializing threads 331, 332
std::chrono
  time event with 259-264
std::clamp ()
  used, for limiting values of
      containers to range 191-194
std::condition_variable
  using, to resolve producer-
      consumer problem 333-336
std::duration class 264, 265
std::jthread 305, 306
std::merge() algorithm 200-202
std::optional
  used, for managing optional
      values 246-249
std::sample() algorithm
  data sets, sampling with 194-197
std::shared_ptr class
  about 284
  used, for sharing objects 275-279
std::thread
  using, for concurrency 300-304
std::transform()
  used, for modifying containers 185-187
std::tuple class 265

std::unique_ptr
  used, for managing allocated
      memory 270-275
std::variant class
  used, for storing different types 253-258
  versus primitive union
      structure 253, 254
STL algorithms
  running, in parallel with
      execution policies 312-314
STL containers
  filling, with iterator adapters 118-121
STL container types
  about 53
  associative containers 54
  container adapters 55
  sequential containers 53
STL iterator adaptors 118
STL iterator traits
  iterators, making compatible
      with 115-118
stream iterators 118-120
string
  concatenating 209-211
  container elements, joining into 176-179
  parsing, with Regular Expressions
      (regex) 241-244
  reading, from user input 227-231
  transforming 215-218
  using, with constexpr 7-9
  whitespace, trimming from 225, 226
string class
  customizing, with char_traits 237-240
strings concatenation strategy
  benchmarks, performing 211-214
  options, selecting 215
  performance discrepancies 214

string_view class
   using, as lightweight string
      object 205-208
structured binding
   using, to return multiple values 38-43
swarm 297
switch statement
   variables, initializing within 43, 44

T

template argument deduction
   using, for simplicity and clarity 46-49
template deduction guide 50
template libraries
   recompilation, avoiding with
      modules 23-28
templates
   creating, with concept and
      constraints 17-22
text
   formatting, with C++20's
      format library 218-224
   formatting, with format library 2-5
threads
   about 300
   initializing, with std::call_once 331, 332
three-way comparison operator (<=>)
   using 11-14
   working 15, 16
timed_mutex 323
time events
   with std::chrono 259-264
ToDo list
   multimap, using for 101-103
trie class
   creating, for search suggestions 380-387

trivial type 326
two vectors
   error sum, calculating 388-390

U

uniform erasure functions
   container items, deleting with 56-61
unique_lock 336
unordered_map
   about 54
   using, with custom keys 79-82
unordered_multimap 54
unordered_multiset 54
unordered_set 54
user input
   filtering, with set container 82-84
   sorting, with set container 82-84
   strings, reading from 227-231

V

value() method 249
values
   sharing, with std::atomic 324-326
variables
   initializing, within if statement 43, 44
   initializing, within switch
      statement 43, 44
variadic tuples
   fold expressions, using for 265-268
vector
   about 53
   elements, accessing 64-67
   elements, sorting 67-69
vector of vectors
   sentence length, finding with 97-101

view
  about 28
  creating in containers, with ranges 28-34
view adapter 28

W

weak pointers
  use case 283, 284
  using, with shared objects 280-282
whitespace
  trimming, from strings 225, 226
word frequency counter
  map, using for 92-96
words
  counting, in file 231, 232
  numbers, converting to 401-411

Z

zip iterator adapter
  building 133-137
  using 140
  working 138, 139

Packt>

Other Books You May Enjoy

If you enjoyed this book, you may be interested in these other books by Packt:

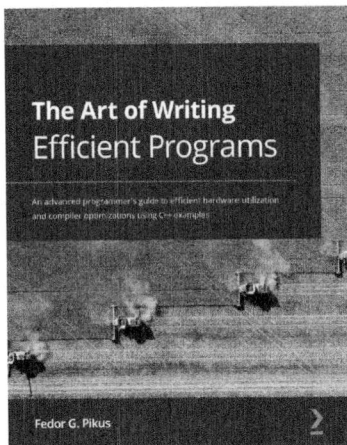

The Art of Writing Efficient Programs

Fedor G. Pikus

ISBN: 9781800208117

- Discover how to use the hardware computing resources in your programs effectively
- Understand the relationship between memory order and memory barriers
- Familiarize yourself with the performance implications of different data structures and organizations
- Assess the performance impact of concurrent memory accessed and how to minimize it
- Discover when to use and when not to use lock-free programming techniques

- Explore different ways to improve the effectiveness of compiler optimizations
- Design APIs for concurrent data structures and high-performance data structures to avoid inefficiencies

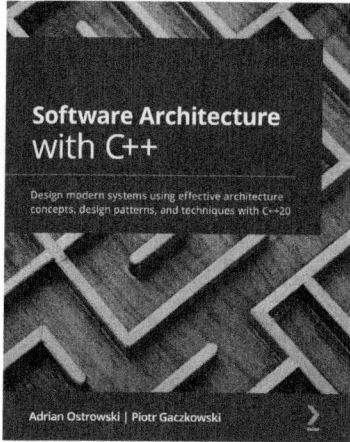

Software Architecture with C++

Adrian Ostrowski, Piotr Gaczkowski

ISBN: 9781838554590

- Understand how to apply the principles of software architecture
- Apply design patterns and best practices to meet your architectural goals
- Write elegant, safe, and performant code using the latest C++ features
- Build applications that are easy to maintain and deploy
- Explore the different architectural approaches and learn to apply them as per your requirement
- Simplify development and operations using application containers
- Discover various techniques to solve common problems in software design and development

Packt is searching for authors like you

If you're interested in becoming an author for Packt, please visit `authors.packtpub.com` and apply today. We have worked with thousands of developers and tech professionals, just like you, to help them share their insight with the global tech community. You can make a general application, apply for a specific hot topic that we are recruiting an author for, or submit your own idea.

Share Your Thoughts

Now you've finished *C++20 STL Cookbook*, we'd love to hear your thoughts! Scan the QR code below to go straight to the Amazon review page for this book and share your feedback or leave a review on the site that you purchased it from.

https://packt.link/r/1803248718

Your review is important to us and the tech community and will help us make sure we're delivering excellent quality content.

Printed in Great Britain
by Amazon